Maurice H Hervey

Dark Days in Chile

An Account of the Revolution of 1891

Maurice H Hervey

Dark Days in Chile
An Account of the Revolution of 1891

ISBN/EAN: 9783742862990

Manufactured in Europe, USA, Canada, Australia, Japa

Cover: Foto ©ninafisch / pixelio.de

Manufactured and distributed by brebook publishing software (www.brebook.com)

Maurice H Hervey

Dark Days in Chile

DARK DAYS IN CHILE

AN ACCOUNT OF

THE REVOLUTION OF 1891

BY

MAURICE H. HERVEY

Special Correspondent of 'The Times'

WITH FIFTEEN FULL-PAGE ILLUSTRATIONS

LONDON: EDWARD ARNOLD
NEW YORK: MACMILLAN & CO.
1892

All rights reserved

PREFACE

WHATEVER may be the verdict in store for this volume, it may at least claim the merit of being a faithful record of the writer's experiences, observations, and convictions. With the exception of the last chapter, the book is based upon notes made regularly and methodically in Chile. And that the author's views upon the merits of the political questions at issue are not those commonly held by his fellow-countrymen is entirely due to the conflicting sources of information upon which those views are respectively based. Whether José Manuel Balmaceda was a bloodthirsty tyrant or a well-meaning, if also ill-advised, patriot, will not be decided, either in or out of Chile, until men's minds shall have overcome the bitter partisan feeling begotten by civil war.

My thanks are due to Messrs. Laird Bros., for kindly lending photographs of the *Imperial* and other vessels built by them, for the purposes of illustration; and to the proprietors of *Black and White*, for permission to reproduce some sketches that appeared in its pages.

MAURICE H. HERVEY.

LONDON, *November*, 1891.

CONTENTS.

CHAPTER I.

OUTWARD BOUND.

Modern Journalism—A Voyage at Short Notice—The *Portugal*—My Fellow-Travellers—Discipline *v.* Gallantry—Dakar—A Moribund King and his Subjects—Rio de Janeiro—Monte Video—Buenos Aires—A Contrast - - - - - - 1

CHAPTER II.

ARGENTINA.

An Interview with President Pellegrini—The Man with the Iron Mask—British Preponderance—A Good Time—I form an Opinion upon the Argentine Situation—'Go on to Chile'—Pellegrini's Opinion of Balmaceda—Sensational Telegrams—The Andes reported infested by Bandits—I engage a Fighting Secretary—And take a Frenchman under my Wing - - - - 14

CHAPTER III.

CROSSING THE ANDES.

A Long Rail Journey—Travelling *en Prince*—Mendoza—A Lift to Uspallata — Fifty Miles on a 'Cowcatcher' — Scenery — Uspallata — A Lost Child on my Hands — Roughing it — A Facetious Muleteer — A Dry Stage — An Independent Yankee — Rio Blanco—Las Vacas—A Goatherd-subscriber to the *Times*—Montes Corrales—Monte de Los Penitentes—A Mule Race—'Corresponsal' wins—Val de la Tolorzia—Cajou del Rio de Las Cuevas—Puente del Inca—A *Posada*—A Night in a Menagerie—The Juncal Volcano—The Summit of the Cordillera—A Slippery Descent—Lake Portillo—A Primitive Hostelry—The Soldier's Leap—The Meeting of the Waters—Juncal—A Wild Drive—Santa Rosa de Los Andes - - - 30

CHAPTER IV.

CHILE AND ITS CONDITION.

Santiago—A State of Siege—Revolutionist Opinions of President Balmaceda—Wanted, Evidence—I hear the other Side of the Question—An Interview with Balmaceda—His Views—A Review of the Situation—A Sketch of Chilian Society—Chile and British Enterprise—Colonel North and his Mission—Dr. Russell upon 'Chile and the Nitrate Fields '—Realized Prophecy—Revolutionary Tactics—I arrive at Conclusions—Right or Wrong? - - - - - - 62

CHAPTER V.

THE TROUBLES OF A SPECIAL CORRESPONDENT.

How to correspond—Telegraph Lines closed—Mails supervised—An Ultimatum to the Government—Pozo al Monte—A Review of Government Troops—Opinion in the Provinces—My Lost Child gets into Trouble—Valparaiso—Opinion there—An Expedition against the Revolted Fleet—A Tempting Offer—I accept—My Fighting Secretary deserts me—And follows in the Footsteps of my Lost Child—Stick v. Bayonet—Political Memoranda—The *Times* and I—' Go, but wire Facts only'—An Interview with Rear-Admiral Hotham—I refuse Good Advice - - - - 112

CHAPTER VI.

MY FIRST CRUISE WITH THE SQUADRON.

A Difference of Opinion—Practice makes Perfect—The Plan of Operations—A Compromise—*En route* for Caldera—We lose our Consorts—Stirring News—Fever on Board—A Warning—The Sinking of the *Blanco Encalada*—The Quartermaster's Yarn—Valparaiso—Captain Moraga's Account of the *Blanco* Exploit—' One Good Turn deserves Another '—The Revolutionists try Orsini Tactics—A Chilian Heroine—The Elections - 158

CHAPTER VII.

MY SECOND CRUISE.

The Plan of Operations—Troops for Coquimbo—Scenes on Board—Coquimbo—British Naval Station—La Serena—Moraga's Advice to Admiral Hotham—*En route* for Iquique—Coaling at Sea—I tranship to the *Condell*—A Contrast—A Desperate Adventure—'The Last Watch'—Captain Cook—Moraga the Wolf—*Un Mauvais Quart d'Heure*—In Iquique Harbour—The Union Jack saves the Rebel Transports—An Alarm—A Difficult Torpedo-shot—Moraga's Dilemma—The Ironclad *Cochrane* bears down—A Harebrained Exploit—What the Prisoners said and did—Northward to sink the *O'Higgins* in a Peruvian Port—A Sea-Lawyer—The *Huascar* and the *Magellanes*—A Naval Skirmish—*Adios*—Moraga the Lamb—A Clever Ruse—Captain Cook saves us—A Naval Duel declined—We rejoin the *Imperial*—Bombardment of Iquique—Bombardment of Taltal—An Attack in Boats—Capture of Taltal—A Banquet and a Bill—Coquimbo—Valparaiso - - - - - - - 189

CHAPTER VIII.

MY THIRD CRUISE.

A Spell Ashore—Chilian News from Abroad—Balmaceda believes in Moral Effect—At Sea once more—A Tempting Bait—A Narrow Escape—Pisagua bombarded—Iquique bombarded—Tocopilla captured—Nitrate-duties for Balmaceda—The British Vice-Consul's Opinion—Antofagasta bombarded—A Deserted Village—Chañaral—The *Condell* in Peril—Reprisals—A Starving Population—Mr. Sherriff's Account—The *Imperial* becomes an Emigrant Ship—A delayed Telegram—Farewells - - - - - 224

CHAPTER IX.

HOMEWARD BOUND.

How I missed the *Liguria*—A Hot Ten Minutes—A Friend in Need—Travelling made Easy—A Meeting—Concepcion—Coronel—I catch the *Liguria*—The Old

Story—Magellan Straits—A Wreck—Monte Video—Rio de Janeiro—Bahia—A Negro Polyglot—Pernambuco—Lisbon—The *Errazuriz*—Plymouth—Home, Sweet Home! - - - - - - 252

CHAPTER X.

THE TRIUMPH OF THE REVOLUTION.

'Back from the Grave'—Smart Paragraphing—News from Chile—The Cumming Incident—The Invasion—A Close Shave—Barbosa the Rash—The Battle of Colmo or Concon—The Attack upon Viña del Mar—Strategy—The Insurgent Army receives Accessions—Balmaceda a Bad Strategist—The Battle of Placilla—Results—*Sauve qui peut*—The *Lynch* caught Napping—A 'Revel of Fiends'—How the Triumph was celebrated in Santiago—Balmaceda vanishes—Señor Montt and the Rump—'Convey, the Wise it call'—A Model Correspondent—Balmaceda's alleged Suicide—Prospects of Future Peace—The Trouble with the United States—How to bring about a Conservative Reaction—Conclusion - - - - - 268

Note on the Chilian Constitution - - - - 310

Appendix A.—The Transandine Railway - - 315

,, B.—The Value of Torpedoes in Naval Warfare 320

,, C.—Chilian Characteristics and Customs - 327

LIST OF ILLUSTRATIONS

	PAGE
PORTRAIT OF THE AUTHOR	*Frontispiece*
PUENTA DEL INCA, ON THE ROUTE OF THE TRANSANDINE RAILWAY	33
ATTACK ON THE 'COCHRANE' BY TORPEDO-BOATS	75
BOMBARDMENT OF IQUIQUE	79
JOSÉ MANUEL BALMACEDA	87
REVIEW OF TROOPS AT VALPARAISO	117
THE ARMED CRUISER 'IMPERIAL'	133
DON CLAUDIO VICUÑA	149
CAPTAIN CARLOS MORAGA	161
A CHILIAN HEROINE	183
THE TORPEDO VESSEL 'CONDELL'	199
THE 'HUASCAR'	235
CHILIAN SOLDIERS	247
AFTER THE BATTLE	285
RUINS IN VALPARAISO	297

DARK DAYS IN CHILE

CHAPTER I.

OUTWARD BOUND.

Modern Journalism—A Voyage at Short Notice—The *Portugal*—My Fellow-Travellers—Discipline *v.* Gallantry—Dakar—A Moribund King and his Subjects—Rio de Janeiro—Monte Video—Buenos Aires—A Contrast.

PERHAPS few persons who daily scan the great London journals for foreign intelligence ever pause to reflect upon the marvellous foresight, energy, and expense necessary to produce results which can be purchased by the readers for a few pence. Let them, however, but consider the number and the length of the telegrams, from all parts of the world, published in any ordinary number of, say, the *Times*, supplemented, as these are, by descriptive letters from correspondents, and they will be constrained to admit that modern journalism spares nothing to maintain its position in the vanguard of modern progress. Let but aught of public interest occur in the most distant quarter of the globe, and forthwith an envoy is despatched to inquire into the matter. Thus it fell to the writer's lot, early in the present year, to be selected for service in South America, when the vexed question of Argentine finance and the recent outbreak of civil war in Chile had become topics of considerable interest to English readers. My orders were clear and concise. I was to get to Buenos Aires as quickly as possible, and I was to report upon what I saw to the best of my judgment. A few inquiries made it plain that the first steamer would leave Bordeaux upon the 4th of February; and within twenty-four hours of receiving my instructions I had bidden farewell to my friends, and was *en route* for Paris. There I had but barely time for an interview with General Mitre, the popular candidate for the presidency of Argentina, to telegraph the results of the said interview to the *Times*, and to catch the night mail for Bordeaux. I had even less time to spare here, for I arrived at 8 a.m., and the Messageries Maritimes steamer *Portugal*, lying some thirty miles down the Garonne, was due to sail two hours later. I followed the mail-bags, well knowing that she could not start until they were aboard, was politely accommodated upon the mail-tender, and got safely on deck at least ten minutes before the good ship steamed away from La Belle France.

A fine boat of 4,500 tons is this same *Portugal*,

and fairly well up to date in the matter of speed. By the captain and his officers I was treated from the first, and throughout the voyage, with the most marked courtesy, the commissaire making himself especially amiable in the important matters of a most comfortable cabin (all to myself) and a seat of honour at table. Doubtless the facts that I was the only Englishman on board, and special correspondent *du grand journal Anglais*, combined to secure for me all these attentions, of which I shall always have the most pleasant recollections. Fortunately, French is almost as familiar to me as my mother-tongue, so that within a very few hours I felt thoroughly *chez moi*.

Life on board an ocean-going steamer has been described so often and so well, by far cleverer pens than mine, that I need not dwell at any great length upon this portion of my late experiences. A few points of comparison between English and French mail services may, however, be of interest to intending travellers. Nor can I wholly overlook my fellow-passengers.

As regards accommodation, attendance, management generally, there is little, or nothing, to choose between the two—both are as good as can reasonably be expected.

With respect to the important (to many persons the all-important) subject of the cuisine, the systems differ widely—in accordance, of course, with national usage. Upon the English vessels three solid meals (breakfast, lunch, and dinner) are provided, whereas their French rivals, condensing breakfast and lunch into one repast, supply but two. People, as a rule, eat a great deal too much on board ship, where the opportunities for exercise are so limited, and the temptations to lie down, or sit, so great. And, for this reason, the French plan is probably the better. Again, the French dishes are far daintier and lighter than their English equivalents, and consequently better suited to most stomachs at sea.

But in one noteworthy particular the English regulations show to distinct advantage : separation of the second-class from the first-class passengers. Upon the *Portugal* both classes had equal access to the promenade deck, and as we had the misfortune to carry a troup of theatrical artistes, male and female, bound for Rio de Janeiro, the presence of certain members of the band, travelling second class, was a very distinct nuisance. So intolerable, in fact, did the noisy, and at times indecorous, behaviour of these young women become, that even the commissaire's sense of gallantry gave way. After several ineffectual warnings, he had no alternative but to relegate the most obstreperous fair ones to confinement in their cabins; after which there was a marked improvement in the behaviour of those still left at large. The directors of the Messageries Maritimes would do well to rectify this serious defect in their otherwise excellently conducted service. It is at present a very distinct obstacle in the way of securing the patronage of English travellers who do not believe in liberty, fraternity, equality—and least of all on board ship.

A few pleasant companions are essential to one's existence at sea; and it so chanced that a trio of foreign financiers needed a fourth to make up that best of all evening pastimes, whist. Into this little set I at once dropped, and we contrived to sustain each other's spirits admirably up to the very end of the voyage.

One never-failing source of amusement lay in the masher-like propensities of the eldest of the trio. Monsieur P——, a gentleman of considerable means, had brought his confidential valet with him, and (there being nothing else to do) made it a point to change his attire at least half-a-dozen times in the course of the day. How many suits he had brought with him was a problem we others attempted in vain to solve. Day after day the changes went on, and, apparently, the same suit never did duty twice. To me, who affect flannels until dinner-time in warm latitudes, there was something almost fascinating in these chameleon-like mutations. You might be pacing the deck discussing the latest phase of the Baring failure with Monsieur P——, clothed in some rare shade of gray. An idea would suddenly strike him. 'You would excuse him for a little moment?' And in an incredibly short space of time he would reappear clad in immaculate white. Yet if, an hour later, you discerned a blue velveteen coat in the saloon, you would discover the owner of that coat, carefully preparing an absinthe, to be Monsieur P——. Of jewellery, also, he had enough to stock an average shop, and rang in the changes with equal originality and effect. No vulgarity about the man. Having an extraordinary taste for dress, and the means of gratifying it, he clearly humoured his fancy for his own satisfaction. Unfortunately, there were no young ladies on board, with the exception of the artistes already referred to, and of these Monsieur P—— had an utter abhorrence. His only rival was a young Peruvian aristocrat—a charming boy enough; but, in the matter of permutations and combinations, Monsieur P—— was master of the situation. I have even seen his youthful competitor wearing the same striped jacket two days running, rather than do which Monsieur P—— would, I am persuaded, have retired permanently to his berth.

Early upon the morning of February 8th the *Portugal* anchored off Lisbon, and, there being ample time, most of us went ashore. But beyond an excellent breakfast at the Braganza Hotel with the local agent of the *Times*, the visit to the Portuguese capital scarcely repaid the trouble of landing.

Upon the 12th we reached Dakar, one of the few French possessions upon the West Coast of

Africa. It does not impress the visitor as a very flourishing township, although the harbour is a fairly good one and the outlet, as we were informed, for a considerable amount of inland trade. The market-square presented a lively ⱴ enough scene, a perfect babel of uncouth cries proclaiming the excellence of the very uninviting-looking beef and evil-smelling fish offered for sale by the gaudily-attired native women. There are a few stores, nearly all kept by Frenchmen; some fairly commodious barracks, and a neglected-looking post-office, in telegraphic communication with Europe. But by far the most attractive sight is a neatly-planned boulevard, well worthy of a more imposing settlement. Dakar boasts (or then boasted) a 'King,' the most decayed specimen of monarchy I ever saw, with, perhaps, the exception of the Port Moresby sovereign, Boë-Vagi. His Dakar majesty's name I do not remember, nor can I find it amongst my jottings; but this can ⱴ scarcely be deemed an irreparable loss to contemporary history. It would seem to be the general custom of European Powers, when a slice of uncivilized territory is annexed, to pension off the heretofore reigning chieftain and allow him to retain the shadow of his former authority; and it is, at least, a more decent policy than the old Spanish system of extirpation. The pension allowed to the titual 'Roi de Dakar' would appear to be inadequate, since a small present of money is greedily accepted at the close of an 'audience.' It does not seem to be in the fitness of things that a nominal monarch, although he be but a deposed savage, should be reduced to gleefully pouching a couple of francs backsheesh. Our Dakar royalty had evidently not long to live, and we understood that, upon his death, the 'King' farce would be discontinued, he being the last of his line. Meanwhile his nominal subjects treat him with a certain amount of rough respect and kindness, making him presents of fish and vegetables, and occasionally enlivening the monotony of Court life by creating a fearful din, which is the local equivalent for a concert. The King speaks a few words of French, an accomplishment of which he is justly vain, and his guttural 'Merci, monsieur!' (accompanied by an outstretched palm) would extract largesse from the most penurious of visitors.

The men are remarkable for length of limb and leanness, in strong contrast to the women, who are extremely obese, short, and, it must be said, abominably ugly—which is, doubtless, one reason why garrison life at Dakar is regarded with such disfavour in the French service.

The voyage to Rio de Janeiro, which we reached upon the 21st, was uneventful: a monotonous existence made tolerable by tobacco, iced drinks, scandal, and an occasional concert wherein our noisy artistes showed to better advantage. Our stay at Rio was but brief, and quarantine considerations forbade our landing. But here our theatrical nuisances left us, and, I hope, had a good time and full houses, for Rio just then was 'booming.'

My diary up to the 26th is a complete blank, and for that date contains the bare entry: 'Arrived at Monte Video.' Here, however, we had ample time to land, and, as it happened, to stay one night ashore. There is always a certain pleasure in playing cicerone, and, being here thoroughly at home, I experienced considerable satisfaction in introducing my newly-made friends to the prettiest town in South America. That, beyond all dispute, Monte Video emphatically is. Picturesquely situated upon the northern bank of the huge estuary geographically known as the River Plate (how reconcile one's idea of a river with a width of one hundred and twenty miles?); laid out upon a plan which admirably harmonizes the *cuadra* system of Madrid with the Parisian boulevard; adorned with memorial statues and fountains which are veritable *chefs-d'œuvre;* boasting of streets full of shops which, whether in the matter of appearance or of dearness, are very good seconds to Regent Street or the Rue de Rivoli; admirably supplied as to hotel, police, and cab service; essentially clean and well drained, and the centre of a flower and fruit province: what more can one reasonably ask for? Anyhow, we all thoroughly enjoyed ourselves, and unanimously voted Monte Video charming.

It was possible to gain a few hours by transhipping to one of the river-boats which ply to and from Buenos Aires. But inasmuch as transhipping one's baggage is a distinct bore and the saving in time trivial, most of us decided to proceed next day with the *Portugal*. And in due course the big ship ploughed her way across the shallow river, and we dropped anchor off Buenos Aires.

I had left the Argentine capital but six months before, soon, indeed, after the short but bloody revolution of July. Matters had then been in a bad way; but with the fall of President Celman it had seemed probable that a change for the better would take place. The victorious Union Civica had set itself, or, perhaps more accurately, had promised to set itself, to the tasks of economy and reform; and including, as it did, amongst its leaders men of known ability and integrity, there really appeared to be grounds for hope. But, alas! these sanguine expectations had been based upon the assumption that the foreign creditor would be forbearing, and allow the distracted Republic time to reorganize its chaotic finances; nor had the nature of the Stock Exchange 'bear' been sufficiently taken into account. Of course, so long as money-markets exist, the warfare between 'bears' and 'bulls' will endure, since it must ever be the object of the speculative buyer of stocks to buy cheap, and that of the speculative holder to sell dear. But, surely, below a certain point it is little short of insanity to prolong 'bearing' tactics, lest securities should become absolutely worthless, and the entire game collapse for want of material to work upon. Yet this is what has actually, over and over again, occurred, and stocks, by no means intrinsically valueless, have been 'beared' into an everlasting *moratorium*. And this is also what occurred with respect to Argentine securities. In vain did the 'bulls,' having, upon this occasion at least, common-sense and logic upon their side, endeavour to stem the downward current; in vain did some of the leading financial newspapers (and notably the *World* in its money columns) counsel moderation and patience. The 'bears' were masters of the situation; they held the knife at the throat of Argentine credit, and they slashed away ruthlessly. They scouted the proposals made by the reformed Argentine Administration as mere devices to put off an inevitable crash; yet better proposals it was not possible to offer, with any reasonable prospect of fulfilment. Paper-bonds, gold-bonds, cedulas, were proclaimed from the house-tops to be mere waste-paper, and a panic-stricken public believed the tale. As a natural result Argentine securities became practically unsaleable, and any further loans an impossibility. The great house of Baring, holding these and kindred securities to the extent of a score of millions of pounds sterling, found it hopeless to unload in the face of a closed market, tottered, and would have fallen, with a crash which would have shaken the commercial world, but for the timely intervention of the Bank of England and its associates. Now, evidently, were the 'bear' gospel correct and Argentine securities worthless, no such intervention would have taken place. The mere fact that it *did* take place afforded proof positive that, in the estimation of the highest authorities upon finance in England, the securities were intrinsically good, even though time might be needed to realize upon them; which was precisely the argument advanced throughout by the *World*, and a few of its clearest-headed contemporaries.

With these considerations clearly before me, I was not surprised to find the general condition of affairs in Buenos Aires worse upon the last day of February (when we landed) than it had been six months before. Trade practically at a standstill; shops, by the hundred, closed, or plastered with selling-off advertisements; the streets swarming with beggars; the erstwhile pandemonium-like Bolsa, a mere gossiping resort for seedy-looking brokers; the native banks degenerated into vulgar pawn-offices, and their foreign rivals intent only upon raking in outstanding liabilities; the best hotels deserted, and places of amusement unable to open their doors: all these, and countless other, 'signs of the times' spoke but too plainly of widespread insolvency. And when I mentally compared the Buenos Aires of 1891 with its prototype a few short years ago, my heart saddened to witness the change that had come to pass. Then, nay, but two years ago, the Argentine metropolis was one of the liveliest, gayest, cheeriest towns in the world. Could this out-at-elbows looking place be the same Buenos Aires which had formerly eclipsed Paris in the brilliancy of its nocturnal illuminations? Was this now-closed theatre the same that had re-echoed to Patti's wondrous voice at a profit—to the diva—of one thousand pounds a night? And where were the countless luxurious equipages, horsed by high-stepping English bays or Russian blacks, that used to throng the route to Palermo Park? Gone, all gone! gone like the money (or the credit) which procured them; gone like the hopes of foreign bondholders, who had supplied the money or given the credit; gone (as I was credibly informed) temporarily to Rio de Janeiro, where a great 'boom' had arisen, and where, no doubt, a still greater crash will, in the fulness of time, eventuate. But, ah me, poor Buenos Aires!

CHAPTER II.

ARGENTINA.

An Interview with President Pellegrini—The Man with the Iron Mask—British Preponderance—A Good Time—I form an Opinion upon the Argentine Situation—'Go on to Chile'—Pellegrini's Opinion of Balmaceda—Sensational Telegrams—The Andes reported infested by Bandits—I engage a Fighting Secretary—And take a Frenchman under my Wing.

MINDFUL of the fact that Argentina and its affairs lay primarily within the scope of my mission, I worked hard for the next few days endeavouring to obtain clear ideas as to the actual situation—a task materially lightened as well by the very nature of that mission itself, as by the numerous letters of introduction with which I had come provided. Local English opinion was well-nigh unanimous: the country itself was sound and progressive enough; all that was needed was time and confidence in the future. This sounded a very old story to one so long familiar with the country, but it faithfully reflected local British belief, and was therefore entitled to some credence. Moreover, the reports from the provinces had been encouraging; good seasons and abundant harvests seemed to be the order of the day. But an interval, possibly a long interval, must necessarily elapse before metropolitan trade could be expected to revive under the beneficial effects of these agricultural blessings. And hence Buenos Aires would probably remain commercially stagnant for some time to come. Upon the whole, this appeared to be a not unreasonable forecast—provided always that Government could be relied upon to persevere in the paths of rectitude. I had many interviews with Ministers, and especially with the Finance Minister, Señor Lopez (whose clever son, Dr. Lucio V. Lopez, appeared to perform most of his father's duties, by the way), and so far as reports, statistics, and apparent candid statement of facts could carry conviction, there seemed to be no room for doubt that the exhausted exchequer was being nursed to the best advantage. Nor can I here omit to acknowledge my indebtedness to the courteous kindness of Mr. H. Chevallier Boutell, manager of the River Plate Trust Loan Company, who was indefatigable in his efforts to procure for me the best and most reliable information.

I paid my first visit to the President in company with Señor Lopez, who very judiciously selected the 'four o'clock tea' leisure-hour for the purpose. (It may be parenthetically noted that afternoon tea has become even more firmly established an institution in South American upper circles than in England.) Dr. Pellegrini, a tall, well-built, intellectual-looking man, somewhere about fifty years of age, received me with great cordiality, introduced me to such of his guests as I did not already know, and proceeded straight to business. He untwisted me very neatly as to London opinion upon a vast variety of points, every now and then glancing towards General Roca (then Minister of the Interior), as though for approval or inspiration. The gallant General's face is the most illegible countenance I have ever beheld: dead-white in colour, rigid as though carved in marble—a face which affords absolutely no clue as to what is passing through the brain; a face such as Napoleon's may have been in his most baffling moods. Only at rare intervals did a movement of an eye-lid, or the ghost of a smile upon the firm-set lips, indicate his appreciation of some point scored by his more voluble chief. For physiognomical purposes his features might as well be hidden altogether, and I mentally dubbed him 'the Man with the Iron Mask.'

It speedily became apparent that the proposed positions were being reversed—that the interviewer was being converted into the interviewed. However, my turn came at last, and I poured my questions in hot and strong. I am bound to say that I was met very fairly: no evasion, very little hesitation. Without entering into details which have no direct bearing upon the subject of this work, I may say that when I took my leave I was more than ever satisfied that the reins of government had fallen into honest and cautious hands.

I was curious to hear General Roca speak in something longer than monosyllables, and, in saying good-bye, asked him the facts of his attempted assassination by a boy, a short time previously.

'The young scamp fired at me through the panels of my carriage. I jumped out, seized him, thrashed him with my cane, and gave him into custody. He is either mad or has been laid on to kill me.'

Certainly this was the most concise possible narrative of an exploit which for many days had filled whole columns of the local press.

No one could fail to be impressed by the fact that, go where one would, the best-dressed men, and the frequenters of such fashionable resorts as still contrived to keep open, were Englishmen. In fact, but for English patronage, it is doubtful if even a single first-class restaurant could have kept open: once more emphasizing the bankrupt condition of the 'sons of the country,' for your Argentine loves fine clothes and the vanities of life. Of course the explanation was simple enough. The Englishman is paid his salary in gold, and the worse the financial crisis, the more paper dollars he gets for the sovereign. The Argentine is paid in paper-money, his salary remaining the same however high the gold-premium may soar. Prices rise, of course, during a crisis, but never so fast or so high as the gold-premium. Consequently, whereas the unfortunate native finds his margin for *menus plaisirs* entirely swept away, the Englishman actually gains by the rise.

And, apart from this, it is clear that the whole of the industrial enterprises in the country are rapidly passing into English or, at least, into foreign hands; to such an extent that, but for the enduring character of the Spanish language, and the well-established fact that the children of English parentage born in Spanish-speaking countries are almost invariably passionately fond of their native soil, one would feel tempted to predict that Argentina is destined, sooner or later, to become a British possession. Certain it appears to be that the Spanish race there is doomed, to be replaced by a new and more energetic race of Argentines, of whom the dominant section will be of Anglo-Saxon blood, but of strongly anti-English sympathies. The language will never die out, for the simple reason that no one familiar with the rich, soft idiom of Spain would ever willingly exchange it for the harsh, comparatively coarse idiom of Britain.

My particular inquiries into the actual economic state of affairs naturally threw me much into the society of my fellow-countrymen, and from them I experienced nothing but unlimited kindness and hospitality. With my work thus made easy for me, and so admirably dove-tailed with enjoyment, I should be ungrateful indeed did I not confess to having had a really 'good time' during my brief stay in Buenos Aires. Given, too, all these exceptional facilities for obtaining the very best information, superadded to an already fairly accurate knowledge of the country, and it is plain that one can arrive very speedily at definite opinions. Briefly stated, mine formulated themselves thus : That things were in a bad way, and likely so to remain for some time to come ; that General Mitre would shortly arrive, and would be enthusiastically received in Buenos Aires by the dominant Union Civica ; that his candidature for the Presidency would be supported by the existing Government ; that he would in due course be elected unless a split later on occurred in the Union, in which case Heaven only and General Roca knew what might happen ; that there seemed no prospect of any disturbance in the near future ; and that the best thing I could do would be to hurry off to Chile. All of which, having been duly cabled to London, brought forth the laconic order, ' Go on to Chile.' This telegram reached me at the very moment when I was discussing the Chilian question with an Argentine brother-pressman, who had been bewailing his hard fate in not having been sent as correspondent to the scene of strife. I had endeavoured to console him by pointing out the alleged dangers of the expedition ; but such dangers being to him, as I gleaned, the very salt of existence, I had duly sympathized with him in his disappointment.

Now, it should be stated that there were at this time, at the Darsena del Sur, two small warships which had excited great interest. They were of the class known to British naval men as torpedo-catchers, were named respectively the *Almirante Lynch* and the *Almirante Condell*, and were about to proceed to Valparaiso, the naval stronghold of the world-famed tyrant and dictator Balmaceda. It was, moreover, reported that several of the warships which had espoused the side of Congress were lying in wait for them at the mouth of Magellan Straits, with the amiable intention of there blowing them out of the water. But the Chilian commanders had openly ridiculed any such possibility : if attacked by any single ironclad, their vessels were heavily-armed and carried (between them) ten torpedo-tubes ; if by a squadron, then they could show a very clean pair of 18-knot heels, and laugh at pursuit. To my mind it was highly improbable that the revolted fleet should allow two such dangerous craft to pass through the straits without some effort to sink them, and I was naturally anxious to witness that rarest of all spectacles nowadays, a naval engagement. So I consulted some of my friends as to the possibility of proceeding to Valparaiso on board one of the torpedo-catchers. Never was proposition worse received. Go ? Of course I could go : they would be but too glad to have the correspondent of the *Times* on board. But had I considered that by so doing I should be identifying myself, so to speak, with the cause of the tyrant? No; this view of the matter had certainly not presented itself to me. It seemed hard lines to miss what promised to be a very novel and interesting scrimmage, merely because people might accuse me of sympathizing with a man whom I knew only, by report, as a savage, and whose portrait I had never even seen. It seemed still harder lines to have to bump across the Andes on mule-back when there was a chance of a sea-passage on board an 18-knot boat. But my friends' verdict was so unanimous that I regretfully gave up the idea.

'Go,' from a great journal to its special correspondent, means 'Go at once'; and that I lost no time in obeying my orders is proved by the fact that, although the telegram only reached me upon the evening of March 5th, I was *en route* within eighteen hours—by the first transcontinental train, in fact. Late at night I betook me to the premises of the leading journals to obtain a few press wrinkles as to the journey, telegraphing, and other details, and also, naturally, to hear the latest news from the disordered country I was about to visit. It appeared that I could get as far as Puente del Inca (upon the Argentine side of the Cordillera) easily enough; that thence I might, if I chose to risk it, get across into Chilian territory; but that Balmaceda had closed all telegraphic communication between Chili and the Argentine. The Buenos

Aires press-correspondents, I learned, had stopped short at Puente del Inca, from which point they telegraphed such items of Chilian news as they could there pick up. The telegrams to hand were especially sensational. There had been several desperate engagements. Balmaceda was besieged in the Moneda at Santiago, and would probably endeavour to escape across the Andes into Argentine territory, if he were not captured and shot. And the mountain-passes were infested by bandits, deserting soldiers, and other desperate characters. It was impossible, *then*, to know that these reports were pure fabrications; and whilst common-sense suggested that, in the absence of telegraphic communication, they could not be depended upon, still they might be exaggerated statements of fact. The brigand item appeared to be especially deserving of notice as being, under the circumstances of a civil war, a very natural outcome. At all events, it clearly suggested a liberal supply of firearms and ammunition. And then there arose the query, Of what use going to Chile at all if it be impossible to send news to the *Times?* No matter. The order was 'Go to Chile,' and the order must be obeyed, brigands or no brigands, news or no news. And after all, it might be possible to get from Valparaiso to the insurgent headquarters at Iquique, and thence cable *viâ* New York. (It did not then occur to me that Iquique, being also telegraphically cut off from Valparaiso, must be, if anything, rather a worse source of information than Puente del Inca.) And what wondrous messages must have inundated Europe from these two telegram factories for many months! I myself was taken in by one—but by one only—which bore every appearance of being official and genuine, and which I repeated to London. One of Balmaceda's crack regiments (the 5th of the Line, I think it was) was reported to have mutinied, murdered its officers, and gone over *en masse* to the insurgents. Yet, before I had well reached Chile, this very regiment had been cut to pieces at Pazo Almonte by the rebels! Wonderful, truly, are the ways of press telegraph agencies! Parisian journalists adopted a system equally reliable, and far less expensive; they simply and persistently invented their Chilian news in their printing-offices.

As one result of a rather restless night of broken sleep, during which, I remember, stumbling mules, precipices, and lurking brigands figured extensively, I paid an early visit to my literary friend who had been so grievously disappointed in his hopes of visiting Chile. I had decided upon taking him with me in the capacity of fighting secretary, special despatch-bearer in emergencies, or for any similar jobs to his taste that might turn up. I found him at home, and gradually (in order to enjoy, to the full, his anticipated rapture) made my proposal. I was not disappointed; he was delighted with the idea—so far as I had gone. Go with me? Of course he would. A journey across the famous Cordillera? The one thing he longed for. Such an opportunity might never occur again. And Señor Guillermo incontinently proceeded to overhaul his wardrobe, and to make selections therefrom. I watched him in silence for some minutes, and then the thought uppermost in my mind found tongue.

'Tell me, *amigo mio*, how are you off for firearms? I suppose you have a regular assortment for handy use?'

'Firearms!' replied Señor Guillermo. 'I don't think that at present I have any. I had a little American revolver, but someone stole it out of my pocket. It didn't much matter, because it wouldn't go off!'

I fairly gasped. A fighting secretary who, at some bygone period, had possessed a *little* revolver, an *American* revolver, and who knew so little about firearms as to be guilty of the ludicrous tautology of adding that it wouldn't go off! Did the man suppose that the Yankee toys exported to Buenos Aires *ever* went off? It was staggering. But, worst of all, he had allowed some person unknown to abstract this harmless but, withal, intimidating weapon from his pocket! One's watch or one's purse, yes—*cela peut arriver des fois*. But one's revolver—in South America!

The thing was past belief. Yet, stay; an idea struck me.

'Never mind,' I said, 'you can stick to the national *cuchillo*, and I'll look after the artillery.'

Señor Guillermo held up a pair of trousers to the light (doubtless with a view to calculating how many hours' mule-riding they might reasonably be expected to stand), and answered very solemnly:

'Señor Corresponsal, I never use a knife except at meal-times.'

This was too much. He spoke in much the same tone as a dyspeptic uses when, bidden to partake of a sherry and bitters, he informs you that 'he never touches anything between meals.'

'You see,' proceeded my new secretary, extending his critical inspection to sundry other garments, 'before I turned my attention to the Press, I was a professor of philosophy, and, long ago, decided that fighting is utterly inconsistent with the teachings of that admirable science. Moreover, it is evident that an unarmed man is really in less danger of being forced into a quarrel than he who carries weapons, a fact which, I am given to understand, is thoroughly recognised in your own enlightened country. And, lastly, to attempt armed resistance to a gang of bandits (should any such present themselves, which I think most unlikely) would be sheer folly.'

It was hard to take all this in at once, and

especially hard to have discredit thrown upon one's bandits.

'Why,' I asked, 'do you doubt the existence of these gentry, in the face of your own correspondent's telegram?'

'Simply,' answered Señor Guillermo, 'because I know Pedro, who sent it, very well. He is a man who rightly esteems his personal comfort above all things. He has often complained in his letters of the overcrowded condition of the small *posada* at Puente del Inca, whereby prices are enhanced and accommodation curtailed. The obvious and only remedy must be to deter any more intending travellers, by means of a judicious scare; and what so likely to do this as a well-flavoured bandit report?'

'Your friend Pedro is a man fertile of resource,' I assented, 'if not of unimpeachable veracity. I trust we shall find the *posada* depleted upon our arrival. *Hasta luego!* And I left my philosopher-secretary contentedly equipping himself for the journey.

Upon returning to the Grand Hotel, I was apologetically asked by the proprietor if it would seriously inconvenience me to allow a French gentleman of his acquaintance to travel with me to Chile. Naturally, I requested an introduction to my proposed fellow-traveller, and, finding him in every way eligible, at once consented. Several other intending travellers interviewed me with the same object, but turned out to be unprepared to start at such short notice. I should, otherwise, have had to captain a small caravan.

Few as were my remaining hours, my English friends found time to rally round me for a sumptuous farewell lunch at the Strangers' Club. Right royally they entertained me. And true though it be that *Scheiden thut Weh*, when the *Scheiden* takes place under such cheering influences, the sting wholly disappears. Then as many farewell visits as I could crowd into the remaining interval. From our Resident Minister, the Hon. F. Pakenham, whom I found vigorously engaged at lawn-tennis at Palermo, I received many valuable hints about Chile, to which he had been previously accredited; but he confessed his inability to enlighten me upon the political merits of the Revolution. My last visit was paid to the President, with whom, as before, I found General Roca. His Excellency was politely sorry that I was so soon leaving Buenos Aires, but added that, of course, from a journalistic point of view, Chile was at that moment a more interesting field for operations.

'Has your Excellency formed any opinion as to the merits of the quarrel between President Balmaceda and Congress?' I ventured to inquire.

'No,' replied Dr. Pellegrini; 'I am not sufficiently well posted in Chilian affairs to enable me to arrive at any very definite conclusions. But President Balmaceda personally I know very well indeed; we are old friends; and whether he be right or wrong in the attitude he has taken up, I have no hesitation in saying that he is one of the most finished gentlemen I ever met. Ask General Roca; he knows more about the matter than I do.'

But the Man with the Iron Mask was very guarded in his brief utterances, as, indeed, he always is. In his judgment, President Balmaceda had no sympathy with the attempts made to increase the powers of Congress at the expense of those of the Executive, and would resist these attempts to the bitter end. Possibly he believed that a ruler, aided by ministers of his own selection, was better able to govern than a roomful of wrangling deputies. 'But,' concluded the General, 'that Balmaceda ever had any intention of supplanting existing Republican institutions by an army-supported dictatorship I do not think probable. He is not the man for a *coup d'état*.'*

With many kindly expressions of goodwill from the President and his Prime Minister, I hurried off to the railway-station, barely in time to catch the train. Mr. Christopher Hill, the courteous

---

* I cannot recall the exact impressions left on my mind which induced me to enter the following remarks in my diary under the date of this interview:

'March 5th, *Memo.*—If ever a South American community should grow weary of the so-called Republican political jumble, which has invariably proved so total a failure south of the equator, and should revert to the One-man-rule system, that community will be Argentina, and the One Man General Roca.' Perhaps the Napoleon-like face and manner of the man inspired the thought more than his words.

manager of the Buenos Aires and Pacific lines, had made all things comfortable for me and my two companions, and good-naturedly accompanied us a short distance. We were fairly *en route* for the Andes.

CHAPTER III.

CROSSING THE ANDES.

A Long Rail Journey—Travelling *en Prince*—Mendoza—A Lift to Uspallata—Fifty Miles on a 'Cow-catcher'—Scenery—Uspallata—A Lost Child on my Hands—Roughing It—A Facetious Muleteer—A Dry Stage—An Independent Yankee—Rio Blanco—Las Vacas—A Goatherd-subscriber to the *Times*—Montes Corrales—Monte de Los Penitentes—A Mule Race—' Corresponsal ' wins—Valle de la Tolorzia—Cajou del Rio de Las Cuevas—Puente del Inca—A *Posada*—A Night in a Menagerie—The Juncal Volcano—The Summit of the Cordillera—A Slippery Descent—Lake Portillo—A primitive Hostelry—The Soldier's Leap—The Meeting of the Waters—Juncal—A Wild Drive—Santa Rosa de Los Andes.

FORTY consecutive hours in a third-class railway-carriage would, it may be supposed, be a test of endurance and of epidermis which few persons would be able to undergo; but forty hours in a suite of luxurious Pullman cars glide by smoothly enough. Monotonous, of course; nothing to see from the car windows on either side but the flat grassy pampas until quite towards the end of the journey. How one longs, after a time, for the sight of even a hillock to vary the dead-level of those interminable plains! An isolated farm-house, usually as primitive in appearance as mud walls can make it, becomes an object of interest, and a herd of cattle excites the liveliest satisfaction; but even monotony is not without charm, provided it does not last too long. And certainly one who has endured a three weeks' calm upon the Line, on board a sailing ship, is little likely to suffer from want of scenery on the Pampas. The service and the accommodation leave little to be desired upon this railway, and the cuisine is very tolerable. Mr. Hill, the general manager of the line, had considerately provided me with a four-berthed dormitory to myself, which was convertible, by the dexterous hands of an attendant, into a snug sitting-room during the day. The only serious inconvenience was the dust, which, despite all precautions, found its way inside in large quantities.

My secretary was in high spirits, finding matter for admiration even in our desolate surroundings. 'Where,' he would ask, 'will you find a country so level, and of such vast extent? For hundreds of kilometres not a hillock and not a stone. Besides, observe how well we are treated! Travelling with a " corresponsal " is, I see, synonymous with travelling *en prince.*'

'Ah, Guillermo,' said I, 'wait until we get outside those mules. They will respect neither the " corresponsal " nor his secretary.' Which foreboding proved, indeed, true enough.

We reached Villa Mercedes at 2.30 p.m. next day, whence, after an hour's halt to stretch our legs, we started for Mendoza, where we arrived at seven o'clock next morning.

Here it became necessary to engage an *arriero* (muleteer-guide), a boy, and twelve mules to transport ourselves and our baggage across the Andes. And here there befell us a piece of luck which saved us nearly sixty miles of mule-riding, in order to understand which, a few words must be said about one of the greatest railway engineering enterprises of even these go-ahead days. Those readers who may be interested in such matters will find full details in an Appendix.*

At the foot of the great range of the Andes, which separates Argentina from Chile, upon the Argentine side, lies the town of Mendoza. Similarly at the foot of the same range, upon the Chilian side, lies the town of Santa Rosa de Los Andes, or, as it is generally termed, more simply, Los Andes. And this range is one of the most impassable in the world. The distance to be traversed, following the only possible track for mule or man, and well-nigh the whole of which has been cut out of the solid rock, is a little over 150 miles, the highest peak crossed being some 13,000 feet above sea-level. The mule-track, narrow and often dangerous as it is, was deemed a triumph of engineering skill, and the route *viâ* the Uspallata Pass has long been famous.

Then there arose a clamour for telegraphic com-

* See Appendix A : The Transandine Railway.

PUENTE DEL INCA, ON THE ROUTE OF THE TRANSANDINE RAILWAY.

munication between the two towns, so as to bring Santiago and Valparaiso in direct contact with Buenos Aires. Two Chilian gentlemen of English descent, Messrs. Juan and Mateo Clark, undertook and successfully carried through this enterprise. And then, having taken careful stock of the engineering difficulties to be overcome, they staggered the scientific world by boldly proclaiming the possibility of driving the iron horse over the Cordillera! At first the idea was received with ridicule; but Messrs. Clark stuck to their guns, converted both the Argentine and the Chilian Governments to their views, obtained the necessary concessions, and the still more necessary capital, and boldly went to work upon their truly colossal scheme.

Now, when we arrived at Mendoza, upon March 8, the iron road had just been completed as far as Uspallata, and it was therefore possible for ourselves and our mules to proceed thus far (about fifty-five miles) upon our mountain journey by train. Mr. N——, Messrs. Clark's agent at Mendoza, courteously placed a special carriage at our disposal, himself accompanying us, together with several young English engineers. It was arranged that the mules should follow by a special train reserved for the conveyance of troops towards the frontier.

At Blanco Encalada, the first stopping-place, some twelve miles up the line, I discovered four of the engineers perched upon the cow-catcher of the locomotive, there being just room for this number.

'Now then, sir,' cried one, 'if you want to get fresh air, and a good view of the Cordillera, take my place here. But keep your head cool going round the curves and through the tunnels.'

I surveyed the narrow ledge upon which I was invited to balance myself, tested it, and, finding that the protruding bars of the cow-catcher afforded some purchase for the heels, accepted the offer with a great show of alacrity, but with considerable inward misgivings. My secretary tried hard to dissuade me, but to no purpose. A shriek from the engine, and we were off.

Oh, the wild delight of that glorious ride! The sun shining brightly overhead ; the exhilarating sensation of rushing through the clear, crisp air ; the distant panorama of the snow-clad Cordillera towering above mountains of well-nigh every imaginable hue ; the spice of danger thrown in to add, as it were, zest to the whole sublime scene! For the first few miles, it is true, the initial sense of insecurity predominated. I was too busily engaged in 'holding on' (or perhaps I should say 'sitting on,' since there was nothing to hold on by), in staring at the stony track along which we were speeding, and in imagining what would happen if some huge boulder should have rolled upon the line, to bestow much attention upon Nature's masterpieces of scenic effect. The first bridge which we crossed, about 200 yards in length, fairly made me start : there, deep, deep below us rushed the river Mendoza, into whose icy waters it would be so easy to fall did but one's heels slip. Involuntarily I leaned well back, but coming, by this movement, into uncomfortable contact with the front portion of the furnace, I, as involuntarily, jerked myself forward again.

'Sit still, sir,' said my right-hand neighbour warningly ; 'it's not safe to throw yourself about on this perch until you're a bit used to it.'

This entirely coincided with my own conviction ; but, in truth, after that first bridge my nervousness entirely disappeared. At our next halting-place, Cacheuta, Señor Guillermo rushed forward to ascertain at what particular spot I had realized his prediction, and fallen off. He embraced me as one returned from a forlorn hope—he even hinted at accompanying me upon the next stage ; but whether it was that my engineer friends drew a line between a correspondent and his secretary, or that they feared two 'new chums' would jostle one another off, or that no one cared to resign his seat, certain it is that one of them told an anecdote which effectually 'choked off' Señor Guillermo, and very nearly drove me back to the railway-car. Guillermo had remarked that, after all, there did not appear to be much danger of falling off.

'Falling off!' exclaimed the engineer ; 'not

much fear of that, because a fellow can see plainly enough what would become of him if he did, and sticks tight. But other accidents may happen. For instance, a few days ago a tourist rode with us on the cow-catcher, just as the correspondent has been doing. But he had quite enough of it after one stage;' and the speaker laughed as at some humorous recollection.

'How was that?' I asked. 'I could ride there all day, travelling through such scenery.'

'How? Well, I'll tell you,' was the reply. 'In the first place, he was a particularly nervous sort of fellow, clutching at one or other of us every other minute; and, secondly, he charged a cow!'

'Charged a cow!' cried Guillermo; 'what on earth did he do that for?'

'Just because he couldn't help it. You see, cows have a habit of straying on to the track, and are very stupid and slow in getting out of the way of a train. Sometimes, indeed, they get into a cutting, or upon a narrow ledge, and *can't* save themselves; and sometimes they are overtaken round one of the sharp curves. We fellows always keep a sharp look-out for the brutes, and if we see that it's going to be a case of " fresh beef," we skip round to the side-ledge of the engine, and hold on by the boiler-rail until the job is over. Upon the occasion I'm speaking of, just as we were turning a corner, we came right upon a tubby old cow. There was barely a second to think and act, and my chum and I used it to the best advantage, leaving the stranger to Providence. We got one glimpse of his huddled-up figure . . . there was a thud . . . and in another instant the front part of the engine was in a fearful mess. Our man looked as though he had been rolled through a slaughter-house. Goodness knows how he contrived to hang on, but he did somehow. Of course, the engine at once slowed down, and we got him off to the guard's van, where he was very glad to change his clothes in favour of a suit of blankets. I don't think that chappie will ever again ride on a cow-catcher.'

I registered a mental vow that if *I* did it should not be in the middle seat. *In medio tutissimus ibis* evidently did not hold good of this sort of travelling.

Time was allowed us at Cacheuta to see the locally-famous baths of La Boca del Rio. These are thermal springs of high temperature, which, oddly enough, rise within a few feet of the river Mendoza ; which latter, being fed by melted snow, is always icy cold. These baths are accredited with wonderful medicinal properties, and it seems beyond doubt that they are of great value in cases of nervous and rheumatic disorders.

My request for a side-seat having been acceded to, with the proviso that, if we should run foul of a cow, I was to ' look smart, and give the middle man a chance,' we started once more upon our winding, upward course. And winding enough, in all conscience, this course is. At a place called La Media Luna (the Half-Moon), the curve is a perfect semicircle, flanked by a precipitous descent, which makes the novice hold his breath. Then a new experience—a tunnel. The sensation of shooting a tunnel, perched upon a cow-catcher, is like nothing else that I ever felt. One seems to have for ever taken leave of the glorious sunlight, and to be pushed, as it were, through the very bowels of the earth, by the panting monster behind one. The din and the darkness so add to the weirdness of the effect that one instinctively feels for one's neighbour's arm, in order to be in touch with a fellow-mortal. Upon emerging once more into daylight, the scene appeared grander than ever—so grand, so sublime, that no feeble word-painting of mine can reproduce it, even in outline. The snow-mantled Cordillera in the background appeared still more stupendous the nearer we approached; the underlying mountains still brighter in hue, with every conceivable shade of colour represented—green, purple, orange, black, red, and thousands of *nuances* for which there are no verbal equivalents; the bridges (of which we crossed eight) seemed longer and higher, and the river below swifter and more boisterous; the tunnels (five in number), if possible, gloomier and more awe-inspiring. Upon one side towered a sheer wall of rock, which one could have touched with the outstretched hand, and upon the other lay a precipitous descent of many hundreds of feet ; the track hung upon a mere ledge of rock wide enough for the narrow-gauge line and no more. Then came cuttings so deep and narrow as to suggest the idea of tunnels with the roofs cut off ; and occasionally, when a light cloud passed across the face of the sun, one could drink in and steep one's soul in the exquisite gradations of hue that swept across the many-coloured hills !

My companions had been over the ground so often that for them these localities had lost the charm of novelty ; but they thoroughly enjoyed my enthusiastic admiration of all that I saw, as good-natured fellows always do, when they see that their efforts to give pleasure are crowned with success. And they actually produced beer (none of your Argentine 'she-oak,' but the genuine red-triangle Bass's pale ale, dear to the heart of all true Britons), and we drank the health of our Queen, and of the *Times*, and of Messrs. Clark, and of our noble selves, until of that delicious beer there remained not one drop. Fortunately, the cows gave us a wide berth, and in the fulness of time we reached Uspallata without other mishap than the loss of a hat (luckily not mine). The line went no further,* and here we had to stay overnight,

* It has since been pushed on to Rio Blanco, twenty-miles further.

awaiting the arrival of the mules. After lunch our kind friends bade us farewell, and started upon the return journey to Mendoza. Before doing so, however, Mr. N—— informed me that a French lad, some sixteen years of age, had been waiting here some days for an opportunity to join some party proceeding to Chile. Would I take charge of him? The boy himself asked me so prettily to allow him to accompany me, that I had not the heart to refuse; but scarcely was the train out of sight when I discovered that my protégé had no clothes but those he stood in, no mules, and but very little money. Evidently I should have to supply him with these necessary adjuncts to travel, and until I heard his story I felt annoyed at having too easily given my consent. Then I relented; the more so as I at once saw that his was one of those hypersensitive, shy natures that *must* fasten on to some stronger will than their own, or come to hopeless grief. I had even some doubts as to his perfect sanity, doubts by no means shared by Señor Guillermo, who assured me that my lost child was clearly as mad as a hatter. *loco de atar* Briefly his story was this: His parents, well-to-do Belgian bourgeois, had sanctioned his making a voyage to Buenos Aires, for his health, in an English ship, and under the care of the captain. Arrived at his destination, having a month to wait for the return voyage and 20,000 francs to his credit, he took it into his head to see something of Argentina, packed up a portmanteau, drew some money, and started off inland, finally reaching Mendoza. Here a wild desire seized him to cross the Andes and have a peep at Chile, and this he furthermore contemplated doing on foot; so leaving his portmanteau in Mendoza, he took train to Uspallata. Here his pedestrian plan had been frightened out of him, and he had stuck—afraid to go forward, yet utterly unwilling to go back. I thoroughly believed the lad's story, and I may add that I have since verified it in every detail. I tried hard to persuade him to return, but this he tearfully but resolutely refused to do. He would follow me on foot, if need be; but follow me he *would*. Finally, I agreed to take him as far as Puente del Inca, where he was to await the return of my muleteer from Chile; and to this arrangement he temporarily consented.

There is not any regular *posada* at Uspallata, though there is a canteen at the station and a fairly good general store where a few travellers can get a shakedown at a pinch. For us the boy in charge of this latter place made special efforts, evidently realizing that the credit of the township was at stake. Upon returning from a refreshing but intensely cold plunge into an adjacent lagoon, it was evident, from the bustle going on, that preparations upon an unwonted scale were in full swing. My lost child (whose name, by the way, was Robert) whispered me that in all his three days' experience he had seen nothing at all like it. At intervals there had reached his ears shrill screams as of fowls in their death agony, and he was almost certain that he had recognised the squeals of a youthful porker *in extremis*. But, most wonderful of all, he had seen a *peon* laying *a table-cloth!* Robert's powers of observation had not misled him. When we, later on, sat down to dine, the table-cloth was there, and we were regaled with chicken soup, roast fowl, and sucking pig, the whole washed down by some very fair Mendoza wine. I had been warned that our experiences of 'roughing it' would commence at Uspallata, but methought I could rough it upon this scale for a lengthy period. To sleep upon, there were stretchers resembling elongated camp-stools, whilst the stock-in-trade furnished a liberal supply of blankets. The couch reserved for me was even adorned with what I took to be a sheet, but which Robert at once recognised as that crowning luxury —the table-cloth.

Next morning we were aroused betimes by our muleteer, who pressed us to lose no time in making a start. To him I confided my wish to take Robert with me if possible. Certainly, he could ride one of the spare mules if a saddle could be procured. But, as regarded the señor's baggage— this, I informed him, need not weigh upon his mind, inasmuch as the young gentleman had brought none. Whereupon the muleteer scratched his head and remarked :

'Of course the señor knows best. But it would be very bad for *our* business if everyone travelled with one shirt.'

And José proceeded to load up his mules, whilst we breakfasted upon the débris of the last night's banquet—the protean table-cloth, which had reappeared upon the board, being removed by general request.* The reckoning paid, a stirrup-cup partaken of, a saddle borrowed for Robert, and we were ready for the road.

'Does your excellency ride well?' queried our guide, who had a true Spanish habit of conferring brevet-rank upon his patrons.

'Moderately well,' I replied cautiously, my Australian and other experiences having, long ago, taught me the unwisdom of vaunting one's horsemanship in a foreign land.

'Ah! I thought so, señor; most English *caballeros* can ride. That is why I have picked out *El Ministro* there to carry you,' indicating a gaunt animal of exceptional stature for a mule. 'He's the best *macho* I've got, and used to be one of the quietest. But ever since he carried Señor Godoy,

* The reader will doubtless remember the analogous experiences of a guest at a French country *auberge*, who was aroused at an early hour, with a request that he would at once get up. 'Why should I get up?' 'Because,' replied the garçon, 'I want to lay the table for breakfast, and monsieur *is sleeping upon the table-cloth.*'

the Chilian Minister for *Londres* (that's why he's called *El Ministro*), he has become proud, and plays tricks occasionally. I dare say he will go quietly enough with your excellency, but be careful of his heels just at first when you mount him.'

This last piece of advice proved not uncalled for. No sooner did *El Ministro* feel my foot in the stirrup than he lashed out savagely, to the accompaniment of a succession of shrill squeals. However, at the second attempt I got safely into the saddle, and, having no intention of risking my neck upon the brute if I could not master him, plunged my spurs into his lean ribs. A battle royal ensued, to the great delight of the onlookers; but in the end *El Ministro* gave in, nor did he ever afterwards give me any trouble.

Quite an imposing cavalcade did our party present as we passed by the station *en route* for Rio Blanco, distant some twenty odd English miles. At the head rode the muleteer's boy upon a small gray mare, to whose headstall was fixed a loud-sounding and not unmusical bell, the mules being trained to follow a bell-mare just as sheep follow a bell-wether. Then came the four members of my party in no particular order, behind us the baggage-mules, the spare mules, driven by the *arriero*, bringing up the rear. Hampered as we were by the baggage, our pace was necessarily slow; indeed, it took us seven hours, without a halt, to accomplish the twenty miles.

For a couple of hours our way lay through a wide plateau, and then we entered a ravine, hemmed in by towering alps of awful grandeur, which endured to the end of the stage. The day was exceptionally warm, and towards noon one's ideas began to take the form of liquid refreshments. I therefore proposed a brief halt for this purpose. But then came the trouble. No such refreshments were to be found. I had several times enjoined on my secretary to be especially careful upon this point; in fact, to consider it *pro tem.* as his only duty. I had myself purchased the necessary fluids. It now appeared that in the excitement of departure they had been left behind. Then I waxed wroth, and I said unkind things of my secretary and of philosophers generally; and wrath begat worse thirst, and I was fain to ask the *arriero* to procure me even a drink of water.

'Impossible, señor,' replied José, 'until we reach the *posada* at Rio Blanco.'

'But, my good man,' I remonstrated, 'we are travelling parallel with the river.'

'*Si, señor*, but we can't get down to it.'

This was but too true. There was the icy-cold, foaming current rushing along a hundred feet below; but the descent was sheer.

I am especially sensitive to thirst, and, I believe, suffered more than the others. But it chanced that a dog—a rather well-bred collie—had followed us, and in noting its distress I well-nigh forgot my own. Poor brute! how it scoured the ground for a stray puddle, where none existed! How, ever and anon, it rushed to the precipitous bank and gazed, with hanging tongue, at the foaming torrent below, as though minded to make one spring and die in water! At last, at a spot where the ravine widened considerably, I perceived a white speck, half a mile away, which I at once knew to be a tent. With a vicious plunge of the spurs, I headed my mule towards the welcome object, my companions pursuing the even tenor of their way, but the collie sticking close to *El Ministro's* heels. It is surprising how fast a mule can gallop, for a short distance, over rough ground. In a couple of minutes I had reached the tent. No one there; the owner, doubtless a railway-navvy, was away at work. But there was a cask of water and a pannikin, and I filled a tin wash-basin for the dog. My wants were soon satisfied, and, oh, how delicious that water was! I left a dollar in the pannikin to express my thanks, and the collie, having drunk its fill, looked up into my face with its great brown, loving eyes to express *its* thanks, and away we scampered, helter-skelter, to rejoin the cavalcade. I told my companions of my discovery, but they were too lazy or not thirsty enough to profit by it.

Some miles further on we observed a man skulking about in most mysterious fashion close to the river-bank. Presently he noticed us, and waved his arms as though he desired to speak with us, at the same time staggering in our direction; whereupon we rode towards him. A queer-looking object! He turned out to be an American mechanic, on his way to Chile on foot. He was half dead with thirst, and had been trying to spy out a track down to the river. Could we give him some water? I explained our own situation, and offered him a lift, upon a spare mule, to the *posada*, then about six miles distant. But this he, not very politely, declined. He did not want my —— mule! He wanted water, and if I had none, why, there was an end of it. Perhaps he could afford a mule as well as I could, or better. If he preferred to walk, what business was that of mine? So I left him, for an ill-conditioned, cantankerous brute, to leave his bones upon the river-bank, if the Fates so willed it. But he did not. He turned up at the *posada* some hours after us.

At Rio Blanco (so called from the milk-white colour of the water which here comes rushing down from the mountains) we stayed overnight. The accommodation, although rougher than at Uspallata, was yet tolerable; and I remember that certain bottles of lager-bier, cooled in the river, were especially good.

Next day (March 10th), having a journey of forty-six miles to accomplish before nightfall, our *arriero* insisted on a very early start. Whilst he was saddling and packing the mules, José incidentally mentioned that he had driven the animals several miles the evening before, to the nearest browsing ground, had slept amongst them, under the stars, rolled up in his *poncho*, and had but just brought them back. A pretty hard life, that of the Andine muleteer.

'And, señor,' said José, with a grin, 'I have re-christened *El Ministro*. He will now be known as *El Corresponsal*.'

'I suppose,' I answered, 'if he should ever carry Balmaceda across the range, he will become *El Presidente?*'

'*Quien sabe, señor?* More unlikely things have come to pass. But take my advice, and don't talk about Balmaceda like that when you get into Chile —*Macho!*—*oo*—*ay*—*Macho!*' And we slowly started upon our way.

We reached a sort of farmhouse *posada* at Punta de Las Vacas at about mid-day, and here we fell into most hospitable hands. The place appeared to be kept by three young fellows, evidently fairly well off, to judge by the number of cows, horses, mules, goats, pigs, fowls, and dogs (of which last there must have been at least fifty), which we saw. One of the proprietors, who, as I understood, was specially interested in goat-breeding, at once explained the reason of the unwonted efforts made on our behalf.

He had, by dint of study and with occasional help from stray Englishmen, learnt enough English to understand the written language fairly well, and derived most of his knowledge of contemporary history from the *Times* weekly edition, to which he was a subscriber. Hence he esteemed it a high honour to entertain a *corresponsal* of the *gran diario*. And when the *arriero* began to grumble at the delay in preparing lunch, he bade him begone with his baggage-mules, for that he would himself conduct the Señor Corresponsal's party to Las Cuevas later on. By this arrangement, we had ample time to do justice to the abundant fare set before us, and for an hour's rest afterwards. The collie was recognised as the property of an English engineer; and though the animal tried to follow us, it was speedily lassoed and chained up. Our host's chums started with us, to see us a part of the way, but eventually accompanied us the whole distance.

Unhampered by the baggage-mules, we were able to cover the ground at a good pace, whilst our guides enlivened the journey by pointing out the most interesting freaks of Nature, which here abound.

To the right arose dark jagged masses of hornblende and schist, the smoother lower portions of which, seamed and scored, gave ample evidence of glacial action. These are known as the Montes Conales.

Further on, upon the other side, stood the most extraordinary rock formation I ever beheld. Upon the slope of a distant hill was an almost perfect counterpart of a huge monastery, whilst lower down certain other groups of rock exactly represented processions of pilgrims ascending the hill. The name Monte de Los Penitentes very happily describes the impression produced upon the beholder; yet, we were assured, upon near approach the illusion entirely disappears. Truly

' 'Tis distance lends enchantment to the view,'

though I never before so fully realized the truth of Campbell's well-known line.

We wasted so much time admiring Los Penitentes that it was deemed necessary to quicken our pace ; and, all being in excellent spirits, a race to a boulder about a mile distant was proposed and agreed to. We were here in a wide valley, and the going fairly good, so we got into line. I fired my revolver as a signal, and away we went. It soon became evident that our guides' mules were fresher and better than ours, with the one possible exception of my tall moke, now christened *El Corresponsal*, and even he was sadly outpaced for half the distance. Now, I had noticed that he had started under me when I fired, and it occurred to me that if I fired again, *behind him*, his mulish brain might be startled into further efforts. The idea was an inspiration. Hearing the report, apparently in the immediate vicinity of his hind-quarters, the brute fairly bounded along, and passed the rearmost of my three rivals. It cost two more explosions to get him past the next man. And now there remained but the leader, some ten lengths ahead, with about a hundred and fifty yards yet to be covered. I noted with satisfaction that he was spurring mercilessly to maintain his lead. Then, when fifty yards from the goal, I fired my last two remaining shots in rapid succession. In a frenzy of fright *Corresponsal* plunged forward, swept past the leader like a whirlwind, and won by half a dozen lengths, about the same distance separating second and third. As for the others, they were 'working their passages' at intervals, Robert (whose saddle, it afterwards appeared, had turned round early in the race) whipping in. There was a general laugh when I explained my novel method of stimulating a mule, which was redoubled when, upon my own confession, I disqualified *Corresponsal*, and awarded the race to the second animal.

Our rapid progress was delayed in the Valle de la Tolorzia, owing to the very uneven nature of the ground. Here the strata seen are twisted and contorted in every conceivable direction, as though Nature had given them birth during an extra violent convulsion. Here, too, as at Montes Conales, the evidences of ice action are plainly visible.

Late in the afternoon we overtook the baggage-mules at Puente del Inca, a marvellous natural bridge, over which the railway will later on pass.

Beneath this bridge are grottos, adorned with innumerable stalactites, and containing thermal springs, which enjoy a high medicinal reputation both in Argentina and in Chile. Much to the surprise of Señor Guillermo, his friend Pedro had departed with the other correspondents for Chile, whence, as we afterwards learnt, they almost immediately returned. We would fain have stopped here overnight, but our muleteers insisted upon pushing on to Las Cuevas, alleging that the distance from Puente del Inca to the summit of the Cordillera was too great for the mules to perform before 10 a.m., at which hour dangerously strong winds commence to sweep the frozen pinnacle. Our Las Vacas friends confirmed this statement; and so, with barely time for refreshment and an all too brief inspection of the beauties of the Inca's Bridge, we made a start for Las Cuevas, the baggage-mules again preceding us.

The sun had set ere we reached the Cajon del Rio de las Cuevas—a chasm of unknown profundity—and as there is scarcely any twilight in the Andes, the last mile of our journey was effected in total darkness. Trusting entirely to the instinct of our mules, though the track here is known to be extremely dangerous, we safely arrived at last at the *posada*. The dinner was quite good enough for hungry travellers to do justice to it; but when the question of sleeping accommodation was broached, and we were shown our quarters, we knew that at least we were ' in for roughing it' with a vengeance. It was a shed used apparently as a lumber-room, hen-roost, dog-kennel, and asylum generally for such animals as preferred a roof to the open air. However, with the help of a liberal supply of blankets, we made the best of it. Having prepared what appeared to be a cosy corner, I was just about to extinguish the light and turn in, when I espied a colony of fowls roosting just above my head. Now, there are obvious and valid objections to these neighbours, and, as I did not care to abandon my corner, I decided to dislodge the enemy. First my own boots and then other people's boots, and then every missile I could first lay hands on, were hurled in rapid succession at those intrusive birds. With wild cries they flew, fluttered, and fell about the room. The dogs, inside and out, hearing the din, joined in with great spirit; two goats, hitherto unnoticed, careered wildly about the place—all was noise and confusion.

'*Mon Dieu!*' cried Monsieur L——, waking with a jump, whilst Robert and my secretary sat rubbing their eyes in bewilderment. '*Mon Dieu! qu'est ce qu'il y a donc?*'

I explained as well as I could, for laughing.

'*Mais c'est infâme!*' cried the irritated Frenchman, making a wild grab at a fugitive fowl hotly pursued by a terrier. '*A la porte toute la bande!*' And, opening the door, he, assisted by the other two, and by the dogs, which vastly enjoyed the impromptu fowl-hunt, made frantic efforts to expel the disturbers of his slumbers. As for me, I could do nothing but roar with laughter. If the row was bad before, it was now ten times worse.

'*Pero, por Dios, caballeros, que hay?*' exclaimed the owner of a shock-head appearing at the door. He speedily understood the situation and duly apologized. 'But,' said he, 'who could expect that the *caballeros* would mind a few fowls ?'

'A few fowls !' cried Monsieur L——; 'why, it's a veritable menagerie !'

However, the intruders were at length expelled, and we finished the night in peace.

With all his efforts, José found it difficult to get us away by seven o'clock next morning, and at the last moment Robert tearfully objected to returning to Puente del Inca (as per agreement), and begged so hard to be allowed to go on with me that, as usual, I gave way.

The ascent to the Cumbre, the topmost point of the Cordillera, and more than 13,000 feet above sea-level, is naturally very steep, and the track is made as tortuous as possible to ease the mules. Hence it was nearly ten o'clock ere we reached the summit, an ice-bound plateau, and commenced the descent upon the Chilian side, which is far steeper than the other. Indeed, so precipitous is the fall, that even the mules could with difficulty keep their footing, and for a short distance it was deemed prudent to dismount and descend on foot. The traveller readily understands how completely impassable this track is in the winter-time, when buried beneath many fathoms of snow. It may be noted that the pass is, ordinarily, quite safe, so far as snow is concerned, between the months of October and May, and is frequently traversed by ladies. The Andine mules are so marvellously surefooted that accidents are of rare occurrence. So the most timid reader, who may deem sublime scenery worth a long voyage, need be under no special apprehension about crossing the Cordillera at the right season.

About 3,500 feet from the summit lies the Laguna del Portillo, as dreary a sheet of water as the world, perhaps, contains, but, surrounded on all sides by lofty hills, picturesque in its very desolation. It is, of course, fed by the snow, which melts in the summer-time. Near the lake is a rough stone shanty, for the shelter of weary or weather-beaten travellers.

Beyond this is a precipitous descent, adorned by a thundering cascade, and known as the Salto del Soldado, or Soldier's Leap. The name was due to some unfortunate deserter, the guide said, who preferred death in this form to recapture. In wild grandeur, it scarcely comes up to Govett's Leap in the Blue Mountains of New South Wales.

The junction of the rivers Blanco and Mendoza occurs in a valley of unsurpassed beauty. One could watch for hours the milk-white waters of the Blanco rushing along to unite with the clear stream of the Mendoza, amid a profusion of luxuriant, if somewhat stunted, vegetation. It has nothing in common with the Vale of Avoca, but is, on a wilder scale, quite as effective a meeting of the waters.

The most conspicuous landmark from the Cumbre, looking in the direction of Chile, is El Juncal, a huge extinct volcano, towards which we had been slowly making our way. At the foot of El Juncal is a capital little *posada*, which we reached at about 1 p.m. Here we had luncheon and heard some good news.

I should have stated that, hearing at Puente del Inca that a carriage-road existed between Juncal and Santa Rosa de Los Andes, I telegraphed to the authorities at the latter town requesting that a conveyance might be permitted to meet me at Juncal. This was necessary, as the passport system was being strictly enforced. We now learnt that a carriage was on its way to pick us up. At three o'clock it made its appearance, an ancient but roomy barouche, drawn by good horses yoked three abreast. After all this mule-work, it was a distinct treat to do the last seventy kilometres on wheels. José undertook to be in Los Andes with the baggage-mules early next morning; and, the driver having changed his horses, away we went at a hand-gallop. Señor

Guillermo confessed to me afterwards that he never regretted anything so much in his life as having abandoned his mule. And, in good sooth, it was a sensational drive.

It must be remembered that we were not yet out of the Andes, that, in fact, we had seventy kilometres of mountain work yet to do before reaching Santa Rosa, which lies at the foot of the Chilian side of the range. It soon became apparent that the vaunted carriage-road was, in the most dangerous places, little better than a mule-track— just wide enough for four wheels. At certain intervals recesses had been made to enable vehicles to turn or to pass each other ; but what would be done if two met at any considerable distance from such a recess, witness knoweth not. As we sped along, it became evident that our driver was a first-rate whip, and confidence revived. But, at first, to lean out and see the wheels passing within a few inches of a sheer descent, reminded me of New Zealand coaching in the olden days, and gave me a cold shiver. When we came to the worst part of the ascent a boy on horseback awaited us to give us a tow. And a stiff climb it was for the game little horses, so stiff that I several times proposed to get out and walk. But this the driver would not hear of.

'No, señor,' he said ; 'it's hard work, but they can do it. I have to work hard ; I dare say your excellency works hard also. You pay for their corn, and they must earn it.' My philosopher secretary affirmed that our driver was a born logician. If so, he presently made it appear that he had another side to his character.

As we were nearing the summit, I heard a snap, and felt unmistakably that some accident had befallen the spring especially responsible for my person. Arrived at the top, I made known my conviction to our jehu. He got down and found that, in fact, one of the many metal layers which, welded together, form a spring (their technical name I know not) had parted company with its fellows. However, a few turns of stout whipcord soon settled that matter entirely to his satisfaction; but not so entirely to mine.

'*Cochero*,' I inquired, 'do you think that spring will stand?'

'*Quien sabe, señor!*' he answered, briskly mounting to his seat. '*Puede ser!*' (*Who knows, sir! Perhaps it will.*) And the boy having disappeared, we commenced the descent at a brisk canter.

This was more than a philosopher could stand. Guillermo, who sat next to Robert upon the front seat, stood up to expostulate. Did the *cochero* want to kill us and himself? In the name of reason, with a broken spring, why not go more slowly? But the 'born logician' would not listen to argument, until, at last, the philosopher lost patience, revoked his former opinion, and even, in his wrath, cast aspersions upon our jehu's pedigree. Whereupon jehu also waxed wroth, and answered :

'See you here, sir : even a dog has but one master at a time. I serve the Señor Corresponsal, and from him only will I take my orders.'

But I, partly, I fear, not to be outdone by Monsieur L——, who was taking matters very calmly, held my peace. And Señor Guillermo remained standing until we came to more level ground, avowedly in order that when the inevitable crash came he might be prepared to spring out. No crash, however, did come, and, upon the whole, I have seldom enjoyed a wheel-gallop more.

At a distance of a few miles from Santa Rosa we stopped at the Custom-house, where we were politely informed that no examination of baggage would be necessary. But were the passports of the gentlemen accompanying me *en règle ?* I had arranged my secretary's, and Monsieur L—— had his, but Robert, of course, had none. Then would the Señor Corresponsal vouch for the young gentleman's respectability ? Of course, he was travelling under my protection. That was quite sufficient, the señor and his friends could proceed ; and after an elaborate series of bows we proceeded. It was nearly nine o'clock when we reached Santa Rosa and drew up at the Hotel Colon. And oh ! the comfort of sitting down once more to a first-class supper, with, above all, the certain prospect of a good bed.

CHAPTER IV.

CHILE AND ITS CONDITION.

Santiago—A State of Siege—Revolutionist Opinions of President Balmaceda—Wanted: Evidence—I hear the other Side of the Question—An Interview with Balmaceda—His Views—A Review of the Situation—A Sketch of Chilian Society—Chile and British Enterprise—Colonel North and his Mission—Dr. Russell upon 'Chile and the Nitrate Fields'— Realized Prophecy — Revolutionary Tactics — I arrive at Conclusions—Right or Wrong?

José did not turn up with his mules and our baggage so early as he had promised—not, indeed, before 3 p.m. There was, consequently, ample time to have a good look round the pretty township of Santa Rosa de Los Andes. Like nearly all the towns in South America, it is laid out in squares, of which a side measures about a hundred and twenty yards. The streets are wide, decently paved, and lined with rows of well-grown poplars. The public buildings are not noteworthy. Beyond a return visit to Don Manuel Nuñez, Governor of the province, who had welcomed me very cordially to Chile, and a rapid inspection of the extensive workshops of the Messrs. Clark (of whose Transandine Railway Santa Rosa is the Chilian terminus), paying off José, and catching the 6.20 train for Santiago, nothing remained to be done. We duly reached the capital at 11 o'clock, and installed ourselves at the Gran Hotel de Francia. Here I said farewell to Monsieur L——, who purposed proceeding to Valparaiso by an early train, and it is satisfactory to record that we parted with mutual regret; but, of course, I still had my Lost Child on my hands, and considerable trouble the dear boy gave me before I finally started him for *La Belle France*.

We were now fairly upon the scene of our future labours, and it behoved my secretary and myself to bestir ourselves. He, being an Argentine, was necessarily strongly prejudiced against all things Chilian, just as Chilians regard with contempt all things Argentine. He had no particular sympathies either with or against the existing Government, and might reasonably be expected to form an unbiased opinion, based upon his own observations. I therefore gave him *carte blanche*, together with a sufficiency of dollars, to pursue his investigations independently of mine. Two heads are better than one, but more especially when one is the head of a philosopher. It was, moreover, further agreed that, should I find communication with the outer world blocked or hampered, he was to bear despatches back to Puente del Inca, whence they could be transmitted *viâ* Buenos Aires, said despatches being previously committed to memory, so as to obviate the danger of carrying compromising papers. This possibly necessary expedient was, indeed, my principal reason for bringing him with me.

Upon the day succeeding our arrival—and, indeed, for many subsequent days—I was favoured with a pretty continuous stream of visitors, all patriotically anxious to enlighten me upon the political situation. It was my duty to listen, and I pride myself upon being a perfect Boswell in this respect. Certainly my endurance was sorely tested: I was interviewed 'from morn till dewy eve'; and if I failed to grasp the logic of the revolutionist arguments, it assuredly was not from lack of instruction. Some of my informants appeared to take my advocacy of the insurgent cause for granted. The bare fact that I was English was almost enough; the fact that I represented the *Times* was, or should be, more than enough. But these deductions I at once overruled. It was true that the sympathies of most Englishmen in England, led by the press, were upon the side of Congress; but it was also true that the opinions of this sympathy-directing press were based entirely upon *ex parte* revolutionary statements, and that even these statements had latterly become so obviously inaccurate and contradictory as to beget a general distrust of all Chilian news received. It was true that I represented the *Times*, but I did so, according to my written instructions, as a perfectly free agent, whether my views should coincide with those held by the leading journal or not. It must be clearly understood that I had not travelled 12,000 miles merely to play echo to Congressionalist statements, and that, although I could not help being somewhat prejudiced in favour of Congress, I would allow no such prejudices to guide me in arriving at a decision. It was easy to denounce Balmaceda as a tyrant, a ruffian, a murderer; but I required evidence of his tyranny, of his ruffianism, of his murders. One gentleman, claiming to be an Englishman and 'in business,' and who, should this book ever fall into his hands, may possibly recognise himself under the initial X——, undertook to supply me with the required proofs in abundance; and I rejoiced to think that I should have such solid material to work upon. He would, upon leaving me, at once proceed to reduce the whole affair to black and white.

'Meanwhile,' he proceeded, 'you can see for yourself on all sides abundant evidence of Balmaceda's tyranny.'

' Where ?' I asked, producing my note-book.

' Well, in the first place, Santiago has been declared in a state of siege.'

It flashed across my mind that I was in a state of siege also.

' Yes,' said I, ' so I understand; but the declaration does not seem to press very hard upon the citizens. A deaf man might live here a long time without finding it out, I imagine.'

'Ah yes, outwardly things appear quiet enough; but it places enormous power in the hands of Balmaceda's police. Why, in the suite of rooms opposite to yours a leading member of our party is confined to the hotel on parole; and a special gaol has been fitted up for political prisoners, where upwards of forty prominent men are at the present moment under lock and key. One of the very chiefs of the revolutionary movement, Carlos Walker Martinez, has been driven to hide himself at the British Embassy to avoid arrest. Is not all this tyranny?'

'Unquestionably,' I asserted, 'this is tyranny; but it is hardly sensational enough for my purpose. Can you, sir, supply me with a single instance of a revolution, ancient or modern, which was not accompanied by such imprisonments, or worse? Detention upon parole in a first-class hotel is a novelty, and so also, so far as I am aware, is the conversion of a British Embassy into an asylum for a person who, on your own showing, is a rebel leader. I must have more than this—a great deal more.'

'And you shall have it, my dear sir,' exclaimed my visitor. 'Read carefully the paper which I will complete and bring you later on. It will convince you—it must convince you—that Balmaceda is the worst kind of monster. I had intended to address it to a friend in England, for publication in an English provincial journal; but it will come with more force through the columns of the *Times*.'

And he departed, I following pretty close on his heels, to escape any more interviewing, of which, for that day, I had had quite enough.

The city of Santiago has been described so many times by others that I do not purpose dwelling upon its beauties and defects; yet cannot I forbear adding my tribute of admiration of the wondrous rock, yclept Santa Lucia, which dominates the town. Originally a stronghold for the primæval handful of Spaniards against the incessant attacks of the warlike natives, in more modern times a mere stony excrescence, it became, thanks to the life-long devotion of the late Señor Mackenna,

'A thing of beauty, and a joy for ever.'

Thither can the wearied citizen or the curious traveller repair, on foot or in carriage, and from the summit enjoy the most magnificent panorama which, I think, the world affords. At his feet lies the entire city of Santiago, as plainly set forth as the scenes in the cycloramas which used to be (and perhaps still are) travelling round the world; behind him, the giant Cordillera, with its eternally snow-capped heights—distant indeed, but which appear so close. And if he be tired after the ascent, or derive appetite from the beauteous scene, an excellent restaurant lies to his hand. What more can mortal expect or desire?

One other noticeable fact struck me in the course of my subsequent drives and walks : almost all the finest public buildings appeared to be quite new, or in course of completion, the explanation whereof was (according to the respective political bias of my informants) that Balmaceda was bringing the country to bankruptcy by his insensate extravagance, or that he was leading Chile to the front rank amongst South American republics.

And here I must ask those of my readers who regard a book upon foreign travel as necessarily a record of more or less exciting incidents and adventures to skip many portions of this chapter, since what adventures I had befell me much later on. Be it remembered that I am, primarily, writing about the Revolution in Chile—*as I saw it;* and clearly a book (however loosely constructed) without some explanation of the political situation would be too much 'like the play of Hamlet without the Prince.' At all events, I can only tell my story in my own way.

I saw nothing of my secretary that night. Doubtless he was pursuing his investigations according to his lights ; or possibly he had fallen foul of the state of siege, and was in durance vile. But I found my Lost Child awaiting me at the hotel, and also the promised manuscript. After dinner I sent Robert off to the theatre (the young dog subsequently confessed to a music-hall), with my addressed card in case he got into any trouble, for he did not know a word of Spanish, and tackled the annihilation of Balmaceda, foreshadowed by X——, taking notes as I read. As a document denunciatory of Balmaceda, his aiders and abettors, the paper left little unsaid; well-nigh every English adjective indicative of moral crookedness was introduced, in the superlative degree. But—it was all assertion. Not one atom of proof was adduced. As an expression of individual opinion, from a revolutionist in Chile to a friend in England, this sort of reiterated abuse might be pronounced forcible, and might carry conviction. But, so far as I was concerned, it was worthless. Evidence was what I wanted, and evidence there was none.

Next day X—— called, with a packet in his hand — presumably a supplementary edition of superlatives. I had meantime made certain inquiries concerning this revolutionist emissary.

'Good-morning,' said he; 'I have brought you a few more notes——'

'Pardon me,' I interrupted, 'are they from the same pen as those you left for me last night?'

'Most certainly,' he replied, 'and upon the same lines. I sat up till——'

'Then, sir,' said I, somewhat rudely, I fear, 'so far as I am concerned, you sat up to no purpose. I asked you for bread, and you gave me a stone. You promised me proof, and you have supplied me with denunciatory rubbish which has, long ago, appeared in every paper in Europe. Take my advice, and, before you mail it home, stick in a few names and a little more detail. Another piece of advice: Don't underrate the intelligence of the Britisher. Your accent betrays you, and your profession is easily found out. Stick to the "Stars and Stripes" (there is nothing to be ashamed of in them); but, candidly, your employers have been very badly advised in trying to palm off upon me a Yankee stock-jobber as an "English business-man."'

(This and the preceding conversation are literally, or very nearly literally, *verbatim*, as I noted them down whilst fresh in my memory.)

Finding no retort ready, he gathered up his papers and departed, to inform all and sundry (as I subsequently heard) that 'the fellow at the Grand Hotel is no more the correspondent of the *Times* than I am.' And after this, beyond sending me copies of their surreptitious paper, *La Revolucion*, the revolutionists left me severely alone, contenting themselves with stabbing me behind my back, by cablegrams and letters to London. This I did not, of course, know till long afterwards. But what if I had known? I was special correspondent of the *Times*. I had not lived long enough to accept a commission as Descriptive Writer for a Nitrate King. I held no brief. And whether or not my conclusions should prove favourable or the reverse to Chilian agitators and their foreign sympathizers, I was resolved that these conclusions should be based upon the evidence of my own senses.

My secretary and I devoted several entire days to a careful study of the events which had culminated in open rupture between President and Congress, pursuing our investigations independently, and subsequently comparing notes. Speeches, pamphlets, etc., setting forth the views of the leaders upon either side, were easily procurable in abundance, and there was the Chilian Constitution itself to steer by. Moreover, I had letters of introduction to several leading residents, who one and all turned out to be anti-Balmacedists, and who, having watched the progress of events for years, were in a position to make out the strongest possible case for Congress. They warned me not to hold too strongly by the Constitution, framed sixty years ago, and quite inconsistent with modern ideas of government, assuring me that there had sprung up a *lex non scripta* largely tempering its autocratic provisions. Now, *leges non scriptæ* are vague, indeterminate factors in legislation, capable of being twisted in any required direction at the will of any temporary Parliamentary majority. I mistrusted these unascertainable, erratic, unwritten laws.

It chanced that a wealthy mine-owner, Señor Alfred Ovalle, had been very intimate with the gentleman who preceded me as *Times* correspondent, and for that reason called upon me. In course of conversation, I learned that after some fifteen years of struggle as a working miner he had at length struck ore so rich that he had sprung at a bound from poverty to affluence, being now known as the 'Chilian Silver King.' Of him and of his amiable family I subsequently saw a great deal; nor shall I ever cease to remember with gratitude the bounteous hospitality invariably extended to me. In politics, he, at this time, held a very open mind. With President Balmaceda he was on such strained terms that he did not visit the *Moneda* (Government House). Indeed, he spoke very severely of the President as a man who, although possessing great natural ability, was largely responsible for the revolution, owing to his susceptibility to flattery, his extreme good-nature, and his utter incapacity for saying 'No' to anyone whom he deemed his friend.

'But, my good sir,' I remonstrated, 'when you speak of the President as "extremely good-natured," are you aware that he is almost universally regarded as a most bloodthirsty, remorseless tyrant?'

'Oh yes, I know that. The *Oposidores* (Oppositionists) have been at great pains to throw dust in the eyes of the foreign press, which Balmaceda has entirely neglected. But bloodthirsty tyrants shed blood. What blood has he shed?* See you

---

* So far [the revolution, apart from the fighting in the north, had been conspicuously free from b. iodshed. Scrim-

here. Two-thirds of the men who stirred up this revolution owe their political existence to the man whom they now turn to rend. If he *had* shot half a dozen of them, all this devil's work would have been nipped in the bud. But there! you can hardly be a fool, or you would scarcely have been sent out here on your present mission. Go and see the man yourself, talk with him, watch him narrowly, and judge whether he be the ogre he is painted.'

This was clearly good advice, and I decided to act upon it. I despatched a note to the principal secretary, asking at what time his excellency could conveniently receive me. An aide-de-camp brought back the reply : the President would be expecting me at four o'clock.

The news had just arrived of the defeat of Balmaceda's troops at Pozo Almonte, and created a great sensation. It was known that Colonel Robles had been killed, and the greater portion of his 1,200 men killed or wounded. This I, of course, at once wired to London, the line being opened for me upon presentation of my card. And

---

mages with the police had, indeed, occurred, and the guardians of order were accused of acting with unnecessary brutality. This seemed probable enough. But, so far as I could learn, but one life (that of a deputy, Señor Ossa) had been sacrificed in these street rows. Of course no notice could be taken of the vague, unsubstantiated charges of outrage, freely alleged to have occurred in various parts of the country, and unhesitatingly believed in by revolutionary sympathizers. One can take nothing on trust in a South American republic.

it may be as well here to state briefly the positions, offensive and defensive, of the rival parties at this time.

Upon January 7 the commanders of the only three ironclads in the Chilian fleet, the *Blanco Encalada*, the *Cochrane*, and the *Huascar*, declared for Congress and revolted. The wooden vessels, numbering about a dozen, had no choice but to follow suit, even had their commanders been otherwise inclined, which is more than doubtful. At all events, Balmaceda found himself without even so much as a cutter. A large number of dissatisfied members of Congress went on board the men-of-war, which in due course proceeded north to attack Iquique. Now, two very important facts must be borne in mind. Chile, being a very long, narrow strip of land, may be regarded as practically all coast-line; consequently the command of the sea is all-important, and Congress commenced with an enormous advantage. Secondly, Iquique is the capital of Tarapacá, the largest and richest of the provinces conquered from Peru in the last war, and is the port whence by far the largest portion of that valuable commodity, nitrate of soda, is shipped; and when it is stated that the export duties upon nitrate yield some $30,000,000 *per annum*, the value of the northern capital as a basis for operations will be at once understood. Why, it may be asked, did not the fleet attack Valparaiso, itself a very hotbed of sympathizers with Congress?

ATTACK ON THE 'COCHRANE' BY TORPEDO BOATS.

The answer is simple. The army (which then numbered only some 6,000 men) stood by the President, and Valparaiso is very strongly fortified. This behaviour of the troops was a great disappointment to the insurgent leaders, who had counted upon their co-operation. However, as matters stood, it was decided to attack Iquique, establish there the revolutionary headquarters, defray expenses by appropriating the nitrate duties, and trust to time and diplomacy for the final result. Iquique was practically unfortified, and in the presence of a powerful fleet was, to all intents and purposes, an open town. Its capture did not, therefore, appear to be a matter of much difficulty. Still, the garrison might offer a stubborn, possibly a successful, resistance, and failure would have a very demoralizing effect upon the insurgent forces. So it was decided to commence operations by bombarding Pisagua, also a nitrate port, situated some forty miles or less further north. This was done, and the town captured.

Next followed a combat at Zapiga, several miles inland, in which the rebels, ill-armed, and as yet ill-disciplined, were routed by a detachment of Government troops, which at once marched upon Pisagua and retook it after some desperate fighting. A terrific bombardment ensued, during which the unfortunate inhabitants suffered untold horrors, and damage was done by fire and shell to the computed extent of at least a million dollars. Pisagua once more fell into the hands of the insurgents. Colonel Robles, who commanded in chief for Balmaceda, pushed forward to retake it, and was met by the revolutionists near a village called San Francisco. After a bloody struggle, in which both sides fought with the ferocity of tigers, neither giving nor taking quarter, the Government troops were totally defeated, leaving two-thirds of their number upon the field. The garrison left at Iquique hastened up to support Robles, and the insurgents profited by its absence to occupy the town.

Having joined the remnant of his troops to those from Iquique, Colonel Robles once more attacked at Huaraz. This time the revolutionists were beaten, and such as escaped massacre retreated upon Iquique, hotly pursued by a detachment of Government troops under Colonel Soto. The town was carried by assault, and had Colonel Robles hastened up with reinforcements, the position of the insurgents would have been desperate. Their sole hope of holding out against the President depended upon the possession of Iquique. At all hazards, therefore, at any sacrifice, the northern capital must be retaken.

Accordingly, on February 17, the insurgent fleet, accompanied by the British squadron 'to see fair play,' commenced a vigorous bombardment. The garrison replied as well as it could; but what avail field-pieces against heavily-armed ironclads? For nearly twelve hours the unequal duel went on,

BOMBARDMENT OF IQUIQUE.

Soto, although wounded, holding out with great determination. By this time a large portion of the town was in ruins, fires were raging fiercely, and a wholesale destruction of the place imminent. But Soto had resolved that, if Iquique *did* fall, it should not be much use to its captors, and pounded away at the ships as fast as his wearied men could load the guns. Considering that a large proportion of the property thus being reduced to ashes and ruins was British-owned, Rear-Admiral Hotham at length proposed an armistice, with a view to some sort of arrangement. To this, Colonel Soto, whose force, by losses and desertions, had been reduced to about *forty men* (why did not the attacking force storm the place in boats?), and who had sent messenger after messenger to his nearest ally, Colonel Robles, praying for reinforcements, agreed, after consulting with the Intendente, Señor Salinas.

At twelve o'clock next day, Rear-Admiral Hotham and Captain Lambton went ashore, and brought off Colonel Soto and Señor Salinas to a conference with the revolutionary leaders on board the *Warspite*.

As showing the fratricidal nature of the struggle, I deem it worth while to translate a letter sent by General Urrutia—the only Chilian general who had deserted Balmaceda—to his old school-fellow and friend, Colonel Soto. I give it rather literally:

'Iquique Harbour,
'Feb. 18th, 1891.

'SENOR J. M. SOTO.

'MY DEAR PEPE,

'Why, being friends, do we to-day face each other as foes, to exchange rifle-shots in a few hours more? Would not an embrace be preferable, which should draw yet closer our former and never-belied friendship? As to my old woman (*vieja*) Lina, the tears will stream down her cheeks when she learns that two persons so dear to her have been at daggers-drawn. Does nothing strike you to save this awkward situation? Could we not have a conference on board a neutral ship?

'What more can I urge, except to bid you remember our wives and children: your children!

'I bid you assure [your wife] Cantalicia, upon my word of honour, that if Fate should part us far, far apart, and if I survive, she will find in me a true friend, eager to do all that may be possible to serve her and her children.

'Can you send me a reply? A farewell, an embrace, from your affectionate friend (*amigo de corazon*).

'G. URRUTIA.'

'I had reason to know afterwards,' adds Colonel Soto, 'what all these fine promises were worth.'

The conference took place. The revolutionists were represented by Señores Waldo Silva, Jorje Montt, and General Urrutia; the Government party by Señor Salinas, Colonel Soto, and Captain Campillo. Rear-Admiral Hotham and Captain Lambton acted as witnesses. A surrender was finally agreed upon, and carried into effect, whereby all the Government troops then in Iquique should surrender their arms. And, as luck would have it, a reinforcement, sent by Robles, had meanwhile arrived. However, a bargain is a bargain, especially if made in the presence of a British Admiral commanding a powerful squadron. And thus Iquique definitely came into the hands of the insurgents.

Unquestionably Colonel Soto committed a fatal blunder in giving up the town. He should have held out to the bitter end. The vital importance of Iquique to the rebels would have justified him in sacrificing his last man in its defence. And reinforcements were only a question of time. But poor Soto was, after all, but a simple-minded soldier. His chief, Señor Salinas, whom I know well, is a timorous civilian who wears spectacles. This small force had dwindled to a mere handful of worn-out, disheartened men. Urrutia's clever letter demoralized him; and he was bluffed out of his seven senses on board the *Warspite.* It is hard to blame Soto. But Robert Clive would have held out.

Warned by past experience, the insurgents resolved this time to retain their conquest. ' Every man that could be found in Iquique or in the surrounding nitrate-workings was persuaded, or bribed, or impressed into their ranks. Vessels were sent up and down the coast to enlist more recruits wherever possible. No effort was spared to organize a force capable of resisting the formidable Government divisions still in possession of the province.

Then occurred a series of blunders on the part of Balmaceda's colonels unparalleled in the history of modern warfare. Robles had 1,200 men within striking distance of Iquique; Gana had 1,500 within two days' march; Arrate had 400 men, farther afield; whilst the Camus division, nearly 2,000 strong, was within four days' march. Against this army the insurgents could barely have opposed 2,500 recruits. The obvious plan was to unite, and fall upon Iquique. But there was no head to direct. Colonel Robles was the senior officer, but understood nothing of strategy, and held the rebels far too cheaply. He took up a strong position at a point called Sebastopol, about seventy miles from Iquique, and sent word to his brother colonels to join him there. But in that waterless, desert region it is not easy to move troops; and, moreover, the other colonels, acting upon individual judgment, had detached portions of their forces to protect coast-towns farther south. Colonel Robles, a dashing leader despite his seventy odd years, grew weary of waiting; water was running short; and so he moved upon

Pozo al Monte (the Well on the Hill), where he was joined by a small detachment of Colonel Arrate's forces. Here, again, he might have awaited the overwhelming Camus division, but he had not patience. The enemy, he learned, was advancing to attack him, and, believing firmly that his troops could make mincemeat of treble their number of recruits, he decided to meet them. Fatal blunder! He had some 1,300 infantry, no cavalry, and but four field-pieces, and (worst of all, albeit he knew it not) *he was short of ammunition.* The insurgents numbered 2,600, some mounted infantry, three field-batteries, and several Gatling guns, worked by the sailors. For a time, despite their inferiority in numbers, the 'regulars' had the best of the encounter, and, wounded badly, Colonel Robles ordered a general advance.* But his adversary, Colonel Canto, was a tactician. Well knowing the sort of troops he was commanding, he had, in anticipation of Robles' charge, detached his cavalry and some companies of infantry to outflank him. ' Colonel Robles led the charge himself and fell, this time mortally wounded. The flank movement was executed at the right moment and the usual massacre ensued. And so resulted the battle of Pozo al Monte.

The other leaders (Heaven only knows why!) abandoned all idea of retrieving poor Robles'

* Of course I am here anticipating. By the first accounts received at Santiago, it was only known that Colonel Robles had been defeated and slain. The details came later.

disaster, retreated eastwards, crossed the Andes into neutral territory, and eventually, after untold hardships, recrossed the range into Chilian territory in the depth of winter.

It must also be stated that between Chile proper and Tarapacá (which, having been conquered from Peru, is hardly yet Chilian) an impassable desert intervenes; and that, consequently, the only way of sending reinforcements from Valparaiso northwards is *by sea*. Thus, President Balmaceda had been debarred from reinforcing his northern garrisons.

Accompanied by Señor Guillermo, I presented myself at the Moneda at the appointed hour, and without delay was ushered into the presence of Señor Balmaceda. First impressions count for something; and I think that no one could have met the Chilian President for the first time without being favourably impressed. Six feet in height, of spare but wiry build, some fifty years of age; in general appearance, in fact, not unlike his brother-President of Argentina. A head that probably a phrenologist would have found fault with; the broad forehead a little too sloping, the chin a trifle weak, the mouth *un tant soit peu* sensual. But the good-humoured gleam in the keen, penetrating eyes, and the smile, half-playful, half-cynical, that hovered about the mobile lips, gave not the faintest indication of the Nero-like qualities attributed to

JOSÉ MANUEL BALMACEDA.

him by his opponents. There is character, too, in a hand-shake, and the President's grip was one to remember for several minutes.

In my notes I find the following *résumé* of our conversation. Quoth his Excellency:

'You arrive at a disastrous epoch in Chilian history, Señor Corresponsal, and I fear you will carry away with you but a poor opinion of our common-sense, or of our patriotism.'

This was evidently a 'feeler,' so I replied by another.

'Subject to your Excellency's correction, the question appears to me to be rather a definite issue upon points of constitutional rights. No country has ever yet worked out its political salvation without such differences of opinion as at present, unhappily, exist between yourself and Congress; nor can Chile hope to be an exception to the universal law.'

The President looked at me keenly for a few moments. I fancied I could read his thoughts: This correspondent is English; he admires no system of government save his own; he believes that I am standing in the way between Chile and the adoption of a similar system. Then he said, speaking very slowly and distinctly, and in a pure Castilian accent, good to listen to:

'What you say, señor, is historically correct, and more especially of England. Your records indicate a continuous struggle between a dominant aristocracy and a liberty-seeking people. And, in course of time, you have contrived to reconcile the pretensions of both. But your ways are not the ways of the rest of the world ; and most certainly they are not our ways. Your hereditary throne, your hereditary House of Lords, and your popular elective House of Commons appear to harmonize with the character of the English nation. But they do not meet the views of younger nationalities, which invariably adopt a republican form of government. Now, here comes the great difference. With you, but one out of the three powers which form your constitutional system is elective. In a republic all three are elective. Your two hereditary powers are, more or less, automata ; that is, neither Crown nor Lords dare oppose a strong expression of the national will. We have no such automata ; least of all is a Chilian president such an automaton, being invested by the Chilian constitution with powers greater even than those of Congress. That his powers are excessive is quite possible, is open at least to argument ; but that they exist is certain, and open to no argument at all. You follow me?' and Señor Balmaceda pointed significantly to the original Chilian constitution, which, framed in gold, adorned a side of the room.

'Perfectly,' I replied; ' your Excellency's Spanish is singularly pure. But it is asserted, upon the other side, that custom and precedent had modified this constitution to an extent which you refused to recognise, and that hence the quarrel.'

'*No es cierto, señor*—such is not the case!' exclaimed the President, somewhat warmly. 'I did nothing that has not been done, over and over again, by my predecessors. This theory of Parliamentary Government is a new idea, a mere pretext of discontented factions to work out their own ends. I am the first representative of the Liberal Party who has ever held office. Ever since 1833 the aristocracy has had a monopoly of the Presidency, and up to my election the presidential powers were never called into question. Moreover, when I was sworn in, I took an oath to uphold and maintain the constitution *as it stands*, without reference to alleged precedents or philosophical theories. Congress, by the express terms of that constitution, has no more right to dictate to me what ministers I shall choose than it has to ordain what food I shall eat or what clothes I shall wear. If I have in any way exceeded my powers, let Congress impeach me when my term of office shall have expired, which will be but six months hence, as by law provided. I did not frame the constitution, nor am I responsible for its provisions. But I *am* responsible before God and man to observe my oath; and this, *por Dios, señor*, I shall do whilst breath remains in my body.'

'It would seem,' I ventured to observe, 'that a revision and remodelling of this apparently somewhat *arriérée* constitution would be the simplest solution of the difficulty.'

'Unquestionably,' assented Señor Balmaceda, 'and this has ever been a prominent feature of the Liberal programme. But the way to effect constitutional reforms is neither to render government impossible, nor to seduce the fleet, nor to play into the hands of foreign capitalists, nor to incite a civil war.'

This was a begging of the whole question, into which, without further study, I was scarcely prepared to enter. So I shifted the subject.

'Does your Excellency think that the struggle will last long?'

'It would have been over ere now,' was the reply, 'had poor Robles displayed more prudence and less impetuosity. He should have awaited the Camus division before he attacked. As it is, my hands are tied for want of ships to transport troops to the north. Our only transport, the *Imperial*, is insufficient, though had we but three or four such vessels, the rebellion would be crushed in a fortnight. We may have to await the arrival of the cruisers *Pinto* and *Errazuriz* from France, unless the new torpedo-catchers succeed in crippling or scaring the insurgent fleet.'

A few other subjects were broached. Amongst other things, I was assured that payment on the July coupons was already provided for. When I took my leave, it was with a distinctly favourable opinion of José Manuel Balmaceda, an opinion fully shared by my secretary. But then, as I reflected, it was his obvious policy so to impress me. And, in any case, I must not allow impressions to influence my verdict.

For several days my secretary and I pursued our investigations, still independently of each other. I shall not here reproduce the very voluminous notes which I made as I waded through a vast pile of polemical literature and files of revolutionary journals. But I cannot well avoid setting down what appeared to me to be a fairly clear *résumé* of the political situation.

When in 1817 Chile threw off the Spanish yoke and embarked upon the then fashionable career of Republicanism, it commenced its national existence by entrusting autocratic powers to the soldier-patriot Bernardo O'Higgins (erstwhile of the County Meath). To him succeeded other generals, also invested with practically despotic power, until in 1833, with the sanction of General Joaquin Prieto, the reigning *Director*, a brand-new constitution was promulgated, which constitution, with trivial modifications, is the one still in force.*
Like most cut-and-dried ready-made codes, it is distinctly of the patchwork order; but as little republican, in its main provisions, as its framers doubtless intended that it should be. It empowers duly-qualified Chilian citizens to elect representa-

* See note on the Chilian constitution, p. 310.

tives to a National Congress composed of a Chamber of Deputies and a Chamber of Senators, provided that such representatives be possessed respectively of incomes amounting to $500 and $2,000 per annum, and be of legal age. In this Congress the legislative power is affirmed to reside, subject to the approval of the President of the Republic. This President is to be chosen by electors nominated by the provinces in the proportion of three such electors to each representative; his term of office is now five years; nor can the same person be elected twice consecutively. In his hands are placed powers which can only be fairly described as excessive. Although bound to convoke Congress to its ordinary session (viz., June 1 to September 1), he can at any time prorogue the session for fifty days. He can summon Congress whenever he pleases to an extraordinary session, and for a specific purpose or purposes, and can prorogue or dissolve such extraordinary session at his will. Moreover, the Chambers, when thus summoned extraordinarily, ' shall occupy themselves with the business for which they have been convoked to the exclusion of all other.'

He can appoint and remove all the ministers, who are six in number, at his sole discretion, and has similar powers with respect to five out of the eleven members of the Council of State, as also with respect to the intendentes of provinces, governors of towns, and diplomatic agents.

He can 'dispose of the forces by land and sea, organize them and distribute them as he may find convenient,' with many other powers and privileges which need not be detailed in this place.

It is evident that such presidential prerogatives are wholly inconsistent with what *we* understand by a system of Parliamentary Government. In fact, the very first article of the constitution states that ' the Government of Chile is a popular representative one' (*El Gobierno de Chile es popular representativo*), of which article the entire constitution is, indeed, an explanation. ' Popular representation' sounds well—rather *too* democratic for most English ears. But, read by the light of the explanatory clauses, it means just this : a large number of people (not manhood suffrage, by any means) may elect their deputy or deputies to the Chamber of *Deputados ;* a smaller number, *i.e.*, those paying higher rates, may elect senators ; and a still more carefully-chosen few are authorized to nominate electors, who, in concurrence with other similarly qualified electors from all parts of Chile, are at liberty to nominate, elect, and finally confirm the candidate for the next presidency. Now, upon the face of it, this arrangement is rotten. It stands to reason that A., being actually President, will use all his enormous influence to secure the return of his friend B. And if any admirer of the system of so-called ' republican' government will be at the pains to inquire into the whole dreary subject, he will find that, with scarcely an exception, in republic-governed countries (and especially in South America) the multitudinous 'revolutions' have almost invariably hinged upon the question : ' Who is going to boss the show next ?' I have borrowed the expression from our humorous cousins, because it just expresses the idea.

We are dealing with Chile. Very well, any reader can form his own judgment from the extracts given in the note on p. 310. They are all that concern the dispute between Balmaceda and the Congress — absolutely all. And the question is simply this : Was or was not Balmaceda right in sticking to the letter of his oath?* Given the constitution and given the oath, the problem reduced itself to a simple matter of comparison and fact. Now, as to the facts both sides were agreed —perhaps for the simple reason that, having but recently occurred, there was no possibility of disputing them. And here they are, briefly, in historical sequence.

Up to January, 1890, all went well—that is, the Liberal Party, which had returned Balmaceda

---

* 'I, José Manuel Balmaceda, swear by our Lord Jesus Christ and upon the Holy Gospels, that I will faithfully fulfil my trust as President of the Republic ; that I will maintain the Catholic faith ; that I will preserve the integrity and independence of the Republic ; and that I will respect, and cause to be respected, the constitution and the law. And so may God aid me and help me. And, otherwise, may He demand of me account of my stewardship.'

to office, still outnumbered the hitherto dominant Montt-Varista-Clerico-Conservative Party. Some grumbling there had been at the President's extravagance in erecting public buildings and pushing ahead public works, instead of saving up the money to redeem the paper-currency, and four Ministries had split upon this very rock, Balmaceda each time replacing them by others holding similar views. Such a Ministry held office in January, 1890, but Congress had taken into its head that, in addition to his lavish expenditure of the national funds upon wholly unnecessary brick and mortar, the President was paving the way for a chosen successor, alleged to be a certain Señor San Fuentes.

Now, this San Fuentes was the idol of a strong section of the Liberal Party, but was cordially detested by other sections of the same party, and these sections (daily increasing in number), rather than have this man forced upon them, threw their lot in, temporarily, with the Clericals and Conservatives, and thus formed an opposition which subsequently rendered government impossible. Henceforth Congress became a skittle-alley, wherein votes of censure were the bowls and Ministers the ninepins. In vain Balmaceda disclaimed all intention of supporting San Fuentes' candidature, and pointed out that, by the law, no Minister could be a candidate; in vain San Fuentes himself solemnly abjured all intention of competing for the

Presidential chair. Congress would have none of him. Balmaceda would not give him up, and in June made him Prime Minister. This was too much for Congress, which now fairly lost its head. Before the new Prime Minister had even opened his mouth in the House, a vote of censure was passed. This was not logical, but it conclusively indicated the temper of Congress. Balmaceda insisted upon the Ministry remaining in office. Whereupon Congress played its strongest trump-card, refusing even to discuss an Appropriations Bill until such time as the President should appoint a Ministry enjoying the confidence of the Chambers. A dead-lock ensued. No taxes could be collected, no civil servants or Government labourers could be paid, and menacing symptoms appeared all over the country. Three weeks later, to avert what looked like a coming popular insurrection, the President yielded, and a Ministry was formed with Señor Belisario Prato as Premier, which Congress accepted as satisfactory. Temporary supplies were voted, and matters re-assumed a more tranquil aspect.

Emboldened by this victory, the Chambers encouraged the new Ministry to legislate with a view to the removal of all intendentes, governors, prefects, and other officials suspected of San Fuentist leanings. But here the President put his foot down firmly. Not one single official would he consent to remove, except for an indictable and duly proven offence. Congress, in effect, sought to secure for itself the same influence in the coming Presidential elections which it proposed to take out of the President's hands, by replacing his nominees with their own. And having the written constitution upon his side, Balmaceda stubbornly refused. He, moreover, pointed out that as the Chambers were then sitting in an extraordinary session, convoked by him for the sole purpose of passing the Annual Supply Bill (which had been left undone throughout the ordinary session), they had no business whatever to wander away from the simple question of dollars. And here, again, he was technically right. But right or wrong, Congress would not hear of money matters until the matter regarding the intendentes and governors should have been settled satisfactorily. Balmaceda was firm; the Prato Ministry resigned; and the President, having appointed a fresh Ministry more to his taste, abruptly closed the extraordinary session to prevent any more votes of censure being passed (October 17th, 1890).

Now, the Chilian constitution provides for the existence of a body called the *Comisión Conservadora* (Constitutional Committee), consisting of seven members, chosen by either Chamber, and whose functions are to see to the due observance of the constitution whilst Congress is in recess, and to tender advice to the President upon such questions as may arise, suggest the expediency of extraordinary sessions, and so forth. This last the *Comisión Conservadora* lost no time in doing; and the President referred the matter to his Cabinet. Should he or should he not convoke another extraordinary session? Ministers did not favourably entertain the idea. Past experience had made it clear that, whatever might be the avowed object of its convocation, the very first act of Congress would be to pass a vote of censure upon the existing Ministry. And it would certainly refuse to vote supplies. Whilst the question was still under discussion, the Constitutional Committee got up a special session on its own account, which deputies and senators were invited to attend, as a sort of rehearsal. And a very lively rehearsal it proved to be. The President and his Ministers were denounced as fit subjects for national execration. He was himself likened to the most despotic of Roman emperors, and was bidden to remember that a Brutus could yet be found for a Cæsar. The notion of voting supplies was scouted; but proposals to pass a special law for the summary deposition of the Dictator were hailed with enthusiasm. It was clear that, unless Balmaceda were prepared for a wholesale surrender of his authority, no good could possibly come of another extraordinary session; and so none was convoked.

This brought matters to a climax. The supplies already voted would lapse upon December 31st.

How carry on the Government until the following June? Unless the President voted a Budget himself and could enforce its provisions, he was clearly a beaten man. Now, he had hitherto given way so often that he was considered to be (even by his own friends) a weak-minded person, incapable of effectively playing a 'lone hand.' It had become known that Congress had many sympathizers in the army and in the fleet prepared, if need were, openly to espouse its cause. Popular feeling in Santiago and in Valparaiso was strongly enlisted upon the same side. Nothing could well appear more hopeless than any attempt upon Balmaceda's part to assert his authority by force. Yet this was what he had at last decided to do, and, having so decided, he gave proofs of an energy and a resolution of which no one had deemed him capable.

Upon January 1st he issued a lengthy and elaborate manifesto addressed to the nation, in which, so far as chapter and verse went, he made out a very strong case for himself. Whether or not the constitution was effete and unfair in its provisions, he avowedly declined to discuss. Whether or not the new theory of Parliamentary government might advantageously replace the popular representative system was also, he affirmed, beside the question. He stood by the bare letter of the existing code, which he had sworn to uphold, and which plainly gave him the very powers which he was branded as a tyrant for using. True, the *Comisión Conservadora* had the right to advise him to summon an extraordinary session, and he was morally bound to heed such advice under ordinary circumstances. But what was the use of convoking Congress to vote supplies when the Chambers would avowedly only meet to discuss other matters, to abuse, and perhaps seek to depose him? It was an open secret that the army and navy had been tampered with, but he was confident they would remain loyal to the established Government. In a few months there would be fresh elections, when the people would have an opportunity of deciding at the polls upon which side its sympathies really were. A few months later and his term of office would expire. Meanwhile he was resolved to do his duty according to his lights.

Within a week of the publication of this manifesto the fleet revolted and declared for Congress (January 7th). The civil war had begun. Balmaceda was now practically a Dictator, and threw himself upon the army, which partly through old-standing jealousy of the fleet, partly through hopes of increased pay and rapid promotion, and partly from conviction, stood to him stanchly enough. A state of siege was proclaimed, and a general dispersal of revolutionary members of Congress followed, most of them finding an asylum upon the war-ships.

Chilian society had for a long time past been in a critical condition. What, for want of a better term, may be called the aristocracy had for many years been floundering in a quagmire of financial difficulties. People whose fathers had been content to lead the lives of country squires, with an occasional run up to the capital, had gradually followed their Argentine neighbours in a newly-developed craze for luxury and extravagance, and many of them had landed themselves upon the very brink of ruin. They, of course, all belonged to the old Conservative Party, of which the component elements were known as Clericals, Montt-Varistas, and Conservadores, the latter being less ultra-Conservative in their views than the others. Now, broken-down aristocrats in Chile at all events, invariably look for assistance to Government, which has charge of the loaves and fishes. And the return of Balmaceda—the leader of their hereditary foes, the Liberals—as President, left them no hopes whatever from this source. When it became clear that Balmaceda would most likely be succeeded by another Liberal, that, in fact, the Government would probably remain in Liberal hands for an indefinite period, all sections of Conservatives had naturally been in despair. Their sole hope clearly lay in causing dissensions in the Liberal ranks, and in annihilating the President's influence throughout Chile.

The clergy had strong grounds for bitter hatred

of Balmaceda. Not only was he strongly suspected of downright Freethought opinions, but he had played sad havoc with the principal sources of ecclesiastical revenues. The establishment of civil marriages had especially smitten them very hard. Their salaries and fees had, moreover, been cut down all round with an unsparing hand. And as the *padres* (in Chile as elsewhere) held unlimited sway over the minds of the female population, a Balmacedist in petticoats came to be almost as rare a phenomenon as was a black swan in the time of Persius.

Naturally the tradesmen and those employed in the thousand and one occupations called into existence by the necessities or caprices of the spending classes sympathized with their aristocratic patrons, and readily attributed diminished earnings to the evil ways of the tyrant. Hence the large number of *Oposidores* to be found in Santiago and Valparaiso.

But, in addition to these direct aids to the revolutionary movement, a majority of intelligent persons espoused the cause of Congress upon conviction. It was absurd, they reasoned, that the destinies of the country should be swayed upon the principles maintained by Balmaceda. Of what use a Congress at all if it could be overridden at the will of a President? If the constitution really gave him the powers which he claimed, then the constitution was utterly rotten, and even a revolution would be a cheap price to pay to secure its abolition.

By the large foreign element resident in Chile, Balmaceda was regarded with very general aversion, and more especially by the British. He was known to entertain many views by no means consistent with the uninterrupted advancement of foreign interests. He had many times hinted that a period must be put to the extensive grants of concessions which had hitherto been so freely made to European syndicates. The wealth of Tarapacá, he had been heard to say, wealth purchased by Chilian blood in the war with Peru, was flowing in a wide stream to London, and in driblets to Santiago. And this idea had been emphasized by Colonel North's not over-successful mission to Chile in 1889, of which an excellent account was written by Dr. Russell, who accompanied him.*

Says Dr. Russell in one passage; 'Señor Balmaceda was on his way to Santiago after the progress through the centres of Chilian life, and of European industry and enterprise, in the course of which he had delivered speeches which had been regarded as the *pronunciamentos* of a new policy: "Chile for the Chilians." It was known that Colonel North had come from Europe to solidify and to extend interests, in respect to any increase

* 'A Visit to Chile and the Nitrate Fields of Tarapacá,' by William Howard Russell, LL.D. London, J. S. Virtue and Co., 1890.

of which President Balmaceda's programme, as reported, might be taken as adverse.' And further on : 'There were, however, signs and tokens that the early declarations of policy, respecting the State properties, attributed to Balmacęda, were considered by the press to be the guiding principles of the Government, and that for the future railway extension was to be reserved for the State.' And that railways were not to be the only enterprises thus reserved is made plain by the following passages : 'The importance of nitrate in agriculture and commerce, and the gradual increase of its production,' said the President, 'warn the Legislature and the authorities not to demur in solving this problem, and to protect effectively the legitimate interests of our countrymen. It is true that we should not exclude the free competition and manufacture of nitrate in Tarapacá ; but we cannot consent that this rich and extensive region should become simply a foreign factory. . . .' It was inferred, especially from his (the President's) speech at Iquique, that he intended, if he could, to close the course to any but native competitors, to handicap those who had been the winners, to refuse industrial concessions in the country to non-Chilian residents, and to reserve the State lands still unappropriated exclusively and inalienably to citizens of the Republic. Although there was no express intimation of any intention on the part of Government to lay hands upon, or, as the phrase in Chile goes, to "expropriate" the railways, it was well known that such a project was in favour with some politicians at Santiago, and some expressions in President Balmaceda's discourses were taken to indicate the likelihood of future action in that disagreeable direction; but no one supposes the President would injure vested interests.'

Dr. Russell throughout employs the style of studied moderation, as befitted the historian of an expedition avowedly undertaken to solidify and, if possible, extend Colonel North's extensive nitrate interests in Tarapacá. But he is at no pains to disguise his conviction that these interests were not consistent with the continuance in office of presidents of the Balmaceda way of thinking. Nor did Colonel North's own expressions of opinion to Englishmen in Chile leave it to be supposed that he in any way differed from the views subsequently expressed by Dr. Russell in his book. Apropos of which book it must be stated that it did not produce a favourable impression upon the native mind in Chile. The author dwells somewhat too forcibly upon the magnificent style in which the 'Nitrate King' thought fit to travel, and a great deal too forcibly upon the extent to which he was dunned by impecunious Chilians. Nor is it quite correct to say that 'the report of his enormous wealth had gone abroad among the people.' People knew quite well, long before, all about his enormous wealth, and where it came from. His career in Chile, previous to his phenomenal rise to nitrate eminence, was an oft-told story; and whilst all marvelled at the wondrous push and luck of the man who had sprung, at a bound, from poverty to boundless riches by simply knowing when the ball was at his foot and kicking it, it was not easy to forget that he had made every farthing of his vast 'pile' out of Chilian soil. His magnificent return was, indeed, a speaking reproof against local want of enterprise, and, as such, was by many resented. Malicious rumours were spread, which to this day are widely believed in. All sorts of improbable stories were put into the genial Colonel's mouth. He could buy up the whole lot, from the President down, with a cheque. To abandon Tarapacá to Chilians would be worse than leaving diamonds to barn-fowls; and so forth. It was openly asserted that the magnificent silver-mounted trophy and the stallions, presented by the generous Colonel to the nation, had been originally intended as gifts to the President, although of this there was not the smallest evidence. Even now the stranger is asked of what sort of regiment is 'Mister North' Colonel? And a catchword reference to the 'North Circus' still raises a laugh. The 'Nitrate King' meant well, and carried out his expedition right royally; but it was an indiscretion.

Still more indiscreet was the oft-heard boast of

the revolutionists that they had the whole nitrate interest at their backs, as well as the moral support of the British Government, and of the British navy. It only remains for them to perpetrate the final indiscretion of informing the world who paid for the *Itata's* cargo, and the repeating-rifles which eventually won the day.

And whilst upon the subject of indiscretion, Dr. Russell was not well advised (in the light of subsequent events) in recording that, at Santiago, 'one gentleman urged the Nitrate King to finance a revolution in a neighbouring State.'

It was now, as it seemed, about time to arrive at some definite conclusions, and a lengthy consultation with my secretary proved us to be agreed upon certain points.

1. That the charges so profusely made against the President personally were most emphatically 'not proven,' and that even his enemies did not lay that besetting sin of South American rulers, the 'itching palm,' to his door; that he was, consequently, by no means to be classed with Rosas, Lopez, Celman, and Co.

2. That he had, upon the whole, a long way the best of the argument, since he stood upon the firm ground of the written constitution, whereas his opponents sought to substitute a system of Parliamentary government not then legally in existence.

3. That he had infringed the constitution—at

least in spirit—by refusing to call another extraordinary session, at the instance of the *Comisión Conservadora*, but that the violent attitude assumed by Congress almost justified such infringement.

4. That victory for the insurgents would infallibly result in subsequent dissensions, consisting as they did of half a dozen sections of dissatisfied Liberals and three sections of Conservatives. Oil and vinegar may be poured into the same dish, but they will never mix.

5. That the triumph of Balmaceda would mean the triumph of but one single party, and would entail no such subsequent disputes *inter se*.

6. That unless Providence for once abandoned the side of the big battalions, the President, with the army at his back, the whole of Chile proper under his sway, and several powerful warships shortly due from Europe, must win in the end.

7. That an established Government has always stronger *prima facie* grounds for the support of right-thinking persons than even the most plausible of would-be reforms, begotten by party cliques and heralded by a revolution.

Mainly for these reasons, and guided by the considerations which have been already stated in some detail, I decided to incline to the side of the President. Subsequent events must decide my subsequent policy. That, in taking this line, for the present, I would be running counter to the commonly-accepted beliefs of the press of the world, including that of my own journal, weighed with me not one straw. I was absolutely the only foreign special correspondent in Chile, and my orders were to use my own judgment. That judgment, such as it was, I used and followed. ✕I believed that Balmaceda would win, and that he was, in the main, in the right—more so, at all events, than the revolutionists. Time (and apparently at no very distant date) would decide whether I was right or wrong in the first of these beliefs ; history would decide whether I was right or wrong in the second.

CHAPTER V.

THE TROUBLES OF A SPECIAL CORRESPONDENT.

How to correspond—Telegraph Lines closed—Mails supervised—An Ultimatum to the Government—Pozo al Monte—A Review of Government Troops—Opinion in the Provinces—My Lost Child gets into Trouble—Valparaiso—Opinion there—An Expedition against the Revolted Fleet—A Tempting Offer—I accept—My Fighting Secretary deserts me—And follows in the Footsteps of my Lost Child—Stick *v.* Bayonet—Political Memoranda—*The Times* and I—' Go, but wire Facts only '—An Interview with Rear-Admiral Hotham—I refuse Good Advice.

IT was all very well to have arrived at some sort of definite conclusions, if only temporary ones ; and it seemed also fortunate, for a variety of obvious reasons, that these conclusions should have assumed a shape favourable to the existing Government. But it soon became apparent that my channels of communication were not clear : my secretary returned with a telegram unsent, and with a supplementary explanatory letter unposted. His explanation was simple. The Transandine telegraph, as already stated, had been closed for some time; and although the officials there had allowed my first message about Pozo al Monte to go through, they had done so assuming, it appeared, that I had special permission to use the line. This, they had ascertained, was not so ; and their latest orders were to pass no messages whatever, even from Government officials, without the *vista* of the Minister for the Interior. As regarded the letter, Señor Guillermo's inquiries had convinced him that the mails also underwent inspection, and that a letter addressed to the *Times* would most certainly be read previous to transmission. Upon personal inquiry, I found my secretary's report accurate in every particular. Now, communication with London upon these terms was clearly out of the question ; and, in a particularly savage frame of mind, I hastened off to the Moneda, to interview the Minister for the Interior. I think I rather staggered Señor Godoy with my vehemence. In very forcible terms I pointed out that, unless I had perfect freedom of communication, my presence in Santiago would be a mere farce. In vain he essayed to convince me that, so far as I was concerned, the *vista* was a pure matter of form. I was obdurate. Then he offered to append his *vista* to any required number of blank forms ; but I would listen to no compromise. Absolute liberty both by telegraph and mail I must have, or I would at once start—for Iquique.

A very meaning smile passed over the Minister's face, one easily read.

'Look here, señor,' I said, 'let us understand each other. With my personal freedom of action, as a British subject, no power on earth dare, with impunity, interfere; and this you must know as well as I do. In Valparaiso there are, at present, three British men-of-war, and, if necessary, I know that I can easily obtain a passage to Iquique upon one or other of these. But, apart from this, your action is not consistent with your speech. You are the President's Prime Minister. Both he and you proclaim that the one thing desirable is that the world should know the truth. I have travelled many thousands of miles to ascertain and report where the truth really is in this revolution. So far, I have formed certain opinions. But I refuse utterly to despatch those opinions subject to the approval of your Government.'

'*Vámos a ver á sa Excelencia!*' replied Señor Godoy, leading me off to the President's study. Here the question was argued out. I again stated my case, this time even more strongly. I adhered to my ultimatum that, failing a total repeal of existing telegraphic and postal supervision in my favour, I would forthwith proceed to the revolutionary headquarters. In the end I carried my point, and, in acknowledging the concession, took occasion to remark very pointedly: 'I rely upon your Excellency's well-known judgment to insist that Government officials will rigidly obey your instructions in this matter. The exercise of any indiscreet zeal on their part, running counter to these instructions, would infallibly place both your Excellency and myself in an exceedingly false position. And now,' I continued, 'that this matter is settled, here is a telegram that would now be on its way to London but for the *vista* difficulty. It concerns the alleged murder of Colonel Robles in the ambulance after the battle of Pozo al Monte.'

'Alleged?' queried Señor Balmaceda. 'Nothing can be more certain. I have here the sworn depositions of Surgeons Middleton and Alvarez, who were attending to him and other wounded officers when the massacre took place.'

These I read through. They were clearly genuine.

'Had the revolutionists allowed the corpse to be sent to Valparaiso,' pursued the President, 'we intended to exhibit it publicly, in order that all men might see the countless bullet-holes, bayonet-thrusts, and unspeakable mutilation, inflicted by these rebel dogs upon a gallant soldier, who was dying of wounds incurred in the discharge of his duty.' And for the first time I saw tears in the 'tyrant's' eyes.*

* This telegram was in due course published in the *Times* and excited considerable indignation throughout Europe. Within a few days (I think upon March 27th) it was copied into the *New York Tribune* with comments from the pen of a Mr. Trumbull, an emissary of the revolutionary party. This gentleman did not hesitate to stigmatize my message as another fabrication of the *Times* correspondent, denying even Robles' death and quoting in confirmation thereof a telegram from Señor George Montt. If Señor Montt really sent any such telegram, he must have done so long after he had himself ordered the removal of Colonel Robles' mutilated body from a

I may add that thereafter I never had any difficulty in telegraphing, nor have I had any reason to suppose that my correspondence was tampered with.

Having considerable curiosity to see how Chilian troops manœuvred, I accepted an invitation sent me by General Gana, the Minister for War, to witness a sham fight and review in the park. From an Aldershot standard, the evolutions were decidedly rough, most of the men being raw recruits. But the skirmishing in loose order showed a great amount of dash; the mule batteries were rapidly brought into position, and fairly well served, whilst a final cavalry charge was really a magnificent sight. Chilians may be said to be 'born in the saddle,' and are splendid raw material for troopers. The horses, especially those of the officers, were so exceptionally good as to lend colour to the common belief that most of them had been requisitioned from the farms and haciendas of the *Oposidores*. *A la guerre comme à la guerre*, as my secretary philosophically remarked.

My numerous expeditions into various parts of the country need not here be chronicled in detail. My principal object, of course, was to ascertain popular opinion in the rural districts; and outside

---

steamer bound for Valparaiso; and after it had been buried, by his orders, in Iquique! This is but one sample of how the Congressionalists 'worked the press.'

REVIEW OF TROOPS AT VALPARAISO.

the capital I could discover scarcely any sympathy with the Congressionalists. All that the Chilian *roto* appeared to know or care about was that Balmaceda had done great things in the way of finding employment for all upon public works, which public works, ever since the meeting of the fleet, had been discontinued. Recruiting parties were very busy, and the large numbers of men thus suddenly thrown out of work made their task comparatively easy. This, indeed, accounts for the extraordinary rapidity with which the Government was able to raise an army of some 40,000 troops. The stories circulated of men forcibly torn from their homesteads to swell the ranks did not appear to rest upon any extensive basis of fact, though I myself saw many cases of enlistment under the influence of drink. But then I have seen the same thing repeatedly in England. This much was quite certain : that the men were well fed, well clothed, and well cared for, as was, indeed, obviously the best policy.

Meanwhile my Lost Child had been upon my hands, and a chronic source of anxiety to me. I at last insisted upon his returning to Buenos Aires without delay, sternly resisting his appeal to be allowed to see Valparaiso and the Pacific Ocean. Very reluctantly indeed he consented. So I supplied him with the necessary funds, taking his draft upon Buenos Aires for his entire debt to me, gave him a letter to the Governor at Los Andes, requesting that gentleman to 'forward the bearer per first caravan bound for Argentina,' saw him safely into the train, gave him my benediction, and returned to my hotel with one trouble off my mind. Alas! I wholly underrated my protégé's marvellous capacity for getting into scrapes. Two days later I received a letter from him, written, of course, in French, of which the following is a literal translation. As a *naïf* recital, written just after the occurrences described, it is, I think, worthy of a place here.

Hôtel Français, Valparaiso,
March 21st, 1891.

'MY DEAR MR. HERVEY,

'When I had bidden you farewell in the train at Santiago, I noticed in my compartment two young Chilians very well dressed, and they very soon entered into conversation with me, speaking French just well enough to make themselves understood. They made themselves extremely agreeable, gave me a glowing description of Valparaiso, where they purposed spending the night, with the intention of returning next day to Los Andes, and assured me that at this latter town many mules were awaiting them. Learning that I proposed to proceed direct to Los Andes from Llai-Llai Junction, they strongly urged me to accompany them first to Valparaiso, pointing out that it would be foolish to leave Chile without having seen its principal port. Finally I agreed to go with them. Arrived at Valparaiso yesterday at 5 p.m., we put up at the Hôtel Français; then whilst I went out to have a look at the harbour with the younger of the two brothers, the elder went to draw some money due to him and to transact other business—at least, he said so. (By the way, he appeared to be about twenty-five years of age, and his brother about seventeen.) I returned to the hotel at 7 o'clock, when we found the elder awaiting us. We dined together and decided to go to the theatre. Then I suddenly discovered that I no longer had my pocket-book! I hunted for it everywhere, and my companions helped to look for it, but all in vain. All my money, all my papers, were in that pocket-book. My friends sympathized with me loudly in my loss, and advised me at once to go to a police-station; and, deeming this excellent advice, I took it, and they accompanied me to interpret for me. The elder of the brothers went straight up to the official in charge and gave him what I supposed to be a full account of my misfortune in quick, earnest tones. Then the official called me up to a bureau and asked me, to my intense surprise, why I had come to the police-station. I understood this, because it sounded very like French. I endeavoured to explain as well as I could; but he did not know a word either of French, English, or German. He then said something which my friends interpreted to mean that I had better await the arrival of the chief of police, a colonel; and he then left the office, accompanied by them. I waited. In a quarter of an hour he returned—*alone.* Sternly he ordered me, with explanatory gestures, to place my revolver upon the desk. (I wondered to myself how he could possibly know that I had a revolver, since it was in the hip-pocket of my trousers and quite invisible.) However, I placed it on the desk, and drawing my long knife from my boot, I placed it beside the revolver in order to prove to this official that I had no evil intentions towards him. But no sooner had I done so than he summoned a soldier, who searched me rigorously and emptied out my pockets. What could it all mean? I made up my mind to keep cool, knowing that I was in the right, even if they proceeded to kill me. So I made no resistance. But I did not fail to tell them, in such few words of Spanish as I could muster, that I knew Mr. Hervey very well, and that he would be extremely angry upon learning how I was being treated. They either did not understand what I said or did not realize what an important personage you are; for all that they did was to turn me out into a sort of yard, there to await the arrival of the chief of police. At eleven o'clock a major arrived, and I was brought before him. He merely repeated the order that I must await the coming of the chief, which would probably be next morning. So I was led off to a cell, containing a wooden trestle, for the night. But as I made no sign of resistance, the door was not closed on me. Several sentinels were pacing up and down with fixed bayonets, so that I had no chance of making a bolt, which I felt very much inclined to do. At midnight the Colonel unexpectedly turned up, or had been sent for, and I was once more brought up for examination. He received me with an appearance of great harshness, and in very bad French told me that I knew Spanish well, and had better speak out at once, that I was merely trying to deceive him, and that unless I forthwith replied in Spanish, corporal punishment would be resorted to. I answered that he might do with me what he pleased, since I was in his hands; but that if he would permit me to telegraph to you, you would at once procure my liberation. This appeared to strike him, and I suppose he really did telegraph to Santiago. At all events, very shortly afterwards he again sent for me, told me that he was satisfied of my innocence, and allowed me to write a telegram to you, which I at once did. Still, it seemed that I was not yet free to depart, for I was invited to finish the night upon a sofa in a sort of officers' common room; and this I did. At 10 a.m. the landlord of the Hôtel Français made his appearance. He told me that it was clear my newly-found friends had robbed me, and that they had cleared off, leaving a portmanteau at the hotel. Explanations followed with the police officials. It now appeared that the elder of the brothers had confidentially told the official in charge that I was a most dangerous emissary of the revolutionary party, masquerading as a French traveller, that I was armed to the teeth, and probably carried important documents upon my person, and that I would inevitably pretend complete ignorance of the Spanish language. This diabolical plot had succeeded but too well; the police themselves now admitted that they had been deceived by a plausible scoundrel. The colonel now asked me what I purposed doing. "Telegraph to Mr. Hervey," was my reply. He then said that there was a difficulty about sending my telegram, and that I had better write, adding that I was now free to go when I pleased. So I accompanied the hotel-keeper back to this hotel, from which I now send you this letter. I eagerly await your reply. What am I to do?

'Yours,
'ROBERT.'

I read this chronicle of disasters over, could not help enjoying a hearty laugh at poor Robert's woeful experiences, and telegraphed him funds to return to Santiago. When he arrived I scolded him roundly, got a telegram through for him to his Buenos Aires agent, who promptly telegraphed funds, and finally shipped him off to Bordeaux, from Valparaiso. I met him again recently, and how delighted the lad was to see me! He is quite a young lion amongst his friends, who never weary of listening to his South American experiences; but he has embellished his police-station adventure past all recognition.

My first visit to Valparaiso was, by mere accident, made in distinguished company. I had arranged to travel by the early morning express, but upon reaching the station found that the train had just started. This was awkward. I detest slow trains, and there would be no other express till evening. However, there was nothing for it but to leave our luggage in the cloak-room and kill another day in Santiago. But just as this course had been decided upon, the station-master accosted me very politely, and informed me that a special train would almost immediately leave for Valparaiso with a Ministerial party, and that he was sure a coupé would be entirely at my service. At that very moment a gentleman, whom I at once recognised as Señor Julio Bañados Espinosa, Secretary-General for War, accompanied by a fairly numerous party, civilian and military, arrived. No further choice was left. Señor Espinosa insisted so strongly upon our accompanying him that, without appearing very ungracious, refusal was impossible. If it were not good policy for a special correspondent to be seen travelling in Ministerial company, and so, in the public eye, tacitly approving the Government action, upon the other hand, it would be still worse policy to identify myself with the revolutionary party by declining a mere act of courtesy. To maintain, always and everywhere, an appearance of strict neutrality is impossible.

Valparaiso is about 120 miles, English, from Santiago by rail, and more than half this distance is taken up by a necessarily tortuous track over an intervening chain of the Andes. Had not our previous journey across the Cordillera somewhat spoilt us for mountain scenery, we could have admitted that the views we now beheld were worth travelling far to see. Behind, in the far-away distance, towered the giant Aconcagua, like some Saul overtopping his big brethren. Over watercourses innumerable, tributary to the Aconcagua River; through deep cuttings, with here and there a tunnel; now speeding along a comparatively level stretch, but generally toiling up steep curves: at length the highest point is reached, and deep below lies one of the fairest landscapes on earth—the valley of Llai-Llai. And then a descent, steeper than had been the ascent, and, if anything, even more tortuous, until the township of Llai-Llai itself is reached, and a halt made for breakfast. Your true Chilian is fond (perhaps rather too fond) of good living; and upon this occasion the repast, having been ordered by telegram, left nothing to be desired. Nor had we, in other respects, aught to wish for.

Señor Espinosa and his companions were excellent cicerones. He himself, in especial, was unwearied in his efforts that nothing should escape notice. He stopped the train to permit us to descend and examine a fine single-span bridge across a yawning chasm of great width, and would have stopped oftener, but for the guard's remonstrances. I think I have never met a man in whom enthusiastic love of, and admiration for, all things pertaining to his native land was so strong. He could not restrain himself. He challenged my admiration, at every instant, upon every conceivable point. Two adjectives were ever on the tip of his tongue: *rico* and *precióso*; and scarcely a rock escaped their application. Once, indeed, he ' put his foot in it.' He observed me staring very attentively at some cattle in a field—the most over-horned, ill-shapen, underbred brutes which, methought, I had ever seen.

'Are they not *ricos?*' he inquired eagerly.

'*Preciósos*, senor,' I assented politely.

'Ah!' he exclaimed, 'we Chilians spare neither trouble nor expense in cattle-breeding. Those, for instance, are all *de pura raza Inglésa!*'

If instant death had been the penalty, I could not have restrained the roar of laughter with which I greeted this astounding assertion. Those overgrown goats *pure-bred English cattle!* And this to a man who has some pretensions to be a judge of stock : *c'était un peu trop !* The blank look upon Señor Espinosa's face warned me that my hilarity was rather ill-timed, if not downright rude; so I endeavoured to save the situation by professing to believe he had been trying to ' take a rise ' out of me. But I fear the zealous Secretary-General never fully saw where the alleged joke came in.

There is not much in Valparaiso to excite interest, nor is the surrounding country in any way suggestive of a valley of paradise. But doubtless the vegetation upon the shores of the bay, with the distant background of hills, struck the early discoverers as a ravishing sight by comparison with the arid northern coast ; and hence the name. I was struck by the greater commercial activity here than in Santiago ; and although I had been assured that the harbour was almost deserted, it appeared to be very fairly well filled.

I was much interested to ascertain what resistance the town might be expected to make in the event of attack by the revolted fleet, and with this object accompanied Señor Bañados Espinosa in several of his tours of inspection. After going over upwards of a dozen forts and batteries, many of them provided with Krupp, Armstrong, Hotchkiss, and other modern guns of heavy calibre, and noting that the gunners made, as a rule, excellent practice, it soon became clear that Valparaiso stood in little danger of bombardment. The revolutionists, indeed, loudly asserted that the fleet refrained from attack solely for fear of destroying the town; but this was merely 'making a virtue of necessity.' The opinions of all naval men, British and others (of whom I spoke with a large number), were unanimous in declaring that for the rebel ships (but three of which were ironclads, and they of old pattern) to venture within range of the shore batteries would be courting destruction.

Public opinion did not appear to be so hostile here to the Government as at Santiago. The general belief seemed to be that the revolutionists, in fencing themselves in at Iquique, were playing a dangerous, as well as a timid, game; since if the Government could succeed in getting out even one powerful man-of-war from Europe, the slow-moving vessels of the fleet would lie at her mercy, and Iquique must fall. Moreover, every day saw fresh accessions to Balmaceda's army, until it seemed that he would soon be at the head of a force invincible from sheer weight of numbers. These impatient partisans of Congress did not sufficiently realize the utter hopelessness of pitting half-armed, poorly-drilled Tarapacá miners against regular troops superior to them in number. Nor were they aware, as evidently the revolutionary leaders were, that every possible impediment would be thrown in the way of the expected warships leaving

France. Indeed, as subsequent events proved, the insurgent leaders throughout played their cards with considerable judgment, aided thereto by the practical sympathy shown to them by foreign nations. By no power were they recognised as belligerents ; throughout the struggle they were, outwardly at least, regarded in Europe as rebels. But their agents and emissaries abroad were active, and not only got a firm hold of the foreign press, but had even the energy to publish a Chilian revolutionary paper in Paris. Foreign Governments shaped their policy in accordance with foreign public opinion thus instructed as to the merits of the quarrel, and gave the rebels every assistance they possibly could short of actually despatching their fleets to their aid.

At the time of which I am now writing, the end of March, Great Britain was the only Power adequately represented by warships, the *Warspite*, *Champion* and *Daphne* being all at Valparaiso upon the occasion of my first visit. A little later on the arrival of the *Baltimore*, shortly afterwards followed by the *San Francisco*, gave due might to the Stars and Stripes. The only other foreign cruiser in Chilian waters was the French corvette *Volta*. Consequently, Rear-Admiral Hotham had had a very considerable amount of responsibility thrown upon his hands in looking after British and German (by the way, *why* German ?) interests along the whole coast-line. Matters had recently become additionally complicated owing to a decree of President Balmaceda's Government, whereby all ports then in the hands of the insurgents (*i.e.*, from Pisagua to Caldera) were declared to be in a state of blockade. It was furthermore enacted that any sums paid to the revolutionary authorities, in the way of duties upon exported nitrate of soda or other produce, would be re-exacted by Government upon the suppression of the rebellion. Against this decree the British Resident Minister, Mr. Kennedy, vehemently protested, pointing out that the mere declaration of a blockade, whilst the revolutionists were in undisputed command of the sea, was quite invalid according to all international law, and that failing an 'effectual blockade,' as understood by civilized nations, any attempt to interfere with British shipping, or to re-exact nitrate-duties already paid, would be regarded as an overt act of hostility to Great Britain. This protest, backed up by the presence of the British squadron, placed the President in the position of having to make the proposed blockade 'effectual,' or cancel his decree. It was decided to try the former alternative, and for two very patent reasons: the nitrate districts were absolutely dependent (being situated in, perhaps, the most sterile region in the world) upon shipping for food, and even for water; the nitrate-duties, worth some two million dollars a month, supplied the 'sinews of war' to the revolutionists, at the expense of the Santiago authorities. Great efforts were consequently being made to send a Government squadron northwards so as to give some sort of colouring to the alleged 'blockade.'

Now, the two torpedo-catchers, *Lynch* and *Condell*, which I had seen at Buenos Aires, had safely arrived at Valparaiso, albeit in a sorry condition. Both had broken down in the Straits of Magellan (for lack of competent engineers), and had they encountered one of the rebel warships, would infallibly have been captured or sunk. However, no such mischance had befallen, and the best engineering skill procurable in Valparaiso was engaged in patching them up. The President had, moreover, some time previously, managed to charter a fast mail-steamer of 3,300 tons, called the *Imperial*, and which had already done good service in reinforcing and provisioning the Government northern garrisons previous to their final overthrow at Pozo al Monte. This vessel it had now been decided to fit out as a cruiser, armed as heavily as possible, and carrying a contingent of troops in the event of a favourable opportunity presenting itself for disembarking at one or other of the nitrate ports. Furthermore, she was destined to act as tender to the *Lynch* and *Condell*, and to assist them in their blockade operations.

This did not seem a very powerful 'squadron' to despatch against a fleet consisting of three powerful ironclads, a fast, well-armed composite cruiser, seven

THE ARMED CRUISER 'IMPERIAL.'

or eight wooden warships, and about the same number of armed transports. But in several important respects the advantage lay with the three Government vessels. In the first place, the slowest of the three, the *Imperial*, having a speed up to fifteen knots, could, if necessary, show a clean pair of heels to anything in the rebel fleet, with the exception of the *Esmeralda*, the aforesaid cruiser; whilst the torpedo-catchers could do from eighteen to nineteen knots when in good trim. Secondly, each of these latter carried five Whitehead torpedo-tubes, in addition to Hotchkiss, rapid-firing, and Gatling guns; being fitted with double screws, they could manœuvre with great quickness, and both had powerful electric searchlights. In resolute, daring hands, what havoc might they not inflict if they got amongst the enemy's ships during a dark night! At all events, it was borne in upon my mind that a novel experiment in naval warfare was about to be essayed, and that this would be an expedition well worth accompanying, should opportunity arise.

The opportunity *did* arise. A chance introduction to Captain Garin, of the *Imperial*, led to a visit to his ship, and there I met the commanders of the torpedo-catchers, Señores Moraga and Fuentes. The conversation naturally turned upon the prospects of the expedition, and I soon saw that all three meant very serious business. Not the smallest shadow of doubt entered into their calculations. It was clear that in one or other of the northern ports rebel ships would be found, and *at night*. What was to hinder the low-lying, leaden-hued *torpederas* from sneaking in and sinking them? If by day they sighted an ironclad, or more than one of the wooden corvettes, they could easily keep out of range. The only real danger was to the *Imperial*, should she encounter the *Esmeralda*, which, when clean, was a somewhat faster vessel.

'But,' I urged, 'suppose that you attack, say, an ironclad in harbour, and that she happens to get her search-light to bear upon you? Or what if she has her torpedo-netting in position?'

'*Bueno, señor*,' replied Captain Moraga, 'if she discovers one of us at several thousand yards' distance and is quick with her heavy guns, it would, perhaps, be unpleasant. But even if she was lucky enough to hit and sink, say, the *Condell* coming up upon her starboard side, she would still have to reckon with the *Lynch* racing up upon her port side. If she sunk *both*, why then, of course, the performance would be concluded. But God help her if either of us gets within five hundred yards of her! As for the nets, they are safely stowed away here in the Valparaiso arsenal. They were forgotten in the hurry of departure.'

I subsequently went over the torpedo-boats. They are sister ships of 700 tons, and may be briefly described as mere boxes of machinery, ordnance, and torpedo apparatus, the very latest masterpieces of the well-known firm of Laird Brothers (who, by the way, also built the *Imperial*). They were constructed to the order of the Chilian Government before the revolution had broken out, and were sent out in charge of specially selected engineers, who alone understood the complicated network of engines, tubes, etc., with which the vessels were fitted. The majority of these engineers quitted at Buenos Aires rather than face the perils of actual warfare. Their places were taken by utterly incompetent men, in whose hands the boats, as before stated, broke down in the Straits, and were with difficulty brought round to Valparaiso. Here some English engineers, who appeared to know something about their business, were secured at exorbitant salaries, and repairs were being effected as rapidly as possible. The torpedoes excited my especial interest. They were the medium-sized Whiteheads, about eight feet long, with a mean diameter of some fourteen inches, charged to a power capable of shattering the thickest armour-plating, and driven by compressed air from the tube which encased them.

'Here,' said Captain Fuentes, fondly patting one of the deadly tubes, 'is a solution of the revolutionary problem, if it be but properly applied. Ah, *canalla!*' (suddenly springing upon one of the crew and cuffing him vigorously), ' is that the way your grandmother taught you to handle a coil of rope?

.... You have no idea, señor, what trouble we have with our crews. The lubbers are very hard to get, still harder to teach, and hardest of all to keep from deserting!'

Judging from the method of instruction apparently in vogue, this did not strike me as very extraordinary.

No allusion was then made to my accompanying the expedition, but I suppose my manner must have suggested the idea, for next day I received a letter from the Naval Secretary offering me, in the name of the Government, suitable accommodation on board the *Imperial*, should I care to join her. My secretary could, of course, accompany me.

Without the slightest hesitation I decided to accept, and replied to that effect for both. Shortly afterwards Señor Guillermo returned from a 'tour of observation.' His notes were uninteresting; in fact, he complained that, for a revolution, matters were very slow and commonplace.

'True, Guillermo,' I assented. 'It requires some faith to believe in the revolution at all. But at length we are going to see something. We are going upon an expedition.'

'Ah! that will be indeed a pleasant change!' exclaimed Señor Guillermo. 'And in what direction are we going?'

'To the north, my friend,' I replied. 'See, here is an official invitation for us both to accompany the Government expedition.'

Señor Guillermo's countenance by no means indicated unmixed satisfaction at the prospect.

'Surely, Señor Corresponsal, you do not seriously propose to risk your life in an enterprise so desperate?'

'My dear Guillermo,' I retorted, 'there is nothing desperate about the affair at all. We shall have a very pleasant cruise—have an opportunity, perhaps, of seeing a torpedo trying conclusions with an ironclad or two, and pick up something really interesting for our note-books.'

'Señor, you entirely underrate the peril,' persisted Guillermo. 'Everyone says the vessels will never come back.'

'A pack of croakers! Why shouldn't they come back? Don't mind what everyone says.'

'But, señor, consider how grieved your friends would be if any misfortune occurred to you,' continued Guillermo. 'As for myself, I have a father, mother, and eleven brothers and sisters——'

'Then,' I interrupted, rather impatiently, 'one would never be missed out of a tribe like that. Anyhow, I am going. Do you mean to say you won't accompany me?'

'Señor, that is the conclusion to which I am reluctantly driven. If you persist in this wild idea, of course I cannot deter you. But most certainly I shall not go. I would far rather remain here (dull as it is) until you return—if you ever *do* return ;' and poor Guillermo gazed at me as at one foredoomed to destruction.

But to this proposal I would not agree, even though he pointed out to me the importance of leaving a representative ashore to telegraph my decease to the *Times*. If he chose to go with me, well and good ; if not, our relations must terminate. Finally, he definitely accepted the latter alternative, and it was decided that he should return to Buenos Aires. I confess I felt somewhat sore at his thus leaving me, and rather encouraged his immediate start for Argentina. He elected to return overland ; and so, having supplied him with funds for the journey, I bade him farewell.

Troubles never come singly./ That same day my horse fell and rolled with me down an embankment, with, however, fortunately no worse result than a severe bruising ; and I wound up the night by a fight with a sentry, which might have had far more serious consequences. The episode convinced me that the ' state of siege ' was something more than a mere name ; though it is but fair to add that I was partly myself to blame, and that it was the only occasion upon which I was ever molested throughout my stay in Chile.

I had partaken of supper with a friend, and was returning to my hotel at about midnight. My route led past the Intendencia (Governor's official residence), and I naturally followed it. A sentry, without his rifle, was on guard, acting apparently as a sort of military policeman. He quickly advanced to meet me, at the same time ordering me into the street. It did not occur to me that this might be an official regulation to prevent persons from approaching too closely to the building at night. So I merely produced a safe-conduct given to me in Santiago, showed it to him, and attempted to pass him.

'*En la calle!*' (Into the street!) he cried, still more peremptorily, and utterly ignoring my safe-conduct.

'*Al diabolo!*' I retorted, pushing him aside.

With an oath he drew his sword-bayonet, and, placing its point fair upon my chest, once more ordered me into the street, with a look which plainly indicated a hardly-suppressed longing to spit me. Quick as thought I dealt him a vicious kick on the shin-bone, and at the same time brought down my loaded cane with all my strength upon his wrist. The bayonet dropped from his grasp, and, with a howl of agony, he turned to extract his knife with his left hand. This movement cost him a second blow (upon the side of the head), which effectually placed him *hors de combat*. Not considering it proper to leave the poor wretch uncared for and, perhaps, seriously injured, I proceeded to the door of the Intendencia, and knocked up the guard. To the officer in charge I explained the case, at the same time presenting my card. He was most courteous, explained that the man really had orders to prevent passers-by from passing close to the Intendencia, but certainly not to do so in an insulting manner.

'However, señor,' he added, a little grimly, 'he shall certainly be punished *for neglect of duty.*'

'Neglect of duty!' I exclaimed; 'say rather for excess of zeal in performing his duty.'

'No, señor, for that no punishment exists. But he shall be punished *for permitting you to pass!*'

I wondered inwardly what promotion would have awaited my late enemy had he been quicker with his bayonet than I with my stick. I waited to see him brought in. Neither wrist nor head was broken, I was glad to find, and a couple of dollars was salve even to his still half-dazed intelligence; moreover, the officer in charge promised to overlook the offence of 'allowing me to pass,' and privately cautioned me to avoid such altercations as being very dangerous.

'That fellow, for instance,' he added, 'is one of our worst savages, and would think no more of bayoneting you than I would of carving a fowl.'

And remembering the fierce gleam of the black eyes, I was very much of the same opinion; moreover, whenever I afterwards had occasion to pass the Intendencia late at night, I took the footpath upon the opposite side of the street.

My acceptance of the invitation to accompany the expedition soon became known, and I suddenly found myself somewhat a notorious personage. By the Oppositionists I was promptly set down as a lunatic, whom my keeper (probably my late secretary) had given up in despair. As to being special correspondent of the *Times*, which every one knew to be a stanch advocate of the revolutionary cause, *that* was simply another craze of my wandering intellect, though it doubtless suited Government purposes to palm me off upon my own valuation. By the supporters of Government I was, upon the other hand, extolled as a model correspondent, to whom dangers were as nothing beside the off-chance of witnessing stirring deeds. 'Of course the Señor Corresponsal does not want to miss the opportunity of seeing the renegade *blindados* torpedoed!' they affirmed. 'Your corresponsal will sink, or be shot like the rest of you!' retorted the *Oposidores*. Opinion at last ran so high that I decided to return to Santiago until such time as the expedition might be ready to start.

Before leaving Valparaiso I received a letter from my departed secretary, written from Los Andes. By an extraordinary coincidence, he also had been robbed in the train, and had been compelled to borrow one hundred dollars from the governor of that town, *on my account!* This was remarkable — so much so that, in forwarding a cheque in repayment, I registered a solemn vow to give a wide berth for the future alike to fighting secretaries and to lost children.

In the train I overheard two Englishmen discussing my unworthy self, they evidently not knowing me by sight.

'Oh,' said one, 'the fellow is *Times* correspondent right enough, unless he murdered the real man and stole his credentials.'

'Well,' urged the other, 'if he is, all I can say is that he is taking a very queer line, backing up this Balmaceda crowd. However, it doesn't much matter. His telegrams have raised such a row in London, that our people are expecting to hear that he is recalled every day.'

Some other severe criticisms upon my monstrous conduct were passed; and then, by one of those accidents common enough in a railway-carriage, I became involved in the conversation, which turned upon home topics. We were travelling by the evening mail-train, and at Llai-Llai there is always a halt of twenty minutes or so for dinner. We gravitated together to the same table, dined, and then, somehow, an interchange of cards followed. The look of mingled amazement and of hopeless apology which greeted the perusal of my name was, to me, a physiognomical treat. Thank God, I can laugh. Fortunately, also, laughter is contagious, and we were soon laughing in chorus. But the cream of the joke came off at Santiago, where (having converted my quondam critics *en route*) we drank a farewell glass to 'the success of the Government squadron.' I may incidentally remark that these gentlemen, like most other Englishmen, knew nothing whatever about the merits of the question at issue. They, like hundreds of others, had been *Oposidores* simply because it was the fashion to be so.

Santiago I found pretty much as I had left it, except that the opinion was rapidly gaining ground that, if the forthcoming naval expedition should prove a success, the position of the insurgents would be a desperate one. Hitherto many people, possibly a majority, had supported them in the full assurance of their speedy triumph. Now that belief had become considerably modified. The revolted ships must, it was argued, be afraid of these new torpedo vessels, or they would assuredly have cut them off in the Magellan Straits. What would happen if these terrible boats, with their marvellous speed and manœuvring power, went upon a mission of destruction? Was the entire Chilian fleet to be destroyed, and by Chilian *torpederas?* Then, too, the new cruisers, *Errazuriz* and *Pinto*, were reported upon their way ;* to say

* Upon the all-important question concerning the despatch of these vessels from France, the Government newspapers lied consistently and persistently. Three months before the final decision of the French Supreme Court overrode the nitrate-inspired hesitation of the Quai d'Orsay, and consigned the ships to their legitimate owners, the Chilian Government, this inspired press followed their course from port to port with unequalled mendacity. They were coaling at Lisbon. They had reached St. Vincent. They had put in—anywhere you like—for provisions. They had had ample time to circumnavigate the globe, but——*they were on the way out!*

nothing of Balmaceda's regiments, which were daily being increased. Truly, matters looked very black for the insurgents, and it behoved prudent citizens to trim according to the wind. And this the clergy, headed by the Archbishop, were also beginning to do.

Political interest at this time centred in the approaching general elections of senators and deputies for a new Congress, in succession to the last Congress, now in revolt, and whose legal existence would cease upon May 31. At first the supporters of the revolutionary party avowed the intention of contesting these elections throughout the country—of fighting the President, as it were, upon his own ground. The Government issued proclamations, enjoining strict neutrality and impartiality upon all intendentes, governors, and other officials, and affirming that every elector should enjoy perfect freedom in voting. But this in Chile, as in all other South American republics, is a mere formula: the party in power invariably brings all the influence it can to bear, so as to secure the return of its own adherents. During the half-century when the Conservatives held office, the same solemn farce was regularly gone through, and it was only owing to the fact that President Santa Maria had personally supported Balmaceda that the Liberals had been able to return their leader to the Presidency and a Liberal majority to Congress. Upon the forthcoming occasion it was hoped by the more sanguine *Oposidores* that the Liberals would rather vote for Conservatives or Montt-Varista candidates than for supporters of Balmaceda, and that thus the new Congress would be as strongly in opposition as its predecessor. But this the Liberals would not do. Such of them as believed in the President's policy would vote for his adherents. Such as did not would refrain from voting at all. Now, the Conservatives and Montt-Varistas stood no chance against even that section of the Liberal Party known as Balmacedists. And when they ascertained that they could not rely upon the other Liberals, they, too, announced their intention of not voting, giving, however, as a reason their conviction that the elections would infallibly be governed and decided at the point of the bayonet. But why not put this conviction to the test, and so prove its truth? Men refraining from voting can surely not be held to invalidate elections made by those who chose to exercise the suffrage. Such, however, were the tactics of the *Oposidores;* and it became sufficiently evident that the Government supporters would have a 'walk over.'

It was, furthermore, clear that whatever claims —based upon moral right and 'unwritten law'— the revolted Congress might be supposed to have to be regarded as the Constitutional Party, those claims would cease to exist upon June 1, when the newly-elected Congress would commence its ordinary session.

Yet further ahead lay the election of the President destined to succeed Balmaceda. Now, this election is much more complicated than the choice of members for Congress. The voters in each department choose three times as many electors as the department has deputies, and these electors must be persons legally qualified to serve as deputies. This is effected upon June 25 in the year of an expiring Presidency. The electors thus chosen in all the departments assemble upon July 25, and choose the future President. Such vast powers are, by the Chilian constitution, vested in the chief of the Republic, that each recurring interval of five years witnesses strenuous efforts on the part of each political faction to secure the return of its own representative. Each such faction has been in the habit of summoning a convention of its supporters, long before the actual voting, to organize measures for the ensuing struggle.

Here, again, it was open to the numerous factions in opposition to the existing Government to have summoned conventions and to have arranged programmes ; but did they do so, it was clear that there would be, at least, as many candidates in the field as there were factions, and that the Balmacedists, voting *en bloc*, would necessarily win the day. Consequently, the only convention actually

DON CLAUDIO VICUÑA.

summoned was that brought together by that portion of the Liberal Party which had stood by Balmaceda. Here, then, was another prospective 'walk over.' In choosing their man the Balmacedists had shown great judgment. Congress had objected to Balmaceda's alleged favourite, Señor San Fuentes, as an utterly unsuitable person. It would equally have objected to anybody else known to stand well in the President's estimation; but in the case of Señor San Fuentes it had been possible to point out that he had formerly been a *stockbroker!* and as few people in Chile had ever heard of an honest stockbroker, this had proved a home-thrust. Indeed, as we have seen, this gentleman had publicly renounced all intention of standing for the Presidency; and he had, since the revolution broke out, retired completely into private life. The choice had now fallen upon a candidate against whom it was well-nigh impossible to urge any plausible objection, Don Claudio Vicuña—a member of a very old and distinguished family; a man whose whole fifty-seven years of life had been passed, *sans peur et sans reproche*, under the eyes of his countrymen; a man who, commencing life as a gentleman of small estate, had gradually, by pastoral and agricultural enterprise, acquired a colossal fortune; a man whose hands had never been soiled by contact with those curses in disguise—guano and nitrate of soda; a man princely in mien, and almost lavish in his hospitality; a man who had heretofore steered clear of politics, but who, during the dispute between President and Congress, had thrown himself heart and soul into the cause of Balmaceda. Against this, all that the *Oposidores* could assert was that he was a silly, vain old man, who, instead of sticking to his sheep and his wheat, which he thoroughly understood, had been seduced by the blandishments of the President (who naturally sought the support of his wealth and influence) into partisanship upon questions of which he understood nothing ; that he had been utterly unable to resist the temptation of figuring as Minister of the Interior, just as he was now unable to reject the dazzling prospect of the coming Presidency, but that he would, if elected, be nothing better than a puppet in Balmaceda's hands. Now, these are charges easily made, but nothing in Don Claudio's successful career indicated folly or weakness ; and, speaking from my own personal and, subsequently, intimate knowledge of the man, I have no hesitation in asserting that he could, so far as common-sense, clearness of perception, and strength of character are concerned, have bought and sold the vast majority of his critics many times over. Him, at all events, a convention of a large section of the Liberal Party had chosen as candidate, and, barring accidents, his election seemed a foregone conclusion.

Of course I telegraphed my intention of accompanying the expedition to London. Two days later I received a reply from the *Times*, affirming that my messages were 'so contradictory to all private and official notices received as to excite ridicule,' and finally bidding me 'return immediately.' The conversation I had overheard in the train at once recurred to me; the very event foretold by one of my critics had come to pass. Very well, I would return; but I could not allow the stigma cast upon my messages to lie unchallenged, so I framed the following terse despatch; 'Your private and official notices are lies. Confirm recall.' This I supplemented by another message, requesting an immediate reply, as the expedition was upon the eve of departure.

The news of my recall spread like wildfire, and the *Oposidores* were in great glee, as, indeed, well they might be. Meanwhile, pending receipt of a confirmatory telegram, I had ample leisure to reflect upon the folly of attempting alone to stem the tide of a foreign public opinion that had for months been carefully educated by revolutionary emissaries and nitrate rings; and being *pro tem.* a 'discredited correspondent,' I was free to drown my troubles in such pleasures as Santiago could furnish.

In four days' time the expected telegram arrived. It was as terse as my own: 'Go, but wire facts only.' Seldom has telegram afforded greater pleasure to recipient than did this one to me. It was not that I had any irresistible longing to risk my life, or even to see an ironclad blown up; but there was the comfortable feeling of triumph over my intriguing adversaries, whose joy would now be short-lived. True, the permission was not couched in very flattering terms. That I was to 'wire facts only' might be taken to mean that I had hitherto *not* been wiring facts; but then, inasmuch as I was the only correspondent in Chile, and the only person with free command of the wires, how could people in London judge of my accuracy except by comparison with the absurd fictions sent from Iquique and Buenos Aires?

Previous to the receipt of this despatch, I had informed the President of the previous message, which he told me he had heard of already. He was politely and, I believe, really sorry that, as he expressed it, I should have 'burnt my fingers telling the truth,' adding that, whichever way the *Times* might finally decide, I was quite welcome to accompany the little squadron if I chose.

When he now learnt that I was empowered to go, still as special correspondent, he was immensely pleased, perhaps regarding it as a sign that opinion in London was veering round in his favour. If so, he was hugely mistaken. As for the *Oposidores*, they simply put it about that the second telegram was a 'put-up' job, several even calling, upon various pretexts, to see and examine the despatch.

Upon April 16th, I left for Valparaiso to take up my quarters upon the *Imperial,* and found that every possible arrangement had been made for my comfort. Two large cabins had been fixed up *en suite*—the one as bedroom, the other as sitting-room. I had the 'seat of honour' assigned to me beside Captain Garin, and was from the first treated by all on board with the utmost courtesy and kindness. We were to have started that evening, but certain finishing touches to the torpedo vessels delayed our departure two days longer. The interval most of us spent ashore, and, as certain private entries in my diary testify, in a thoroughly enjoyable manner.

I profited by the delay also to pay a visit to Rear-Admiral Hotham on board the *Warspite*, and with him I had a long conversation. He did not hesitate to avow that his own sympathies, and those of almost all his officers, were strongly in favour of the revolutionists. But when asked upon what grounds these sympathies were based, the only explanation offered was, many of the officers in the revolted fleet had been trained in the British navy, and that a certain amount of friendly feeling had thereby been engendered between the British and Chilian naval services. Of the merits of the political questions at issue he admittedly knew nothing beyond what he had been told by the insurgents and their partisans. But, in his opinion, the mere fact that naval officers, trained to habits of discipline and of obedience to authority, should have gone the length of openly espousing the cause of Congress, was sufficient proof that the cause was a just one. The Admiral had heard of my projected departure with the torpedo vessels, and strongly dissuaded me from going.

In plain terms he pointed out the very grave risks that would have to be run, and that all the probabilities were in favour of the three Government vessels being sunk or captured, cautioning me that, if taken prisoner, I could not hope that my nationality would save me from the fusillading which would ensue. Finally he offered me, if I wished to visit Iquique, a passage thither on board the *Champion*. Nothing could have been kinder than both the Admiral's words and manner; and I thanked him very gratefully. But I begged him to remember that I had promised to go with the squadron, and that if I withdrew at the last moment men would say 'the *gringo* was afraid.' This consideration clearly had weight with him; and, finding me determined, he gave up his well-meant efforts to dissuade me, and wished me *bon voyage*. An inspection of the magnificent cruiser concluded a very pleasant interview.

Having a steam-launch at my service, I went on to have a look at the American cruiser *Baltimore*, which had quite recently arrived. I found the officers, from the captain downwards, very distinctly partisans of the Government. They regarded the alleged causes of the revolution as mere flimsy pretexts, and believed that the whole affair had been worked up by agitators on behalf of the European nitrate syndicates. As regarded the expedition, it was the general belief that, properly handled, the torpedo vessels should sink the hostile ships wherever they found them. I remember a very prophetic remark made by one officer, Lieutenant S——y : 'If,' he said, 'the *Lynch* and *Condell* come to close quarters with the rebel flagship, I wouldn't care to be aboard her.' / Now, the rebel flagship was the *Blanco Encalada*; six days later the torpedo vessels *did* come to close quarters with her, and—well, all the world knows the result. I should have admired the *Baltimore* perhaps more had I not just quitted the *Warspite*. Both are classed as first-class cruisers ; but the British ship is incomparably the better-armed and better-manned, to say nothing of having some 2,000 tons more displacement.

A dinner with the captain and officers of H.M.S. *Daphne* agreeably wound up my last day (for the present) in Valparaiso.

CHAPTER VI.

MY FIRST CRUISE WITH THE SQUADRON.

A Difference of Opinion—Practice makes Perfect—The Plan of Operations—A Compromise—*En route* for Caldera—We lose our Consorts—Stirring News—Fever on Board—A Warning—The Sinking of the *Blanco Encalada*—The Quartermaster's Yarn—Valparaiso—Captain Moraga's Account of the *Blanco* Exploit—'One Good Turn deserves Another'—The Revolutionists try Orsini Tactics—A Chilian Heroine—The Elections.

NEXT day, April 18th, at 11.30 a.m., the three vessels steamed in company out of Valparaiso Harbour, as everyone ashore believed, direct for Iquique. This, indeed, was also the general belief on board the *Imperial*; and being myself in the confidence of the leaders of the expedition, I was considerably amused by the calculations of the junior officers as to the exact number of days and hours it would take us to reach the northern capital. Our real immediate destination was Quintero Bay, distant only some thirty odd miles from Valparaiso. Here it was proposed to remain a couple of days for the purpose of torpedo practice, big-gun firing, etc. I may mention that there had been a very stormy council-of-war before this judicious preliminary had been decided upon. Captain Moraga, of the *Condell*, held the command-in-chief, but he invariably consulted the two other commanders before taking decided steps. He had been for wasting no more time, but for an immediate advance north, and attack wherever opportunity should offer. Captain Fuentes, of the *Lynch*, insisted that his torpedists and gunners were raw hands, and needed, at least, a couple of days' practice. Captain Garin supported Fuentes; and a hot discussion ensued. At length, Moraga point-blank refused to concede the point; whereupon the other two threatened to resign their commissions. Admiral Viel was appealed to, and he persuaded Moraga to consent to the proposed delay. But a certain amount of friction existed after this between him and the others. And much as I afterwards learned to esteem Moraga, I certainly think they were right upon this occasion. Indeed, a few days more fully vindicated Fuentes' judgment.

What with torpedoes, big guns, quick-firing guns, Gatlings, rifles, etc., the time passed noisily enough. Upon the evening of the second day after our arrival, an important telegram was brought overland from Valparaiso to Moraga. Reliable information had reached Government that the insurgent troopship *Aconcagua* (a sister-ship to the *Imperial*) was on her way to Caldera, under escort of two ironclads. His orders, therefore, were to proceed north, and await a chance to enter Caldera Bay and sink these vessels.

I was with Moraga when he received this message, which he read to me, at the same time exacting my word that I would not divulge its purport. He then signalled for Fuentes and Garin to come aboard the *Condell*, remarking that the expedition showed promise of a lively commencement.

' But, *comandante*,' said I, ' if you and Fuentes attack these ships, what share will the *Imperial* have in the business ? Will it be possible to see what goes on from her deck ?'

' I do not expect that any of us will see very much,' answered Moraga, ' because we shall attack at night. Of course, the *Imperial* will not accompany us inside the harbour ; she will cruise about outside until we rejoin her. That is just what I want to arrange with Garin.'

' Then may I tranship to the *Condell ?* I am anxious to see as much of the operations as may be possible.'

' Well, I hardly know, Señor Corresponsal. You see, the President's last instructions to me before we left were, " *No exponga el Imperial y sobre todo no exponga el Señor Corresponsal.*"* Now, if you shift to the *Condell*, clearly I shall be disobeying orders in allowing you to run unnecessary risk.'

I did not much relish the prospect of perhaps

---

* ' Don't expose the *Imperial*, and, above all, the Señor Correspondent, to any risk.'

CAPTAIN CARLOS MORAGA.

missing the whole performance, and was still urging my plea when Fuentes and Garin made their appearance. Moraga read them the telegram, adding grimly:

'Now, then, Fuentes, you'll have a chance of some more torpedo practice.'

'Yes,' retorted the commander of the *Lynch*; 'and I hope my fellows will aim a bit better than yours did to-day'—alluding to some very bad trial discharges from the *Condell* that morning.

'That's what we shall see, señor,' said Moraga. 'In the meantime, let us decide upon our plan of operations.' And he produced a chart.

A long discussion ensued, in which the secretary to the squadron, a remarkably smart Anglo-Chilian, named Sartori, had a great deal to say. A very good fellow this same Sartori, and high in favour with Moraga, but regarded with considerable jealousy by the other officers.

Garin did not much like the inactive *rôle* assigned to the *Imperial*, but it was clearly all that she could do under the probable circumstances. He was to stand off as close as he deemed prudent and await results. Failing intelligence within forty-eight hours of the attack, he was to assume that the enemy's ships had not yet arrived from the north, and was to proceed north himself, slowly, towards Iquique, a northern rendezvous being fixed upon. The three vessels would proceed together to Caldera.

This being settled, I again submitted my claim. All opposed my leaving the *Imperial* except Sartori, who only saw one objection to my joining the *Condell*: there was not even a spare bunk on board. Both *torpederas* were, indeed, much overcrowded. Garin at last solved the difficulty by proposing that the Corresponsal should go to Caldera in the *Imperial* and, upon the evening of the attack, tranship to the *Condell*. And with this compromise I had to be content.

No one was sorry when we left Quintero, which might at any moment have become a regular trap, should any hostile cruisers have heard our firing and discovered us. But fortunately they did not care to come so far south.

And here I shall, for convenience, continue the narrative of my experiences at sea in the form of extracts from my diary, supplemented by such explanatory remarks as may be needful:

April 21. — Left Quintero Bay at 8 a.m., the *Condell* and *Lynch* hugging the shore, the *Imperial* standing out about six miles. A very keen look-out is kept for warships or blockade-runners. The orders are, it seems, to capture or sink any vessel found in Chilian waters with nitrate or arms in her cargo. At 4 p.m. passed a steamer, which hove to in obedience to a blank discharge from the 5-ton Armstrong bow-chaser. She proved to be the *Theben*, a German, of Hamburg, bound from Guatemala to Valparaiso. Her papers and cargo corresponding with her alleged course, she was allowed to proceed. No lights are carried at night. We travel in total darkness, the saloon and cabin ports being heavily curtained.

The *Imperial* is a most comfortable ship. In addition to all the modern luxuries in the way of costly furniture, etc., music-saloon with piano and harmonium, and large and well-fitted cabins, she is fitted with a spar-deck running her full length, which makes a fine promenade. The cuisine is by no means bad, and the wines very tolerable. We carry about seventy riflemen, a crew of nearly one hundred, and about thirty officers of various grades. I notice that five out of seven quarter-masters are English, as are also all the engineers.

April 22.—Still heading north. Our consorts are still standing quite close in-shore. Sighted no other vessels all day. After it had become dark, and we had lost sight of the *torpederas*, we arrived off Caldera and hove to, awaiting signals from the *Condell*. But none were made, though there were two false alarms in the night, and the officer on watch believed he heard firing in the direction of Caldera before daybreak.

April 23.—At early dawn all eyes were directed towards land, from which we were distant some eight miles, but not a sign of any vessel was to be seen. All on board in a state of great excitement throughout the day, and anxious to look in at Caldera. But Garin's orders to await signals were imperative, and though he was, perhaps, even more anxious than the others, he obeyed them to the letter. Upon this the safety of the *torpederas* absolutely depends, since they only carry coal for a week, steaming at high speed, and rely on the *Imperial* to replenish their bunkers. As the day wore on, the opinion gained ground that the expected enemy's ships had not yet arrived, and that the torpedo-catchers were lurking in some inlet until the forty-eight hours agreed upon should have expired.

At dinner I proposed the health and memory of St. George, and upon learning that he had been an excellent horseman with a very pretty taste for a fight, he was unanimously voted a very good fellow, and the toast was duly honoured.

Late at night I found the captain, first lieutenant, and the colonel (Pedro Campos) commanding the troops on board earnestly discussing the situation, and I was unanimously called in to make a fourth. Assuming that the rebel ships had not yet arrived, they could not be very far off, and would probably time themselves so as to enter Caldera Bay early next morning. If daybreak should find the *Imperial* within range of the guns of an ironclad or of the still more dreaded *Esmeralda*, she would be in a position of great peril. If, on the other hand, she stood out to sea, she might miss a signal from the *Condell*. It was finally decided to stand out about five miles further, with a full head of steam on, and trust to a sharp look-out for timely warning. The probable whereabouts of the *torpederas* was next discussed, and the weight of opinion favoured the theory that, having drawn Caldera blank, they were lying *perdues* in some inlet, and would proceed slowly to the northern rendezvous next morning. (Alas for theory! The *Condell* and *Lynch* were at that very moment steaming in half-crippled condition back to Valparaiso, after sinking the rebel flagship and crack ironclad, the *Blanco Encalada*, and leaving us to Providence and our own devices.)

April 24.—Still no sign of any vessels, and early we proceeded slowly northwards. Late in the night we made out a steamer's stern lights and gave chase, but they suddenly disappeared and we lost her in the darkness.

April 25.—Overtook the Peruvian steamship *Maria Rosa*, bound north, and brought her to. She was (rather indiscreetly, I thought) allowed to go on her course without any examination of her cargo.

April 27.—Steaming very slowly, we were overtaken by the German steamship *Diana*, from southern ports. She, like the others, was stopped and examined, but, having nothing contraband on board, was, upon the return of the search party, signalled 'clear.' Instead of steaming ahead, she deliberately passed close under our stern, and then, stopping her engines, signalled us to send off another boat. This was at once done, all wondering greatly what 'was up.' We were not long kept in suspense. Our boat returned almost immediately after reaching the *Diana*, the men pulling like fiends, the officer astern standing up, waving a paper and yelling like one possessed. We held our breath to listen. Then two words were borne to us by the breeze : CALDERA, BLANCO. The forefinger, pointing in jerks downwards, told the rest—*the Blanco Encalada had been sunk in Caldera Harbour!* Heavens! what a yell, what a succession of yells went forth! A British cheer is a stirring sound to listen to, but for downright deafening noise it can't touch a Chilian *viva* from two hundred Chilian throats. Everyone embraced everyone else (I thought what a pity it was we had no nice Chilian girls on board to share the general enthusiasm), and yelled himself hoarse. Then, as the boat drew nearer, two fingers were held up, and the word *Huascar* became distinguishable. The *Huascar* gone also! Oh, this was too much! Sore as all throats must by this time have been, the yells were redoubled, and the embracings presented the appearance of a general wrestling-match. My bad luck threw me into the titanic embrace of Colonel Campos (reputed to be the strongest man in Chile), and I esteemed myself fortunate in escaping with a broken eyeglass and a stud embedded in my flesh. Then the boat came alongside, the paper was quickly passed up to Captain Garin, and he read aloud its contents. It was but a brief telegram printed upon a sort of handbill, but it was startling enough :

'The valiant Captain Moraga has just returned to Valparaiso in the *Condell* with news of which all loyal Chilians may well be proud. At 3 a.m. upon the 23rd inst. he, with the gallant aid of Captain Fuentes, of the *Lynch*, attacked and sunk, by the application of torpedoes, the flagship of the revolutionary fleet, *Blanco Encalada*. Another ship, believed to be the *Huascar*, was only attacked, and it is believed also sunk. Then the *Lynch* engaged in a desperate action with the transport *Aconcagua*, but unfortunately sustained severe damages to her machinery, as did also to a less extent the *Condell*. The *Aconcagua* escaped, hotly pursued by the *Imperial*.'

This last astounding item sent me off into one of my incontrollable fits of laughter, which I had to bolt into the chart-room to smother. And I mentally put the whole story down as one of those *bolas* for the manufacture of which Chilians are so justly celebrated. Not so the others. All the rest of the events recorded were true. The very fact of the disappearance of the *torpederas* and the non-appearance of the hostile ships was clear evidence. The officer who *thought* he had heard guns now stood forth quite positive that he had heard them. What more could anyone want? The only one who appeared to share my doubts was Garin.

It appeared that the captain of the *Diana* had not been certain of our identity until he saw the ship's name astern; hence his delay in giving us the tidings. Out of compliment to him, the German flag was saluted, several volleys fired, cheers given and returned, and the *Diana* proceeded north, in all probability to discharge her freight at Iquique.

It was generally expected that we would forthwith return to Valparaiso. But Captain Garin's doubts were too strong. Even assuming that the report was substantially correct, where was the *Lynch*? Might she not have gone north to the rendezvous, trusting to the *Imperial* for coal? And what would be her fate if she did not find her then? If she had followed the *Condell* back to Valparaiso, both vessels could there refit, refill their bunkers, and start again northwards. The *Imperial* carried a month's supply of coal and provisions, and could come to no dearth. Besides, she alone would be doing the necessary blockade-cruising. Garin's judgment was sound enough, but the prospect of cruising off Iquique until the *torpederas* should see fit to join us was not a tempting one.

It was clear that Moraga must have found a chance to attack too unexpectedly to allow him time to communicate with Garin. Over and over again I bewailed my hard fate in not having carried my point, and joined the *Condell* at Quintero.

The very action I had so anxiously wished to see had, probably, taken place, and I had seen no more of it than a man in Fleet Street. I was tolerably easy as to the transmission of the news to the *Times*, having arranged with a Mr. Loewenstein, an Englishman, and also a pressman, to act for me in my absence, and having, thereto, secured the necessary permission from Government. But I had not seen the exploit, and I felt disconsolate. Garin tried to console me by pointing out that at 3 a.m. Moraga himself could have seen very little; but this was sorry comfort, for Moraga, at least, was there. I envied the stokers on the torpedo-catchers.

April 28.—Off Iquique; standing out to sea some forty miles, and barely moving. Gun-drill and rifle-practice all day.

April 29.—Nothing. Ominous rumours that the bottled beer is running short. The champagne also has disappeared so rapidly that the doctor has reserved the balance for the use of the sick. Had slight touch of fever.

April 30.—Fever no better. Dr. Bravo (a most attentive young medico) congratulates himself upon his foresight with respect to the champagne. I congratulate him also. We congratulate each other and have some of the 'medical comfort,' he also feeling at times feverish. He agrees with me that quinine taken alone is lowering to the system. Weather unpleasantly hot.

May 1.—Colonel Campos has got the fever also, and Major Santiago doesn't feel well. If this sort of thing continues the entire mass will be fever-stricken. The doctor hints darkly that he doesn't believe them, and whispers his suspicion that it's all a trick to get at the champagne.

' As to Campos, señor, I felt his pulse, and he no more has any fever than——' (I wonder if an unpardonable indiscretion will blurt out a *personal* pronoun !) ' than . . . Garin has !'

At this very moment a steward informs Dr. Bravo that the captain desires to see him. Presently he returns.

' *Por Dios, señor !*' he exclaims, ' this is past belief. *Garin has the fever too !*'

After this fevers went out of fashion, with the champagne.

May 4.—The past three days have, like most of their predecessors, been a period of absolute time-killing ; not even a stray steamer to bully. But to-day we sighted one, and gave chase. She was a smart boat, and we overhauled her very gradually. When well within hearing distance she paid no heed to two blank discharges, and Garin, losing patience, was on the point of sending a ball after her, when she hove-to. She proved to be an English vessel, the *Puno*, and, for variety's sake, I accompanied the boarding party, wearing (it being somewhat fresh) a naval cloak and a yachting peaked cap. Whilst the formality of overhauling the ship's papers was being gone through, I got into conversation with the chief mate.

'You're English, aren't you?' he inquired.

'Yes,' I replied; 'I am the *Times* correspondent.'

'Then, sir, perhaps you can tell me what right that armed mail-boat has to stop a British vessel on the high seas?'

'I regret to say I cannot,' was my answer; 'unless it be that long gun you see projecting over her bows.'

'Well, sir,' rejoined the mate, 'it's a good thing for her there's no British man-of-war in sight; and, what's more, it will be a very bad thing for *you* if she chances to be captured by one of the revolutionary cruisers.'

'Quite possibly, my friend, but then you see she is not going to be captured. It's quite an arranged matter that she'll be blown up first.'

The mate looked at me doubtfully.

'Well, sir,' he said, 'I wish you safe out of it.'

'Thanks,' I replied. 'And now tell me the truth of this Caldera business.'

He did more; he brought me several newspapers containing details of the affair, and which I took back with me to the *Imperial*. Upon examination it appeared that but one ironclad, the *Blanco Encalado*, had really been sunk, that the *Huascar* was not in Caldera at all, but that some idea survived that a small vessel called the *Bio-Bio* had gone down also. The *Lynch* had returned to Valparaiso, whereupon Captain Garin at last decided to return to Valparaiso too ; and we shaped a southerly course forthwith, standing well out to sea.

May 5.—At daybreak a large ship was sighted upon the port quarter, which shaped a course in pursuit of us, apparently. Judging from her outlines and manifest speed, she was strongly suspected to be the *Esmeralda*, and the *Imperial* was sent along at top-pressure. In about three hours she was out of sight, having presumably abandoned the chase. All on board entertained a very wholesome dread of this ' crack ' cruiser, which upon the last voyage of the *Imperial* had come very near to sinking her. An English quartermaster gave me the following rather graphic account of the incident :

' Well, sir, you see it was just this way. We left Valparaiso upon the first Saturday in March to land a regiment at a place called Camarones, right away up north, beyond Pisagua. We got there right enough, but on entering the harbour found one of the enemy's corvettes waiting for us. The *Imperial* had not got her big Armstrong bow-chaser then, and was, of course, not a match for even a small warship. However, nothing would satisfy the captain but to exchange a few shots. So we let fly our port guns at about 3,000 yards range, and then, slewing round, tried the starboard pieces. But the shots all fell short. Then the corvette replied, sending shot after shot whizzing just over our heads, and steaming towards us. Her guns were evidently too good for us, and so we cleared out at full speed. Well, sir, we next tried to get the troops ashore at Antofagasta, where we arrived late at night upon the 11th. The captain presently sent a steam-launch, well manned, to reconnoitre. Antofagasta was then, of course, still garrisoned by Government troops ; and as the launch seemed in no hurry to return, the port dingy was sent ashore, and we went inside the harbour and anchored. At the first streak of dawn a big hull was made out in the southeastern corner of the harbour, half hidden behind a sort of small promontory, and not half a mile away. In a few minutes she was recognised. It was the *Esmeralda!* I never saw an anchor heaved so smartly as ours was that time, and away we ran westward. The *Esmeralda* made us out just as we got way on, and blazed away with all the guns she could bring to bear. Most of us thought it was all up with the *Imperial*, 'cos you see, sir, although she's a smart boat, the *Esmeralda* is a couple of knots faster, and, having two screws, can work her guns to perfection. It was so early, too, that the cruiser would have a daylight chase for fourteen hours or more. However, our only chance was escape, and trust to Providence. Luckily it took the *Esmeralda* some time to get steam up properly, and we got a good start of about six miles before she held her own. Then she began to gain on us, and the captain went himself to urge the engineers to crack on more steam. That was the cry, sir, all over the ship,— *mas vapor!* But the engineers were doing their best, and the gallant ship was quivering all over like an over-driven horse. Presently we saw a white puff of smoke, and a shot struck the water fair in our track, but a good bit astern. An hour later another shot was fired, but also fell about the same distance short. Our hopes revived : we were holding our own, and, unless some accident occurred to our machinery, we might yet prolong the race until nightfall. It was evident that the *Esmeralda* was in bad trim, for her, and, indeed, it was pretty well known that her bottom was very foul, for lack of a dock wherein to clean up. At about 6 p.m. we fell off so much in pace (owing, as they said, to raking out the furnaces) that several shots passed over our heads. But soon afterwards we went faster than ever, and got fairly out of range again. Wasn't it the Duke of Wellington that prayed for night, sir? Well, he never prayed harder than we chaps did. And it came at last, dusk, then dark, then black—thank God there was no moon! The *Esmeralda* kept her search-light flashing about, but when we altered our course to the northward she didn't seem to know it, for she still headed due west. At daybreak she was out of sight, and we veered round to the south again, making Coquimbo Harbour two days later. Nothing saved us that time, sir, but the *Esmeralda's* foul bottom.'

May 7.—Arrived in Valparaiso port at 10 a.m. Enormous crowds were assembled upon the wharves and upon the adjacent high ground to witness the return of the Chilian *Alabama*. At least a dozen bands were playing the stirring national hymn, and all the flags in the place seemed to have been brought into requisition. The *Imperial* had been reported as having been sunk by the *Esmeralda* off Iquique, and the authorities had been extremely anxious on her account; hence probably all the fuss made, for certainly our people had done nothing to distinguish themselves. Not caring to figure in the show, I slipped into a small shoreboat, and, making a detour, landed unnoticed at the stairs, just in time to see my late companions, in full uniform, and preceded by the inevitable band, march off in triumph to the Intendencia.

I at once sought out Mr. Loewenstein, and from him learnt that he had at once telegraphed the *Blanco* affair to the *Times*, which had replied, asking for full details by post. These, too, he had sent. This was a good hearing, though I still felt very sore at having missed the great event.

I next visited Captain Moraga, and strongly upbraided him for breach of covenant; but he protested that events had so fallen out as to make the

12

delay incidental to any communication with the *Imperial* impossible, that had he waited even a few hours the attack must have failed. However, he promised that next time I should have a fair view of operations, and meanwhile he related all that he personally knew of the affair.

Captain Moraga's Account.

'The last we saw of the *Imperial* was upon the evening of the 22nd, when, as you know, we were not far from Caldera. About dusk a boat from shore hailed the *Lynch*, and, from a notice thus sent, Fuentes learnt that, if we wished to catch any of the hostile squadron at Caldera, not a moment was to be lost, inasmuch as three vessels had already left that harbour. Fuentes signalled me, and then came on board, to arrange upon a plan of attack. This was quickly agreed upon. We were to pass Caldera after dark, and at about 3 a.m. to enter the harbour from the north, my vessel leading by about two hundred yards. Once inside, we were to make for the rebel ships, I upon the starboard and he upon the port side ; creep up as close as possible, and let drive the torpedoes.

'At 3.30 a.m. the *Condell* entered the bay, the *Lynch* following close behind. In the dim light it was presently possible to make out one large ship, and astern of her a smaller one. The former I felt certain was either the *Cochrane* or the *Blanco* ;

the latter I took for the *Huascar*. Parting company, our two vessels manœuvred so as to bear prow-on upon the big ship, and upon opposite sides of her.

'At about one hundred yards' distance I ordered the bow torpedo to be discharged. It missed its mark, passing astern, but, as the look-out man reported, striking the smaller ship. Putting the helm hard up, I ordered Lieutenant Vargus to let go the foremost of the starboard torpedoes, which was reported as having struck the ship in the bows. The second starboard torpedo followed on. Just then the ironclad opened a heavy fire upon my vessel, having apparently no suspicion that the *Lynch* was the other side of her; and I went full speed ahead. Meanwhile, the *Lynch* crept up unobserved, and at pistol range put a torpedo fair into the ironclad amidships. In less than three minutes she sank.

'As we were leaving Caldera, we met the *Aconcagua* making for the harbour. Seeing us, she turned and fled westward, opening fire upon us at the same time. Then, seeing that our speed was so superior to hers as to make escape hopeless, she again turned and made for Caldera, still firing away, in hopes, doubtless, of attracting the attention of her consorts inside the harbour. She was crowded with troops, so I ordered that no Gatling guns were to be used, but only the Hotchkiss and rapid-firing guns. She fought manfully against the two of us for an hour and a half, when she ceased firing and stopped her engines. She carried no flag, so that we accepted this as a sign of surrender, and also stopped our fire. At this moment a ship, which we at once recognised as the *Esmeralda*, was seen in the distance, apparently steering so as to cut off our retreat. Both the *Condell* and the *Lynch* had suffered severely in the action with the *Aconcagua*, the vibration caused by the discharge of our own guns having burst many of the steam tubes, so we abandoned the prize and steamed as well as we could southward. Shortly afterwards we saw that the approaching man-of-war was the *Warspite*; but by the time we returned for the *Aconcagua*, she had crept under the guns of the forts. I should add that throughout these forts had kept up a heavy but ineffectual fire upon us. Our losses were one killed, ten wounded. Two hundred and forty-five men were drowned in the *Blanco*. What the losses on the *Aconcagua* were we do not know; but certain it is that, but for the unlucky appearance of the *Warspite* at the moment of surrender, we would have brought the transport, with the regiment on board, back to Valparaiso.'

'Ah well,' I replied, 'better luck next time for both of us. When do you again start upon the warpath?'

'In two or three days,' said Moraga; 'and if you come another trip, I'll promise that you shall enter Iquique harbour on board the *Condell*.

There are about fifteen transports, besides men-of-war, in the nitrate capital, so we shall have lots of sport. We are to do some bombarding of the coast towns also.'

The interval I decided to spend in Santiago, which I much preferred to Valparaiso. That afternoon I received the following note from the doctor of the *Imperial*:

'*Imperial*, May 7th, 1891.

' Dear Señor Hervey,

' I desire greatly to visit Santiago, but all leave is stopped. Could you not have a touch of " fever," and get me ashore ?

'Yours,

'J. BRAVO.'

Upon the good old principle that ' one good turn deserves another,' I obtained, without much trouble, the required leave for the worthy medico ; and we travelled to Santiago together.

There had been lately a good deal of Orsini bomb work going on. Bombs had been hurled at the windows of the President's library, amongst groups of newly-elected senators, ministers, and other Government supporters. I arrived in the very nick of time to observe the results of the latest attempt. It is not considered ' bad form ' to call even as late as 11 p.m. at a house of which one has the *entrée*. I had jestingly promised a member of Don Claudio Vicuña's family that my first visit upon my return should be to—*him*; and as the train reached Santiago at 10.30 p.m., I decided to effect a 'surprise call,' taking the house *en route* to my hotel. But on approaching Don Claudio's residence, my coachman was stopped by a strong patrol of mounted police, and I had some trouble in substantiating my right to pass. I found the family in a state of considerable agitation, though I was cordially welcomed.

'Come, señor,' said Don Claudio, 'and see the latest sample of revolutionary tactics.' And he led me to a long room he used as a sort of study, one window of which gave upon the street. The street window and the contents of the room nearest to it were shattered. Upon a table at the further end lay a metal ball with a short projecting tube, which I at once recognised as the sort of bomb one sees at Madame Tussaud's.

'This evening, at about six o'clock,' pursued Don Claudio, 'during my absence at the Moneda, my daughter was writing some letters for me at this table. Suddenly she heard a crash of broken glass, followed by a loud explosion at the street end of the room. There has been so much bomb work lately that she instinctively guessed what had happened. But before she could collect herself sufficiently to make a rush for the door, a second bomb was hurled in, and rolled almost to her feet, providentially without exploding. This she picked up and threw out of the other window

A CHILIAN HEROINE.

into the *patio*. Then seeing that some brown paper was smouldering in a half-open box of rifle cartridges, she quickly dashed a large jug of water over it. By this time the servants had rushed in, and succeeded in extinguishing the fire, which had caught the curtains and elsewhere. But my brave girl, recollecting that I had gone out unarmed, took my big Colt revolver, and started forth alone to meet me on my way back from the Moneda. " Here, papa, take this," she said; and then she told me what had occurred. Not bad for a sixteen-year-old niña, eh ?'

' I assure you, Don Claudio,' I replied, ' that my indignation at this savage outrage is, if possible, exceeded by my admiration of the señorita's wonderful courage and coolness. This is the work of fiends, not of men ; yet it is almost impossible to believe that even fiends would strike at the life of an innocent girl. The attempt must have been directed against you.'

' Ah, señor, they know that they could strike me most fatally through my darling,' said Don Claudio sadly. ' If they merely seek my life, they could easily take it any day. I walk the streets, generally unarmed, and always without an escort, at all hours of the day and night. I have repeatedly and publicly challenged assassination ; but, you see, my foes strike at my home, at those most dear to me, not at myself.'

Having but one clear day in Valparaiso, Don

Claudio insisted upon my dining *chez lui* next evening, when, as he gracefully put it, 'the English hero of the press will have an opportunity of renewing his acquaintance with the Chilian heroine of the *bombas*;' though, indeed, I failed to see where the 'hero' part came in.

My time was fully taken up next day in receiving and paying visits. My engagements made up a rather varied programme, viewed politically. Three Oppositionists breakfasted with me; I lunched with my friend Señor Alfredo Ovalle, took afternoon tea with the President, dined *chez* Don Claudio Vicuña, and wound up with supper amongst some of the most violent partisans of the revolution. Thus, I certainly had opportunities of hearing both sides of the question; but I neither heard nor saw anything to induce me to alter my previously-formed opinion, either as regarded the merits of the quarrel or its probable results.

It should be added that the Oppositionists disavowed all connection with the Orsini bomb attempts, and there can be no doubt that the more respectable among them were in no way connected with those outrageous attacks; still, the fact remained that upon the very day fixed for an interview between leading revolutionists and Ministers —a friendly attempt made by certain foreign representatives to bring about peace—a party of Ministers and senators, including the Premier, Señor Godoy, narrowly escaped assassination by

Orsini bombs in the public streets in broad daylight, upon their way to the proposed conference, which latter, thereupon, fell through. Clearly a section, at all events, of the Opposition did not desire any amicable settlement. The revolutionary chief, Señor Carlos Walker Martinez, who, upon the strength of a safe-conduct, had emerged from his hiding-place, the British Embassy, and two other delegates, profited by the opportunity to place themselves under the French flag, and secured passages in the French corvette *Volta* to Iquique.

The elections had, for the reasons set forth in the previous chapter, resulted in the almost unopposed return of Liberals favourable to the Balmacedist theory of government, though of course the legal existence of the new Congress would not commence until June 1st. The revolted Congress still legally existed, but having enjoyed its necessary three months of ordinary session, from June to September, 1890, its legislative functions had ceased with its last dismissal. It is most important to remember that, by the express terms of the Chilian constitution, the President is not bound to convoke Congress for more than these three months in any one year, and that failing such convocation by him, the members have no more right to assemble for legislative purposes than would have an equal number of mule-drivers.* This may be as radically unsound

* See 'The Chilian Constitution,' Art. 82, sec. 5, in Appendix

a system as one may choose to assert ; but it is, for all that, the plain, clearly-expressed law of Chile. The Rump of the Congress had as little right to call itself the Chilian Congress at Iquique, as the Home Rulers would have, during a recess, to call themselves the Parliament of the United Kingdom in Dublin.

CHAPTER VII.

MY SECOND CRUISE.

The Plan of Operations—Troops for Coquimbo—Scenes on Board—Coquimbo—British Naval Station—La Serena—Moraga's Advice to Admiral Hotham—*En Route* for Iquique—Coaling at Sea—I tranship to the *Condell*—A Contrast—A Desperate Adventure—'The Last Watch'—Captain Cook—Moraga the Wolf—*Un Mauvais Quart d'Heure*—In Iquique Harbour—The Union Jack saves the Rebel Transports—An Alarm—A Difficult Torpedo-shot—Moraga's Dilemma—The Ironclad *Cochrane* bears down—A Harebrained Exploit—What the Prisoners said and did—Northward to sink the *O'Higgins* in a Peruvian Port—A Sea-Lawyer—The *Huascar* and the *Magellanes*—A Naval Skirmish—*Adios*—Moraga the Lamb—A Clever Ruse—Captain Cook saves us—A Naval Duel declined—We rejoin the *Imperial*—Bombardment of Iquique—Bombardment of Taltal—An Attack in Boats—Capture of Taltal—A Banquet and a Bill—Coquimbo—Valparaiso.

THE sinking of the *Blanco Encalada* had produced great 'moral effect' throughout Chile, and, as we afterwards learnt, had created a panic in the revolted fleet. It was therefore decided to renew the attack, and, if possible, to sink a ship or two in Iquique Harbour itself. A few more such lessons would, it was thought, bring the insurgents to their knees. It is tolerably certain that but for the active and passive help given to the revolutionists by foreigners, and more especially by the British, continued resistance would have been impossible, absolutely dependent as the northern towns were upon sea-borne supplies. But the help was given, and given liberally. Steamer after steamer left Valparaiso, Talcuhano, Coronel, and other southern ports, laden with coal and provisions of all sorts, clearing nominally for Callao or some other neutral port, but always contriving to call in at, or to be intercepted off, Iquique. Sometimes, indeed, the insurgents made a mistake, and 'intercepted' the wrong vessel, as when Rear-Admiral Hotham compelled them to restore the coal forcibly taken from a German collier, and to salute the German flag by way of apology. But then this German skipper was an exception. Why, it may be asked, did not Balmaceda temporarily stop all exports from Chilian ports? Because such a course would have completely ruined the already severely-crippled southern trade, and because supplies could still have been sent to Iquique from Buenos Aires or from Peruvian ports, to say nothing of awkward complications with foreign Governments. And so the Government had to look on whilst British and German steamers loaded up stores in Valparaiso for the rebels at Iquique. It was open to the President to prevent the entry of these vessels into northern harbours, if he could maintain an effectual blockade; but how could he do this with the entire fleet against him? This was the active assistance rendered to the insurgents. Passive aid took the form of an absolute refusal upon the part of shipowners to sell or lend a single steamer to the Government. The South American Steamship Company had indeed supplied the *Imperial*, but this they had been compelled to do by the terms of their charter. No others could be procured for love or money. And it being impossible for troops to cross 200 miles of desert, Balmaceda was effectually debarred from hurling his legions upon the revolted districts. His hopes for the moment therefore centred in the possibility of destroying the two remaining ironclads, *Cochrane* and *Huascar*, and the cruiser *Esmeralda*, by means of the *torpederas*. Failing this, he could only await the arrival of the new warships from France, and the off-chance that his agents in Argentina, Uruguay, and Brazil might succeed in buying up a few transports. Meanwhile he had decided to keep a large force stationed at Coquimbo (about 160 miles north of Valparaiso), in readiness for future operations.

The *Lynch* had not yet undergone the needful repairs consequent upon the damage inflicted upon her by the guns of the *Aconcagua* at Caldera. She was therefore left behind, with orders to follow on as soon as possible to a rendezvous agreed upon off Iquique.

Upon May 10th the *Imperial* and the *Condell* steamed out of the harbour, amidst loud *vivas* from the assembled spectators. The spar-deck of the transport had been assigned to the troops, numbering 500 men. A halt was made at the village of Papuro, distant some twenty miles, for the purpose of embarking 800 additional men and two batteries of artillery. By the time this reinforcement was on board, the spar-deck, extensive as it was, was literally packed with humanity. Most of the soldiers appeared to have two or more wives, and each wife a liberal supply of children, so that what the total number of souls came to it was hard to guess within a few hundreds. A small portion of the deck abaft the chart-room was corded off, and a narrow pathway to one of the companion-stairs kept clear by sentries, but the music saloon amidships was quite inaccessible, and had, indeed, to be locked up to save it from desecration. Poor devils, what a good-humoured, merry lot they were! It gave one appetite to see with what gusto the coarse fare served out (and heaven only knows how this was effected) was devoured! Huge mounds of bread, bucketfuls of beans, and countless junks of half-raw meat appeared and disappeared in interminable relays. And when, later on, all had 'camped' for the night, what a scene presented itself! Men, women, rifles, children, knapsacks, dogs, in indescribable admixture. It was good to see how the men had given up their *ponchos,* and often even their coats, to make their female comrades and the *ninos* more comfortable—for bedding there was absolutely none. I saw one hapless terrier, securely bound, serving as an impromptu pillow for a baby, the mother's head reposing upon the breast of her husband, who in turn reposed upon a comrade's outstretched limbs. My friend the quartermaster viewed the scene with a look of intense disgust. 'By George,' he muttered, 'there'll be a week's work cleaning up after *this* lot !'

Fortunately this invasion did not last long, for next day we reached Coquimbo, and the task of disembarkation at once began. The method used of slinging the horses into the tenders struck me as so needlessly brutal that I suggested to Colonel Campos to shove the remainder of the animals overboard and let them swim ashore ; and, upon my assurance that it was sometimes done in our service, when the beach is good and not too far distant, my proposal was adopted. It was amusing to see the *puzzled* look of some of the horses when they found themselves afloat ; they seemed unwilling to leave the side of the ship, but soon struck out for shore, where all arrived safely.

A fine harbour this at Coquimbo—large, well sheltered, and with deep water up to within a furlong of the shore ; for which good reasons it was long ago selected as a depôt for the British

Pacific Squadron. We found the Union Jack very much *en évidence*, the *Warspite, Champion,* and *Daphne* all lying within musket-range, whilst nearer still was permanently moored that relic of bygone days, the *Liffey*, dismasted, and now used as a supply-ship.

Of course, a party of us went ashore, where we were most hospitably entertained by the officers of the garrison, of whom I more particularly remember Colonels Carvalho and Errazuriz. After a regimental lunch one usually sees things *couleur de rose*, but I confess that Coquimbo struck me as a particularly ugly town. Upon the opposite side of the bay is a town of more ancient date (in fact, some 300 years old), called La Serena—a few years ago, ere the French syndicates brought about a crash, an important centre of the copper industry, a metal which abounds in the neighbourhood.

Nunc tantum sinus et statio male fida carinis.

In fact, only vessels of very light draught can approach this side of the bay at all. A dreary place, Serena, which one reaches by rail from Coquimbo. It seemed to be heavily garrisoned; indeed, Colonel Carvalho informed me that the two towns between them mustered 11,000 troops. Here we dined, and, as usual, very well, returning on horseback along the beach, which at low-water affords a splendid ten-mile stretch of hard sand for a gallop.

Captain Moraga always referred with great

bitterness to the inopportune appearance of the *Warspite* at Caldera, whereby the *Aconcagua* had been enabled to escape capture; and he now strongly urged upon the British Admiral the expediency of keeping clear of northern ports, especially Iquique, for at least a fortnight, lest, should he again mistake the *Warspite* for the *Esmeralda*, a regrettable disaster might ensue. He made no secret of his intention to scour the northern ports and to torpedo any hostile ships he could discover. Rear-Admiral Hotham took the advice, as Moraga informed me, in very good part, and promised to keep his squadron in southern waters for the period named. Whereupon the *Imperial* and *Condell* started together for Iquique.

Beyond stopping and searching one sailing-ship, nothing of any interest occurred during the run north. Upon May 14th the two vessels hove to about sixty miles west of Iquique for the purposes of filling up the *Condell's* coal-bunkers and deciding upon a plan of attack. Coaling at sea must be a difficult operation in anything like rough weather, since even in the smooth water prevalent in these latitudes the task is a tedious one. Whilst it was in progress I accompanied Captain Garin on board the *Condell*, taking a portmanteau and some bedding with me. I had previously sent Moraga a line, reminding him of his promise to allow me to accompany him in his next attack, whereto I had received the following reply:

Condell, May 14*th*, 1891.

'MY DEAR SEÑOR HERVEY,

'I shall probably attack to-night. Come by all means, if you wish to, but I warn you I can only offer you a sofa to sleep on. You know how glad I shall be to have you with me. So if you really are inclined to put up with a rough welcome and share a little danger with your friends on board here, come along. Bring some bedding, especially pillows.

'Yours cordially,
'C. MORAGA.'

Garin, Campos, and the others had tried hard to dissuade me from going; but this, as I told them, was mere jealousy because they couldn't go also. And so off I went. I was most enthusiastically welcomed by the officers of the *Condell*, who regarded my visit in the light of a personal compliment, and especially by the navigating officer, Captain James Cook (a descendant as well as namesake of the great navigator), who remarked to me : " They say ashore that an English sailor has no right to be aboard a Chilian war-vessel, and I've had some doubts about it myself. But if a *Times* correspondent comes too, why, it must be all right.'

A brief council of war was held in the little saloon, wherein it was agreed that the *Imperial* was to cruise upon the present parallel of longitude and within two degrees of latitude, keeping a sharp look-out for both us and the expected *Lynch*. And then, so soon as the last sack of coal had been got on board, we parted company.

Compared to the *Imperial*, the *Condell* seemed like a little tug-boat. She was, moreover, a distinctly dirty vessel, it being impossible upon deck to escape a liberal coating of soot and coal-dust. Yet withal her diminutive ' saloon ' was very cosy, and the cuisine even better than that of the *Imperial*. The promised sofa was soft and comfortable. In a very few hours I was quite at home.

At about 4 p.m. we spoke an English barque just out from Iquique, and most probably nitrate-laden. But, as Moraga wanted information, no questions were asked about cargo. We learnt that the news of the *Blanco* disaster had produced a great scare, that every possible precaution was being taken to protect the entrance to the harbour by means of chains and sunken torpedoes in electric communication with the shore, and that a small torpedo-launch had somehow been procured for night-patrol duty. It was also stated that the men-of-war never remained in harbour during the night, standing out to sea and returning in the morning. All this was serious news if correct. Moraga determined, therefore, to reconnoitre that night with a special view to ascertaining whether or not the report concerning the men-of-war were true. And here I may again quote from my diary.

May 14.—At dusk the *Condell* steamed full-speed towards Iquique. Onward through the gloom, like a gray shark, a keen look-out being kept for any out-going war-ships, which with her tremendous speed the *torpedera* might successfully attack even in motion. At all events, Moraga had decided to risk it, should any turn up. At about midnight a light was reported, which was presently recognised as Iquique lighthouse. When about three miles off, speed was slackened and the harbour cautiously approached until, with the aid of night-glasses, a fair idea of the shipping could be obtained. Seven or eight sailing vessels, a few small steamers, but no sign of war-ships or transports. Clearly nothing to be gained by entering the port, so Moraga ran out seaward upon the off-chance of sighting one or other of the absent ironclads.

May 15.—Spoke *Imperial* about forty miles south-west at 10 a.m. She reported having learnt from a schooner that the *Huascar* is at Caldera, and that the *Cochrane* is expected at Iquique with a flotilla of transports. The skipper of the schooner being apparently friendly to the Government cause, Garin believed his information to be substantially correct. Whereupon Moraga decided to revisit Iquique that night and, as he said, 'sink something, were it only a pontoon, just to put the fear of God in their hearts.'

May 16, 1 *a.m.*—Moving at half-speed straight

THE TORPEDO VESSEL 'CONDELL'

for the harbour. As we draw close, it seems to me that the rays from the lighthouse will betray our whereabouts, but although the *Condell* passes it within a few hundred yards, no signal of alarm is given. This seems a somewhat desperate venture, what with chains, booms, submarine mines or torpedoes, etc., to say nothing of the forts and possibly the *Cochrane*; but Moraga is resolved to sink *something*, and so onward we go. In half an hour more we shall be in the thick of it; not sooner, because we are feeling our way with great caution. It occurs to me that a cigarette and B. and S. (possibly my last in this vale of tears) would not be amiss, and not being officially tied to the deck, I obey instinct and descend to the saloon, profiting by the occasion to jot down these notes. A few minutes later Señor Sartori came down to fetch something.

'Well, I'll be hanged!' he exclaimed. 'Writing *now!* You had better shove your papers into a bottle well corked, if you are so anxious to record the "Last Moments of a Correspondent." *That's* not a bad idea, though,' he added hurriedly, helping himself to the Martell and disappearing up the companion-stairs.

With some difficulty I groped my way forward and ascended to the bridge, where Moraga, Cook, and others were gathered. Every man was at his post, and a death-like silence pervaded the vessel as she slowly approached the shipping.

'I wish they would hurry up,' I whispered to Captain Cook. 'This suspense doesn't agree with me at all.'

'Perhaps you'll wish it had lasted a little longer presently,' growled Cook. 'And look here! *whatever happens*, don't you leave the ship. I mean, even if they sink us.'

'Oh, by Jove!' I answered. 'If it comes to sinking, I shall clear out for those rocks over there. I'm a good swimmer.'

'Were you Webb himself, you'd never reach them. *The water here is just alive with sharks!*' And hurriedly turning to Moraga, he said '*Ahora, señor!*' (Now, sir!)

A rapid vibration of the engine-room bell, and in another minute we were racing into the harbour at top speed. Close in shore it was just possible to make out two lines of vessels, one behind the other. Only one vessel at all resembling a man-of-war could be discerned, and her we fortunately identified as the *Baltimore*. Indeed, from the sudden appearance of many lights on board of her, we concluded that she must have seen us and wished to assist us in recognising her. Moraga was savage, and called the rebel warships all the hard names he could think of.

'A nice fleet this, Señor Corresponsal, is it not?' he asked bitterly. 'To abandon the port it is supposed to protect! However, when the *Cochrane* returns in the morning, she'll find that the wolf has been here during the watch-dog's absence;' and he pointed significantly to the vessels moored in line. Then, as we got up close to them, he suddenly dashed down his glasses, wrenched the telegraph-handle round to 'Steady,' and proceeded to curse as only a Spaniard in a real rage can curse. The cause of his wrath was soon obvious. The front line consisted of sailing-ships moored broadside on and in close order, so as effectually to cover the second line, consisting of six or seven fair-sized steamers—evidently the expected transports. What was to be done ? It was clearly impossible to get at the transports without sinking at least one of the sailing-ships. A hot, quick discussion ensued.

'D—— them!' exclaimed Moraga savagely. 'What right have these foreign vessels to shove themselves between me and my prey ? Who could blame me if I sink one of them?'

In a very few words I pointed out that these vessels were, to a certainty, British or German, and that to *torpedo* one of them would infallibly involve the Government in a war with Great Britain. Cook backed me up, and vowed he would have neither hand nor part in sinking a British ship. Sartori took the same view. And finally our enraged commander gave in. But a shot at something he would have, and one vessel, apparently a disused steamer, and believed to be employed as a supply-ship, was made out standing apart from the rest. At less than one hundred yards the bow-torpedo was discharged at this vessel, and was reported by the look-out man (a negro, renowned for his good sight at night) to have struck her in the bows. At this moment a rapidly-moving light was seen approaching the *Condell's* port quarter, and several rifle-shots were heard from the shore. It seemed probable that the light belonged to the torpedo-launch we had heard of, especially as it almost immediately was hidden; and should a general alarm be given and a search-light be brought to bear, the forts might open fire upon us. But, above all, no good could could be done if the *Condell* remained in the harbour all night. And so the engines were reversed, and she steamed astern, full speed, out to sea.

But when about two miles out, Moraga again stopped the engines and, summoning his principal officers to the saloon, reopened the question of attacking the transports. It was too intolerable, he said, to have run all this risk for nothing, or next to nothing, with all those transports waiting there to be sunk. He did not wish to exert his authority as captain and order a return into the harbour, if it were the unanimous opinion that it would be foolhardy. But would no one support him in his desire to have another try? No one did. I think all had had enough nerve-testing for one night, especially as the captain had no new plan to suggest for getting at the transports without sinking a sailing-ship. Possibly he himself only asked opinions so as to exonerate himself from any possible future charge of having missed an opportunity. Anyhow, the idea of returning was abandoned, and I am not ashamed to confess that I was very well pleased that it was so. But upon one point Moraga was determined. He would wait outside the harbour till daylight so as to get a clear view of the shipping.

At 7 a.m. a large steamer was sighted coming from the west, which was soon made out to be the *Cochrane* returning after her nocturnal cruise. But her advent caused no uneasiness, as it was well known that she could steam no more than nine knots an hour. Then ensued a series of very saucy manœuvres on the part of the *Condell*. In full view of the big ironclad and of the people ashore, she went close enough to the port for us to obtain, with the naked eye, a distinct view of the shipping and of the town. When I saw the somewhat intricate course he must have followed, in the dark, to reach the back-lying vessels, I paid a mental tribute to the pilotage of Captain Cook. And there plain enough was the *Baltimore*, but no other warships. After a fairly long inspection, it was deemed time to keep out of the way of the approaching *Cochrane*, then some three miles off. Meanwhile, a small steamer had been approaching from the north, and as Moraga wanted information upon various points, he steamed off to meet her, the *Cochrane* altering her course in pursuit. A challenge blank-shot was fired, but the steamer, emboldened, doubtless, by the near presence of the ironclad, paid no heed. A second blank discharge was likewise disregarded. With a grim smile Moraga fired a shot with his own hand, which passed within a few yards of her bows. Then she hove to, and ran up the Union Jack. She was a small vessel called (I think, but am not sure) the *Juanita*, engaged in the water-carrying trade. Her skipper happened to be an old friend of Cook's, who presently hailed him thus :

'D—— your eyes, Bill! why didn't you stop? D'ye want a hole made in your hull?'

'D—— *your* eyes, Jim Cook! what the deuce are *you* stopping for? Don't ye see that big chap over there? He'll put a few holes in *your* hull, if ye stop here much longer. A pretty game you're up to, and no mistake, a-piloting a d——d pirate! You ought to be durned well ashamed of yourself, Jim Cook!'

Fortunately, Moraga does not understand a word of English; but Sartori, as I have said, is half an Englishman.

'Look here, my friend,' he called out, 'you had best keep a more civil tongue in your head. What ships are at Pisagua?'

'You'll precious soon find out, if you're going up that way,' was the reply.

'*Que dice?*' inquired Moraga.

'Oh, the fool knows nothing!' answered Sartori evasively. 'And see, Señor Comandante, the *Cochrane* will be within range in a few minutes.'

'*Bueno!*' said the captain coolly; 'we'll be off as soon as we have spoken that little boat over there,' indicating a small row-boat hugging the coast. 'And, by the way, hoist this signal to the *Cochrane*.'

Sartori showed me the slip, upon which was written, 'Have a communication for commander,' as he went to the flag-box.

The row-boat tried hard to escape, but to no purpose, there being deep water right up to the rocks. A hail, followed by a warning rifle-shot, brought the boat's head in our direction.

'Quicker!' thundered Moraga; and very soon the boat was made fast alongside, and the occupants, five men and a boy about six years of age, scrambled on deck.

The *Cochrane* was now within easy range, but, to our surprise, did not fire. Forgetting the boat alongside, the order was given 'Full speed ahead!' and away we went, with the result that the boat swamped and was cut adrift. The unfortunate captives were horror-stricken at the loss of their boat, and loudly bewailed the disaster.

'Never mind, lads,' said Moraga, 'accidents can't be helped, and I'll make good the value of the boat. Come, now, answer these questions, and turn out your pockets.'

Then ensued a lengthy cross-examination, which elicited the information that things were in a very bad way in Iquique, that provisions of all sorts were at famine prices, work almost at a standstill, and money so scarce that almost every tradesman was issuing his own *vales*, or paper-money. Of these *vales* the captives had a miscellaneous assortment, signed by all sorts of persons. The owner of the boat had almost sixty dollars in notes, payable at Valparaiso by the Bank of London and Tarapacá; and these notes, he affirmed, were the only ones esteemed to be of any real value, because everyone knew that the English nitrate syndicates were financing the revolution. They all believed that the *Huascar* and *Magellanes* were at Pisagua (about thirty-five miles north of Iquique), and that the *O'Higgins* was in the Peruvian port Pacocho.'

'How much of this rubbish do you earn a month in Iquique?' queried the captain, indicating the *vales*.

About thirty dollars, it seemed.

'*Bueno*,' he said; 'now I'll give you fifty dollars of good sound Government money if you'll join my crew, besides a suit of clothes apiece, and as much as you can eat three times a day.'

Without the least hesitation this offer was joyously accepted by all—the prospect of plenty to eat apparently outweighing even the promised dollars. It was furthermore agreed that the value of the boat would be paid at Valparaiso. A special meal was ordered for the poor fellows, who seemed to be starving ; and a few minutes later I got a glimpse of the youngster gorging himself in the galley, and evidently upon the best possible terms with the cooks.

Moraga decided to proceed due north, and to attack the *O'Higgins* at Pacocho that very night.

'But,' I remonstrated, 'that's a Peruvian port, and therefore neutral.'

'I don't care about that,' was the reply. 'The Peruvian Government long ago decreed that the rebel ships were not to seek refuge in their ports, and this *O'Higgins* has no business being there ; but as the place is unfortified, and has no guardship, it is evident that the authorities there are unable to enforce the decree. I shall enforce it for them.'

'This is very bad international law, captain, I'm afraid.'

'Perhaps it is,' acquiesced the captain, ' but it is very good sea law, especially when backed up by a couple of torpedoes.'

Meanwhile the *Cochrane* was toiling away astern of us, our speed being regulated so as just to keep out of range of her big guns. She hoisted no reply to our signals, but followed us steadily. This conduct was as unaccountable as her previous neglect to fire upon us when within range, since her commander must have known that the *Condell*

14

could have left him out of sight in half an hour. The generally accepted theory was that he wished to get well away from Iquique before opening up communication with us. I was extremely curious to know what the nature of the communication to be made might be, and threw out a hint to that effect.

'Well, I'll tell you, Señor Corresponsal,' said Moraga; 'but don't spread it about. I suppose you have heard that the revolutionists sent an emissary to me offering me $200,000 to join them with this vessel?'

'Yes,' I replied, 'I have been told of that, and of your handing your tempter over to the police.'

'*Bueno*,' he went on, 'now I am empowered by Government to offer the commander of the *Cochrane* one million dollars if *he* will join *us* with *his* vessel. That would finish the rebellion at once.'

'I see,' I assented. 'But how can you make the offer? Surely not by signal for all his officers to understand?'

'No, of course not,' rejoined Moraga. 'If he replies "All right," I must try and find a crew and an officer who will venture to await the *Cochrane* in a boat under the white flag.'

'And failing that?'

'Failing that, I must risk it myself . . . unless——'

'Unless,' I concluded, laughing, 'the Corresponsal hoists British colours and goes instead, eh?'

'That's about it,' assented Moraga, echoing my laugh, but looking me very hard in the face.

The position was becoming a little embarrassing. The risk, such as it might be, I did not mind; but I felt the utter impossibility of having any share in bribing an officer to betray his trust, rebel and all though he were. A midshipman (Moraga's son) saved me the necessity of explanation by descending into the saloon to announce that two steamers, supposed to be warships, were leaving Pisagua Harbour, apparently to cut us off. We soon made them out to be the *Huascar* and *Magellanes*, and the *Cochrane's* reason for following us became more plain. Knowing that her consorts would be informed by telegram from Iquique of the *Condell's* route northward, she reckoned upon their pouncing out at us, and perhaps by a lucky shot crippling us, when, of course, she would be 'in at the death.'

By altering his course a couple of points to the westward, Moraga might easily have distanced all three ships without running the smallest risk. But he must have his joke. He held straight upon his northerly course. 'They're burning lots of coal,' quoth he; 'let us see if we can't tempt them to burn a little powder also.' And he deliberately ordered the engines to be stopped. 'When they put a shot over our heads,' he explained, 'we'll move on a bit and lead them a dance to Pacocho if they care to follow.'

The *Magellanes*, a wooden sloop, opened fire first, she being a somewhat faster vessel than the *Huascar*. There is a certain fascination in being made a target of. You watch the puff of white smoke which announces that the iron messenger is on its way, followed, after an interval, by a ' boom,' faint or loud according to the size of the gun, the distance, and the direction of the wind, and then you mark eagerly where the shot falls. The whistling rush of a ball overhead has an especially thrilling sound until one gets used to it. Of course at long range the odds are greatly against any particular shot striking the ship, and incomparably greater against it striking an individual on board, so that the sense of personal danger is not much felt. We sat upon a skylight smoking and criticising the *Magellanes'* performance, whilst she sent us three messages in succession, all of which fell short.

'I don't think much of *her* guns,' commented Moraga. 'She can't be more than 3,000 metres off. Let us see.' And, carefully sighting one of the Hotchkiss pieces, he fired. The little *Condell* shivered all over, these guns being really too heavy for a vessel of her light build. The shot passed just over the sloop's bows. A second shot passed clean over her, whereupon she steamed off towards her consort. The *Huascar* then began to speak, and to more purpose, shot after shot falling around us and ahead. ' No use wasting powder upon an ironclad,' said the captain. 'I'd fight that wooden tub all day, but I can't stand the *blindado.*' And the engines were again set going. The *Huascar* kept firing away fiercely, and for some minutes made really good practice, several shots falling within twenty or thirty yards of the *torpedera,* but, as luck would have it, none striking her. Soon they began to fall short, and for about two hours we kept at just a safe distance, the ironclad blazing away as fast as her gunners could load. Her commander appeared to have lost his head at sight of the *torpedera,* and no great wonder, since he had previously commanded the ill-fated *Blanco,* owing his life to the fact that he was ashore in Caldera assisting at a banquet when his ship was blown up. The fire was kept up until we could hardly make out the shots falling miles astern. At last even he gave it up, and we saw all three ships heading back towards Iquique. From beginning to end, the *Cochrane* never once fired a shot.

That night we arrived off Pacocho, and were about to enter the harbour, when an extraordinary thing happened. One of the engineers came to Moraga and very humbly begged to be allowed the use of a boat so soon as the *O'Higgins* should be struck.

'A boat ? What for, man ?' asked the captain.

'My brother is on board the *O'Higgins, Señor Comandante,*' explained the suppliant ; 'and if he is drowned it will break mother's heart. Give me one chance of picking him up, small as it is.'

Moraga looked at the man for several seconds, and then swore at him roundly.

'Why didn't you tell me this before, you big-hearted fool?' he asked.

Then, turning to Cook, he merely bade him put the vessel's head about and shape a course to rejoin the *Imperial*, and at once disappeared downstairs.

'Did anyone ever meet such a mixture of wolf and lamb?' ejaculated Cook, half disgustedly.

But the engineer went his way rejoicing, and spread the fame of the *Comandante's* good-heartedness throughout the ship. A strange character, this captain of the *Condell!* After the Peruvian War, in which he had highly distinguished himself, he had retired from active service to devote himself to a quiet country life. But by nature a stern disciplinarian, he had upon the outbreak of the revolution and the mutiny of the fleet at once offered his services to the Government, which eagerly accepted them. He had travelled overland to Buenos Aires to bring round the torpedo vessels, and was now risking his own life and his boy's life in a desperate effort to cripple the rebel fleet. He had distributed his share of the *Blanco* prize-money (about $20,000) amongst his crew—an example followed by most of his officers; but he was absolutely merciless towards any breach of discipline—a man equally loved and feared.

May 17.—About abreast of Iquique, *en route* to our rendezvous with the *Imperial*, spoke two small schooners just out from that port. The crews were very sulky, and reluctant to give information. It was ascertained, however, that, as a result of the *Condell's* nocturnal visit, the crews of the transports had refused to remain on board at night for the future, whilst in harbour, 'until those devil's ships, *Condell* and *Lynch*, should be captured or sunk,' and that a battalion, which it had been intended to despatch to Caldera, had absolutely declined to embark. Also that two new forts had been lately erected, and in positions which made it plain that we must have passed unseen within fifty yards of one of them; that additional sunken torpedoes were being laid down; and that two more steam-launches had been detailed off for night patrol duty. The pontoon had been struck too far forward (close to the cut-water) for the torpedo to do more than damage her. The *Baltimore* was avowedly waiting to seize the *Itata*, which had escaped from California with a cargo of arms and ammunition for the revolutionists. To prevent this seizure, two fast steamers had been despatched to meet the *Itata* and warn her captain to land his cargo elsewhere.

At 10 a.m., made out the smoke of two steamers going south, and cracked on high speed to overtake them. So soon as we got near enough to identify them, the larger vessel was pronounced to be the *Imperial*. The smaller one, some distance astern, and not easily distinguishable against the high brown coast-line, was assumed to be the *Lynch*. What could they be up to, thirty miles east of the rendezvous parallel? Then, as we came still nearer, it was evident that the smaller vessel was *not* the *Lynch*, having but one funnel. Then a puff of white smoke from her bows, followed at intervals by other puffs, apparently explained matters: one of the enemy's ships was pursuing and firing upon the *Imperial!* And, judging from her slow rate of progress, something must be amiss with the Government transport. The excitement on board was intense, as the bugle sounded to quarters and the guns were manned for action. Under forced-blast the *Condell's* engines drove the little ship along at a speed of nearly nineteen knots—a dangerous strain in the patchwork condition of her tubes. Captain Cook—a long telescope glued to his eye—had hitherto expressed no opinion. Suddenly he removed it, and quietly remarked:

'*Señor Comandante*, that's not the *Imperial* at all. It's her sister-ship, the *Aconcagua*. The other is the *O'Higgins*, which cannot have been at Pacocho, after all.'

Captain Cook was known to be almost infallible when he expressed a decided opinion. With a muttered curse, Moraga ordered the engines to be slowed down, and altered his course away from the pursuing ship and towards the fugitive vessel. Almost immediately the latter altered her course also, so as to head towards us, and opened fire with her bow-chasers. The ruse was now apparent, and a very clever one it was. Indeed, but for Captain Cook's coolness and judgment, it would have succeeded perfectly, and the *torpedera* would have found herself under a double fire.

'*Caramba!*' cried Moraga. 'It shall never be said that the *Condell* turned tail upon a transport, and it will take the *O'Higgins* ten minutes to come up.' And, without firing a shot, he bore at full speed down upon the *Aconcagua*. But the latter had not bargained to tackle the *Condell* singlehanded, and very promptly sheered off to meet her escort.

'*Por Dios!*' exclaimed the captain. 'If only the *Lynch* were here!'

But alone even he dared not risk fighting the pair.* Our course was therefore shaped westwards; and four hours later we picked up the *Imperial*.

---

* It should be remarked that vessels of the *Condell* type are not intended to act as fighting ships, as, indeed, the name 'torpedo-catcher' sufficiently indicates. A shot, or even a rifle-bullet, striking one of the five large torpedoes on deck, would cause it to explode with, of course, destructive results to the vessel. The risk run every time the *torpederas* came under fire was, therefore, far greater than that of an ordinary warship. Indeed, they were used throughout in a most foolhardy manner.

Captain Garin at once came on board; but he had nothing of interest to report, nor had he seen any sign of the *Lynch*. He was specially anxious that I should rejoin his ship, whilst Moraga was equally pressing in his invitation to remain where I was. I hardly knew which way to decide, so as not to give offence to either. But as it appeared that both vessels were to proceed in company upon a bombarding expedition down the coast, I compromised by proposing to return temporarily on board the *Imperial*, with the option of rejoining the *Condell* should she undertake any specially interesting work. And so I once more enjoyed the luxury of my two cabins.

At 5 p.m. the *Imperial* hove to outside Iquique Harbour, and opened a heavy fire upon the forts and barracks, very carefully avoiding the populated portion of the town and the shipping. The *Condell* had sneaked round from the north, and, getting under cover of some high land, was soon busily at work also. Of course, no definite results could be expected from this demonstration, which was intended chiefly as an insulting reminder of the powerlessness or cowardice of the fleet; nor do I suppose much damage was done, if any at all. The forts could not effectively reply, as we easily kept out of their line of fire, whilst the *Condell* was quite concealed from their view. After about an hour and a half of this noisy and somewhat bravado business, the two vessels proceeded southwards, parting company, with a rendezvous opposite a town called Taltal for the 21st.

May 21.—The *Condell* rejoined the *Imperial*, and the two vessels anchored in Taltal Harbour at 9 a.m., within rifle-range of the shore. The place was known to be unfortified, and consequently there had been no intention of bombarding; but no sooner were the ships at anchor than fire was opened upon the *Imperial* from the beach, from a couple of field-pieces, supported by a rattling discharge of musketry. One shot carried away a portion of her bowsprit, whilst the bullets were flying all round. In a trice the two ships replied; and a shell from the *Condell* exploding upon the beach, a general stampede of the garrison took place towards the interior of the town. The guns were now brought to bear upon the local Intendencia, and then Moraga signalled that the troops were to land and capture the place. Never saw I men more delighted than the soldiers on board at this unexpected chance of a scrimmage. So far as could be judged, the shore garrison numbered about two hundred men; and as Colonel Campos had only sixty available after providing for the service of the guns, some very warm work was imminent. Campos himself was in high glee.

'Come along, Mauricio,' he cried, 'and see how my children here will make that rabble run!'

This was a liberal proposal enough; but what right had I to accompany the attacking party?

Besides, it is no joke to go under fire without the privilege of returning shot for shot; but, on the other hand, *noblesse oblige*. If I remained on board, might it not be said that the *gringo* was over-careful of his skin? One of the ship's surgeons (we had two this trip) solved the problem for me. 'Here,' he said, 'tie this red cross on your arm, and come and help me.' A minute later we were both in the Major's boat, Campos leading by several lengths. Four boats started in all, each carrying fifteen men. The garrison were very slow to profit by the advantage given them of having boatloads of men to shoot at. The shore was almost reached before they opened fire; but in a few seconds four men were wounded (two very badly), all in the leading boat.

'*Esperad canalla!*' (Wait a while, you dogs!) cried Campos, standing erect in the stern, and shaking his sword at the foe.

The men hardly waited for the boats to touch land, so impatient were they to get at the enemy. The garrison did not wait, either, but fled precipitately, hotly pursued by the invaders.

Moraga had meanwhile landed some thirty men lower down. The two forces presently united and formed into column. Parading the men in the Plaza, Moraga announced that the penalty for any outrage to a peaceful inhabitant, or intoxication, would be instant death. The Intendencia was found to be in a sadly ruinous condition, from the effects of the shells which had been put into it. A clean sweep was now made of all official documents; the telegraph instruments were smashed up, and all discoverable Government property (including the two field-pieces and a miscellaneous collection of old-fashioned rifles) confiscated.

A telegram addressed to the Intendente from Iquique, and dated the previous day, created much amusement, which was increased by an explanation given to me by an English resident. The telegram announced that the *Condell* had been sunk by the *Huascar*, and that the *Imperial* had surrendered to escape a similar fate. This glorious news had been communicated to the leading residents at once, but it was decided not to make it public until next day; for be it noted that May 21st is a high holiday in Chile, being the anniversary of the death of Captain Prat, the Chilian Nelson, who, losing his ship the *Esmeralda* (a wooden vessel) in a desperate engagement with the (then) Peruvian monitor *Huascar*, was slain in a heroic attempt to board the ironclad; and thus at Taltal it had been arranged to give additional *éclat* to the festival by publicly proclaiming the good news received from Iquique. Preparations for a sort of banquet had been in progress, when the identical vessels supposed to be lost for ever to the 'Dictator' Balmaceda had suddenly made their appearance in the harbour. A more ludicrous *démente* has surely seldom been given to unscrupulous liars.

The banquet (perhaps for lack of time for preparation) was a hollow fraud so far as eatables were concerned; but a very fair assortment of fluids was discovered in the local club. My English acquaintance overcame my scruples to follow the example of Campos and the others, who were indulging in 'free drinks' *ad lib.*, by gravely entering my name in the visitors' book, being himself a member. This gentleman's description of the condition of affairs at Taltal was a very gloomy one; in fact, it was, like all the other northern towns, commercially stagnant and ever hovering upon the brink of famine. The houses were very gay with bunting, in honour of Captain Prat; but, as he said, the cupboards in most of them were dismally empty. The inhabitants, he affirmed, cared little which side won, but were extremely anxious to see an end to the struggle.

It was dusk before the troops re-embarked, many of the inhabitants imploring Moraga to leave them to protect the town, alleging that, upon the return of the runaway garrison, all sorts of excesses would be committed. But this, of course, the commander could not do, the Government having no intention as yet of definitely re-occupying the place.

Just as I was leaving the club, the manager, a Frenchman, politely handed me the following 'little bill,' earnestly begging me to remit it to the President:

'The Club, Taltal, May 21st, 1891.

'List of articles destroyed or consumed after the capture of the town :

'1 oil-painting	$550
7 small do., @ $40	280
4 sets billiard-balls	560
Sundries	280
Wines, spirits, etc.	600
	$2,270 '

I thought the man a little out of his mind, but undertook the commission, and in due course executed it. Whether or not a cheque was ever sent from Santiago, I never heard.

May 23.—Touched at Coquimbo.

May 24.—Arrived at Valparaiso. British shipping gay with bunting in honour of her Majesty's birthday, which I invited my friends, naval and military, to celebrate with me ashore. We celebrated.

CHAPTER VIII.

MY THIRD CRUISE.

A Spell Ashore—Chilian News from Abroad—Balmaceda believes in Moral Effect—At Sea once more—A Tempting Bait—A Narrow Escape—Pisagua bombarded—Iquique bombarded—Tocopilla captured—Nitrate-duties for Balmaceda—The British Vice-Consul's Opinion—Antofagasta bombarded—A Deserted Village—Chañaral—The *Condell* in Peril—Reprisals—A Starving Population—Mr. Sherriff's Account—The *Imperial* becomes an Emigrant Ship—A Delayed Telegram—Farewells.

I HAD pretty well made up my mind to tempt Providence no more in northern waters, but rather 'to take mine ease' at mine inn,' and await the progress of events. With this intention, I betook myself to Santiago and endeavoured to ascertain what form the said events would be likely to take. The end of the struggle appeared to be as far off as ever. The army at the disposal of Government now numbered about 40,000 men, and, although Oppositionists boasted that most of the regiments would desert at the first favourable opportunity, my own observations led me to form an entirely different opinion. It was asserted also that the revolutionists in the north were only awaiting the arrival of several large consignments of repeating rifles, sent to them by their foreign sympathizers, to attack Balmaceda upon his own ground; that they had secured the services of a skilled German tactician, Colonel Körner, and were quite confident of ultimate success. What was quite certain was that, until additional ships were secured, the Government could not send a sufficiently strong force northward to capture and hold Iquique; and as yet there was no reliable information concerning the cruisers, nor had any additional transports been procurable.

I think the Balmacedists were somewhat disappointed that no more ironclads had been sunk, and found vent for their feelings in a severe denunciation of the cowardly conduct of the rebel ships in abandoning the harbours at night. But, after all, it was the chief business of these ships to avoid being blown up, and the plan followed was the safest that could have been devised. For instance, had the *Cochrane* been in Iquique harbour the night the *Condell* entered, she would, almost to a certainty, have shared the fate of the *Blanco*. It appeared that the reason the *Lynch* did not start to join us last time was the serious illness of Captain Fuentes, who, the doctors said, had been poisoned. He certainly looked very ill, poor fellow.

Of course, I revisited all my old haunts and looked up my many friends, thus contriving to kill

15

a few days pleasantly enough. I derived especial amusement from the perusal of the ' Chilian news' published in various foreign journals. For downright fabrications I divided the first prize between Buenos Aires and Paris, the New York papers being a good way ahead of their London contemporaries, which, however, at times broke the record. Thus, one of the English illustrated papers published sketches of the bombardment of Valparaiso by the revolutionary squadron, accompanied by a vivid description of the event. The person who made the sketches had clearly never seen Valparaiso. But this was a mere detail compared to the all-important fact that *Valparaiso had never been bombarded at all!* And when I reflected that these were the sort of fabrications so 'contradictory' to my messages, I began to realize how really ridiculous I must have made myself. I could imagine the tame effect of a telegram sent by me announcing perfect quietude in Santiago, as compared with an Iquique or Buenos Aires despatch describing wholesale massacres in the streets, or Balmaceda fleeing for his life to the Moneda.

During our absence an attempt had been made to secure a Government torpedo-launch, the *Aldea*, for the insurgents. Three of the crew had been bribed, with some of the spare nitrate money, to run away with the launch, which was to be met out at sea by a warship. The poor wretches fulfilled their part of the contract, but having only six hours' coal, and the man-of-war not turning up, the launch was recaptured by the *Lynch*, which had started in pursuit. The three men were tried by court-martial, and of course shot. Yet the Oppositionists worked up tremendous sympathy for these bribed traitors, and perhaps some day will erect statues to their memory.

A long interview with the President did not do much towards clearing away the mists which seemed to overhang the near future. He could take no definite steps towards crushing the rebellion so long as the command of the sea remained in insurgent hands. He must await the arrival of the ships from France, which he admitted had not yet started from Havre, but which he was confident would very soon be released by order of the judges of the French Supreme Court, 'who,' he added bitterly, 'may be supposed to be above being influenced by nitrate rings, or bribed by Jewish holders of Peruvian bonds.' This latter allusion was not quite plain to me, but he explained it. What truth may lie either in the allusion or in the explanation, I do not know. I merely give the latter as I got it.

' You are aware that by the treaty which closed the Peruvian War in June, 1883, Chile became possessed of Tarapacá definitively, but that, as regarded the two other provinces, Tacna and Arica, she only received them for ten years, at the end of which time the inhabitants were to decide by a plebiscite whether they should remain under the Chilian flag or revert to Peru. Now, the total loss of Tarapacá, and the possible prospective loss of Tacua and Arica, meant little short of national ruin to Peru, which had so long been enriched with the nitrate deposits in these provinces. Her only hope lay in recovering the two provinces when the ten years should have expired. And, of course, the hopes of her foreign creditors lay in the same direction, since thus alone could they ever expect to be paid. It cannot be unknown to you, Señor Corresponsal, that by far the largest of these foreign creditors, the man who has practically held Peru under his thumb for many years, is a wealthy Hebrew capitalist of Paris. Now, for nine years these provinces have been governed from Santiago, that is, by governors and other officials appointed by Chilian presidents, and the policy pursued has always tended towards securing a majority of votes in favour of Chilian nationality at the approaching plebiscite. *Beati possidentes,* you follow me ?'

'Do I overstep your Excellency's meaning in inferring that the presence of Chilian administrators might be expected to influence the direction of the popular vote ?' I inquired.

'I believe that some such idea prevails both in Lima and in Paris,' answered Señor Balmaceda, with a significant smile. 'At all events, it is no secret that I have personally used every means in my power towards retaining the provinces. You will, therefore, understand that my continuance in office, and the possibility of my being succeeded by another sharing my views, were regarded as very distinct obstacles in the way of Peruvian hopes. In the confusion attendant upon this revolution, Tacua and Arica have passed away from the control of the central Government, and are being administered by nominees of the fragmentary Congress at Iquique, if indeed they are administered at all. These people must, at any cost, keep upon friendly terms with Peru, since they are dependent upon the good offices and connivance of the northern republic for the very bread which they eat. And thus the revolution (especially should I and my Government be overthrown) affords a rare opportunity to Peru of regaining her influence in her lost provinces during the year preceding the decisive plebiscite. Upon no other grounds is the action of the French Government, in detaining ships ordered and paid for by the Chilian Government, intelligible. But we shall see what the French judges have to say upon the subject.'*

* The President correctly foreshadowed the judgment of the French Courts, which decided that the *Errazuriz* and *Pinto* were the property of the established Government of Chile, and must forthwith be handed over to the agents of the President of the Republic. But the decision came too late to save Balmaceda.

'Does your Excellency suppose that the insurgents would await the arrival of the war ships?' I inquired. 'Would they not rather risk a descent upon the south, once the departure of the vessels from France became known?'

'Yes,' replied the President, 'that would be their only chance; but for every man they can muster I can put four into the field. I have no fears on that score. Meanwhile the *torpederas* must again go north and intensify the moral effect produced by the recent expeditions, if they cannot manage to sink a few ships. I shall order Moraga to bombard every fortified port upon the northern coast. What think you of these attacks? You have witnessed some.'

'Well, candidly, your vessels are not powerful enough, or numerous enough, to inflict much damage,' I answered.

'But I do not wish to inflict much damage,' retorted Señor Balmaceda. 'I merely desire to let the northern populations understand what they may expect later on, and to prolong the scare caused by the sinking of the *Blanco*. And who knows? Perhaps the *Cochrane* and the *Huascar* may yet be caught napping.'

'Perhaps so,' I assented, rising to take my leave. 'But at present they appear to believe in the English proverb, that "discretion is the better part of valour."'

Upon June 1st the newly-elected Congress commenced its first session, the President opening it in person, and delivering a clever but somewhat over-lengthy inaugural speech, wherein he went over much old ground, and indulged in sanguine hopes for the near future. The first act of the new Chambers was to pass a sort of Bill of Indemnity, legalizing all decrees issued by Señor Balmaceda since the dismissal of the previous Congress. They then proceeded to discuss the question of reforming the existing constitution in accordance with modern ideas—a question which bade fair to keep them fully occupied for many months to come.

That same evening I received an urgent wire from Captain Garin, stating that the squadron would start next morning, and begging me to make one more cruise on the *Imperial*. A second followed from Captain Moraga, to the same effect. I was still undecided, when in walked Colonel Campos, to inform me that he had run up to Santiago on purpose to fetch me, deputed thereto by the officers of the squadron in conclave assembled.

'You've got to come, *amigo mio*,' quoth the stalwart Colonel, 'and that's all about it.'

And so it was settled. We decided to have a 'look round' Santiago that evening, and to start by the express next morning, telegraphing the decision to Moraga.

From my diary :

June 2.—Left Valparaiso on board *Imperial*, accompanied by *Lynch* and *Condell*. Three deserters flogged—*pour encourager les autres*.

June 3.—Coquimbo. Went ashore, and experienced same hospitable treatment as before. Seeking to return on board at 12 p.m., we could find no ship's boat awaiting us. So we lowered a boat suspended upon davits on the jetty, impressed four waiters to row, and shoved off. Passing the *Lynch*, were challenged by sentry. Having no bull's-eye lantern, could not give the night-signal (two long flashes followed by one short one), and passed on, whereupon the sentry fired. We raced on past the *Condell*, where the same thing happened, and the guard being aroused, a perfect hail of bullets was sent in our direction, but none struck the boat. The impressed waiters were so frightened, that Campos had to threaten them with his revolver to keep them going. Nearing the *Imperial* we were again challenged.

'*Imperial!*' roared Campos.

'Halt, *Imperial!*' cried the sentry. 'The password?'

'Confound it,' muttered the Colonel, 'I've forgotten it!'

'Never mind,' suggested Colonel Errazuriz, who was with us, and was somewhat ' on ' ; ' never mind, I'll give it to him. *Ratones!* (Rats!)' he yelled.

Crack went the sentry's rifle, the bullet crashing through the gunwale amidships.

'*Carrajo!*' roared Moraga. 'Don't you know my voice?'

'*Si, comandante,*' replied the sentry; 'but your orders always are to allow no one to approach the ship without the password.' And up went the rifle to his shoulder.

'Confound you for a fool!' said Moraga. 'Call out the officer of the guard.'

'*Mey bien, mi comandante,*' was the reply.

In a few minutes the officer made his appearance, and we were relieved from the dilemma. But nothing would induce our scratch boat's crew to return ashore that night.

June 4.—Left at night for north; the *Imperial* ablaze with lights on purpose to attract the notice of hostile cruisers, whilst the *torpederas* followed in total darkness. The idea, of course, was that, if challenged or fired at by an enemy's ship, the *Imperial* was to signal her surrender, whilst the *Condell* and *Lynch* were to torpedo the man-of-war. A clever idea enough, albeit somewhat risky. It was to be kept up the whole way north to Pisagua.

June 8.—This afternoon all three vessels opened fire upon Pisagua, the forts and the *Huascar* replying; but the ironclad did not leave the harbour. This time a good deal of damage must have been done, shell after shell falling close to the barracks and forts. The spar-deck of the *Imperial* was smashed through astern by a ricochet shot, one of her boats destroyed, and her ensign carried away.

No one seriously injured; a few wounds from splinters.

June 9.—The same fate befell Iquique, and, so far as could be judged, with considerable effect. It would have been easy to have created awful havoc amongst the shipping, but this, owing to the presence of foreign vessels, was carefully avoided.

June 10.—Proceeding southward, the vessels entered the undefended harbour of Tocopilla, and a party was landed to occupy the town. Two sailing-ships had just loaded up with cargoes of nitrate, and the duties thereupon (amounting to $47,000) were exacted. Mr. Williams, the British Vice-Consul, complained that the revolutionary authorities would certainly re-exact these dues; but this, as Moraga justly remarked, was no business of his. 'Those fellows at Iquique care little what they do, so long as they rake in the dollars,' added Mr. Williams. He subsequently begged me to take a message from him to the senior British naval commander at Coquimbo, and gave me his card thus endorsed:

'Tocopilla, June 10th, 1891.

'THE SENIOR OFFICER, H.M. PACIFIC SQUADRON.

'SIR,

'Please send one of H.M. ships at once to this port. It is most essential.

'W. H. WILLIAMS,

'British Vice-Consul.'

THE 'HUASCAR.'

The Intendente had fled, but his wife had sought refuge with Mrs. Williams, a charming dame, with a pretty taste for 'writing to the papers.' During the confusion consequent upon our arrival, the local thieves had stolen several articles from the Intendencia. Whereupon Mrs. Williams sent me a note by her husband, saying :

'They have stolen her blankets, pillows, and other things. Ask Mr. Hervey if he can get them back, or I'll have a lovely notice on the Balmaceda crowd.'

Unfortunately I was unequal to the rôle of detective-policeman, so that no doubt the threatened 'lovely article' duly found its way into the columns of some home journal.

June 11.—Reconnoitred Antofagasta and exchanged about a dozen shots with the forts, but no landing was possible, the place being strongly garrisoned. Proceeding along the brown, bare coast-line, we passed Blanco Encalada, literally a deserted village, for of some hundred cottages not one showed signs of being inhabited. A very picture of desolation, these deserted tenements on that barren, arid shore !

Dined on board *Condell*, and slept on the sofa.

June 12.—Early this morning the *Condell* and *Imperial* entered Chañaral Harbour, the *Lynch* keeping watch outside. There being a strong ebb-current, it was deemed expedient to anchor, and the *Condell* took up a position about 150 yards from shore. We had previously seen a train starting, presumably bearing away the Intendente and the garrison to a place of safety. A second train now followed, and the *Imperial's* big Armstrong bow-chaser was discharged. It was a prettily-directed shot, knocking the engine over like a ninepin! Then, almost simultaneously, a flash, a thundering report, and the rush of a projectile just overhead, between the funnels of the *torpedera*: a battery within 150 yards of us! In a trice the gallant little *Condell* was vomiting forth a perfect torrent of missiles upon the spot whence the discharge had proceeded. But the battery replied no more. Then the boats were ordered out, and a landing effected. Cleverly placed amongst the rocks were found an old-fashioned seventy-eight pounder, and a smaller piece, of at least equal antiquity. The gunners had all disappeared, but it was conjectured that they had been unable to resist the temptation of earning a million dollars by a shot at such close range. Had they fired point-blank, they could not have missed; but the gun had a slight elevation, and it was this that saved us. Meanwhile, the *Imperial*, seeing our apparent danger, and, indeed, as we afterwards heard, giving us up for lost, commenced a furious cannonade, which, however, ceased upon seeing our boat go ashore. By the townsfolk here Captain Moraga was received with enthusiasm, and having promised a passage to Valparaiso to several anxious inquirers, the news soon spread that all who chose could obtain free passages by the *Imperial*. Such a scramble as ensued! Whole families turned out of their houses, carrying furniture, bedding, utensils, etc., towards the little jetty. I soon ascertained the reason of this: the entire population was literally starving. An extremely pleasant-spoken English gentleman, a Mr. Sherriff, invited me to enter his house, when he gave me a most harrowing account of the sufferings of the unfortunate people, an account fully confirmed by the ladies of his family. All the able-bodied men had long ago been impressed to serve in the revolutionary ranks at Iquique. No ships ever called —no supplies were ever sent.—The Congressionalist leaders had simply seized the bread-winners, and had abandoned the aged and the women and children to starvation. The ladies (and, oh, how pleasant to see refined, well-dressed Englishwomen in this abandoned place!) assured me that their lives were made miserable by the wretchedness they saw around them; for, of course, do what they would, they could not relieve all. The gaunt, wolfish look of the people one saw in the streets told its own tale also; and now, when we came to count up heads, nearly eight hundred famine-stricken wretches were clamouring to be taken on board.

Captain Moraga at once made it known that this number was greatly in excess of what the *Imperial* could accommodate ; decent women could evidently not be huddled together like troops and camp-followers. Finally, he decided that not more than three hundred would be taken, and that those first on board would have priority of claim. ' That will hurry them up,' he whispered to me. It certainly *did* hurry them up, and what few boatmen there were were mobbed by the frantic crowd. Some few offered to pay their passages to Valparaiso, and methought Señor Sartori pricked up his ears inquiringly ; but the notes tendered were all Iquique dollar-bills or *vales*, and, of course, worthless, so the proposal was magnanimously rejected. The boatmen reaped, if not a golden, at least a very profitable harvest, naturally selecting those passengers who bid highest for their services. One old lady, who had caused her piano to be brought down (upon Heaven knows what wild idea of getting it on board), was fain to barter the instrument for seats for herself and family. Household gods of every description were being offered upon all sides. It was a regular scramble, and ' Deil take the hindmost !'

Upon the outskirts of the crowd I noticed two young girls, evidently sisters, apparently orphans, leading, as I supposed, their little brother between them. Both were very pretty, and the elder not more than eighteen. I suppose I looked inquiringly at them as I passed, for the elder followed me, and, bursting into tears, besought me to get them on board. Father and mother both dead; they had no money; but they had an aunt at Coquimbo. Now, it is very hard to say 'No' when two lovely black eyes are tearfully urging one to say 'Yes'; and when the other sister added two more equally charming orbs to the battery, I gave in at once. But how get them on board? An idea struck me.

'Come along, then,' I said; 'jump into the boat which I will show you, and cover yourselves as much as you can with my cloak.'

And I cautiously stole round to where Moraga's gig was in waiting. His son, a great pet of mine, was middy in charge.

'Carlos,' I explained, 'I want you to take me and these young ladies off to the *Imperial*.'

'Do you, Señor Corresponsal?' replied Carlos, with a knowing grin, for which I could have boxed his ears; 'I dare say you do. But what would my father say if he came here and found the gig gone? He'd flay me!'

'Nonsense, Carlos,' I persisted; 'I'll come back with you and take all the blame.'

'Oh, all right then—come along;' and very gallantly handing the girls (whom I at once covered up with my cloak), into the stern, away we went, the crew all on the broad grin.

Luckily Captain Moraga was too busily engaged

to notice us, and we soon reached the *Imperial*, where I safely deposited my fair freight. I explained how matters stood to Garin, and he very good-naturedly caused the ship's boats to be manned and sent ashore, accompanying me back himself in Moraga's gig. We left the girls and the youngster doing ample justice to an impromptu lunch, the first decent meal, doubtless, they had seen for many a long day.

Moraga never alluded to the absence of his gig, to Master Carlos' great satisfaction, and was glad to see the *Imperial's* boats arriving. A rough selection was made from amongst the remaining applicants, and in less than two hours the stipulated number were on board the transport, whither I also returned with Garin. It was horrible to see the avidity with which our new passengers devoured raw rice, raw peas, and even raw potatoes, whilst the cooks were preparing a meal for them. They were classified so far as possible, about thirty of the more respectable being admitted to the saloon, whilst the rest were located forward. I gave up my own cabins to my protégées, and was more than repaid when the elder archly regretted that Coquimbo was not a few thousand miles further off!

June 13.—Called at Coquimbo and disembarked about one-third of our passengers, including, alas! my pretty young friends. They found their aunt all right, and the old lady entertained my inseparable chum Campos and myself most hospitably. The troops here and at Serena now numbered nearly 14,000 men.

June 15. — Entered Valparaiso Harbour at 10 a.m. Ashore I found a telegram awaiting me from the *Times*, requiring me to start at once for London with certain documentary evidence.

The Andes being quite closed up with snow, my only route lay viâ Magellan Straits, and upon inquiry at the office of the Pacific Steam Navigation Company, I found that the first mail-steamer, the *Liguria*, would leave upon the 25th instant. By her I accordingly secured my passage. This second recall did not greatly surprise me, for I had not gone back one single inch upon my original estimate of the political merits of the quarrel, and I still stood alone in that estimate amongst foreign journalists. A review of back numbers of leading English journals (including the leviathan which I had the honour to represent) made it abundantly clear that more weight was attached to the fabricated intelligence received from Buenos Aires and Iquique than to the bare facts transmitted by me from Santiago, especially supplemented as the former were by grossly inaccurate communications from enthusiastic Oppositionists in the Chilian capital. These gentlemen made no secret of the fact that they were leaving no stone unturned to counteract the pernicious influence I might be supposed to exert. The surreptitiously-published insurgent organ, *La Revolucion*, continually boasted that, despite the Balmacedist sympathies of its correspondent, the *Times* still supported the Opposition, and quoted long extracts in proof thereof. The local organ of British opinion, the *Chilian Times* (owned and conducted, oddly enough, by a German), which had contrived to escape suppression by 'holding a candle to the devil,' went as far as it safely could in the same direction. I was in a hopeless minority of one. It was hard lines to miss the *dénouement* of the drama. But the decree of recall had gone forth, and I perfectly understood why. My mission, so far as European opinion was concerned, had been a *coup manqué*.

The news of my approaching departure had not on this occasion leaked out through the telegraph-office, but became known by the fact of my having engaged a cabin on the *Liguria*. Chilians are extremely warm-hearted, and I got wind of a series of farewell banquets to be given in my honour, which drove me into rural retirement for a week, such demonstrations being obviously so many trump cards in the hands of the Oppositionists. A couple of dinners *en famille* with the President and with Don Claudio Vicuña could not, with due respect to their exalted stations, be declined; and these were all I would accept, apart, of course, from partaking of the hospitality of Senor Alfredo Ovalle and other friends in a private position.

The departure of the *Liguria* had been postponed

to the 26th, and upon the previous day I bade farewell to Santiago. The President received me alone and with the utmost cordiality.

'You are leaving Chile,' he said, 'because your judgment has led you to lean towards my side in this civil war, and doubtless the black shadow which has been cast upon my reputation will also bedim your own.'

'Possibly, your Excellency,' I replied; 'but that troubles me very little. I have throughout followed my own judgment, based upon what I read, and heard, and saw. What care I for the opinions of persons who either know nothing of the questions at issue, or who have personal interests to serve? And now may I venture to offer you some parting advice? Do not underrate the fighting power of the troops at Iquique. Your officers, from the generals down to the corporals, have the idea that one regiment of well-drilled Government infantry is a match for double its number of what they call armed miners; and equally armed, equally led, so I have no doubt it would be. But these armed miners, inferior as they are in numbers to your large army, are being trained by a German expert, a well-known strategist, and they are, or soon will be, provided with repeating-rifles. Now, one regiment, thus armed and thus led, is worth three regiments equipped with your *fusils-Gras* or Martini-Henry. You have not a single general who understands modern tactics; your Peruvian War veterans are out of date———'

'Pardon me, *Señor Corresponsal*, but I would like General Barbosa to hear so candid an opinion of his capabilities;' and the President tilted back his chair to press an electric bell.

'One moment, your Excellency. I am speaking to you now as a friend and well-wisher who is leaving you, not as an impertinent critic to the President of Chile.'

Señor Balmaceda did not ring.

'That I believe, señor,' he said; 'pray proceed;' and he looked at me straightly, candidly—inviting truth, candour.

'I have not much to say, your Excellency,' I went on, warming up to my work; 'but that little amounts to this: the insurgents will not await the arrival of the *Errazuriz* and the *Pinto*, which, added to the *torpederas*, would mean annihilation to the revolted fleet. So soon, therefore, as you receive *certain* information that these vessels are on their way to Valparaiso, look out for an attack.'

'*Pero, por Dios*, señor!' exclaimed the President, 'do you know what you are saying? I have 41,000 infantry, 4,000 cavalry, and upwards of 200 field-pieces! They, with their paltry 7,000 or 8,000 rabble, attack Chile! The thing is absurd!'

'*Puede ser absurdo*,' I persisted; 'but if those ships start, they will attack—they *must* attack or

CHILIAN SOLDIERS.

die like dogs in Iquique. It only concerns you to provide against that attack. And if my calculation be correct, given their arms and their generalship, you will need odds of five to two against them to win. At anything like even numbers, your men will be shot down like rabbits.'

Señor Balmaceda left his chair and paced the room. At length he said:

'*Señor Corresponsal*, have you ever been a soldier?'

'No,' was my reply; 'but I have seen something of soldiers' work. I speak merely as a civilian, who believes that a repeating-rifle is more than a match for a breech-loader.'

'I understand,' he replied, still walking to-and-fro. 'And what is your advice, then?'

'Simply this,' I answered: 'keep all your men within twenty-four hours' reach, and guard all your railway-bridges. Withdraw the forces from Coquimbo, because Coquimbo is not in rail communication with Santiago. The troops there would be simply isolated, and the town is worthless from a strategic point of view.'

'*Amigo mio*,' said Señor Balmaceda, stopping short, 'you mean well—that I know. But in these matters I am in the hands of my generals; and their views do not correspond with yours. What you urge seems reasonable, when one reflects. Yet I cannot act upon it. How can I, indeed, oppose a civilian opinion against the unanimous counsel of the leaders of the army ? Politics I understand, because I am a lawyer. Warfare I leave to them, because they are soldiers. *Y ya esta !*'

'Well,' I concluded, 'I hope all will turn out well. However it turns out, one *gringo* at least will always remember you with sincere regard. *Adios, Señor Presidente, y que le vaya muy bien !*'

'*Adios, pues !*' replied the President. 'Stay— keep this in memory of your friend José Manuel Balmaceda. It is my bribe to the *Corresponsal* of the *Times !*' And, with the grace of which he was so consummate a master, he handed me a pretty morocco letter-case containing his portrait and autograph.

That was my last interview with the 'Bogieman' of London journalism—the great leader who stood between the Chilian people and the triple curse of a bankrupt oligarchy, a depraved Papist clergy, and the insatiable greed of *parvenus* foreign nitrate adventurers.

From Don Claudio Vicuña and his *señora* I received the most cordial wishes for a pleasant voyage, coupled with a hospitable invitation to return to Chile as their guest as soon as I could, and view the country under fairer and peaceful auspices—an invitation which, seconded by the charming heroine of the Orsini bombs and by a round-robin from her brothers, it seemed well worth another long voyage to accept. But, alas! we none of us then foresaw the dire ruin that would erelong overwhelm that happy household.

Poor Colonel Campos mourned over me as over a brother.

'Don't go, Mauricio,' he urged. 'Tell your *gran diario que vaya al diablo!* Ask the President for a commission, and see the thing through.'

But this thing might not be, though I had great difficulty in making the gallant fellow understand *why*.

Upon the 26th I left Santiago by the early mail for Valparaiso. But early as it was, my friend Alfredo Ovalle V. accompanied me to the station, to see me off and to bring me the last adieux of his family. He had been elected senator in the new Congress, and had already come to the front as an ardent advocate of constitutional reform. Poor fellow ! the mere fact of having accepted the position of senator was destined to cost him dear, little as either of us suspected it then.

I looked back sadly enough from the car-window so long as Santiago remained in sight ; for I was leaving many dear friends behind me, and unaccountably gloomy forebodings took possession of me as to how, when, and where I should see any of them again.

CHAPTER IX.

HOMEWARD-BOUND.

How I missed the *Liguria*—A Hot Ten Minutes—A Friend in Need—Travelling made Easy—A Meeting—Concepcion—Coronel—I catch the *Liguria*—The Old Story—Magellan Straits—A Wreck—Monte Video—Rio de Janeiro—Bahia—A Negro Polyglot—Pernambuco—Lisbon—The *Errazuriz*—Plymouth—Home, Sweet Home!

A CLERK at the office of the Pacific Steam Navigation Company had informed me that the *Liguria* would sail at 6 p.m. Consequently, after farewells innumerable, I started shortly after five o'clock in an eight-oared cutter to go on board. The steamer lay about two miles out, so that there was ample time. Scarcely, however, had the boat left the pier, when the *Liguria* fired a gun and steamed off. I stirred my boatmen up and they pulled manfully, whilst I signalled as well as I could from the stern. At first we appeared to gain, though she showed no intention of stopping. Then she put on speed, and, after a four-mile race, the case looked hopeless. Still there remained the chance that her commander would understand that the pursuing boat must contain a passenger, and that he would stop to pick that passenger up; and to lose one's passage was a serious matter. So I urged my crew to persevere.

'Look, señor!' cried the stroke, suddenly stopping, and thereby causing the others to stop also.

I looked, and saw the familiar white puff, followed by a splash in the water about fifty yards ahead of us. One of the forts was practising upon us.

'Go on!' I said. 'Those chaps couldn't hit a boat of this size in six months.'

But not an inch would they budge. I expostulated, coaxed, bribed; but all to no purpose. Then I exhausted my fairly copious vocabulary of Spanish maledictions upon them, my at no time very angelic temper rising to boiling-point as I saw the *Liguria* placidly steaming ahead. Still they would not move. Finally I resorted to very strong measures. Producing my revolver, I swore by all the saints in the calendar that I would empty it amongst them if they any longer disobeyed me. Stroke, not liking the look of the weapon a few feet from his head, growled out a sickly '*Vamos, pues!*' and we got way on once more. A very lively ten minutes followed. I was almost certain the *Liguria* had slowed down, and 'coached' my crew vigorously, whilst the fort tried pot-shots at unpleasantly frequent intervals. At last the men finally threw up their oars, as who should say, 'Now then, señor, do your worst!' Of course, I had to give in, and ordered them to return ashore. So soon as the boat's head went round, the firing ceased.

I landed at the jetty feeling, and doubtless looking, uncommonly foolish. All my luggage was on board the *Liguria*, and there would be no other mail-steamer for a fortnight. There just remained one hope. The *Liguria* would call at Coronel, and it might be possible by taking train to overtake her there. A time-table soon dispelled this hope. She would be off again before to-morrow night's train could arrive.

Now, although the agent at the shipping-office stoutly maintained that he had told me five, and *not* six o'clock as the hour for sailing, I took it into my head that I had purposely been left behind as a sort of rap over the knuckles for my Balmacedist leanings. I know not what suggested the idea, but it took firm root. '*Rit bien qui rit dernier*,' was my soliloquy as I entered the Intendencia and sent the following telegram to the President :

'*Liguria* has sailed without me. Can you detain her at Coronel ?'

In ten minutes the reply came back :

'Most certainly. I have ordered a special train to bring you up to Santiago, where you will find my own travelling-car awaiting you to take you to

Talcuhano or Coronel, as you may prefer. God preserve you, and a prosperous voyage !

'BALMACEDA.'

So matters were looking up. The *Liguria* had had *her* joke ; now I was to have *mine*. I telegraphed my thanks to the President and proceeded to the railway-station, where I found that the station-master had already ordered an engine to get steam up. In half an hour I was off, *en grand seigneur*.

I reached Santiago very early next morning, had a bath and a capital breakfast in the station-master's house, and at nine o'clock took possession of a most luxurious saloon-car, *en route* for Talcuhano, where the *Liguria* was to be detained. All day the special sped along, and seldom indeed have I travelled so enjoyably. Everything that could be desired in the way of 'creature comforts' had been provided most liberally, and special precautions had been taken to clear the line. Several times we passed passenger and freight trains respectfully drawn up upon a siding, and great was the craning of necks from carriage-windows to see who the distinguished creature might be that was thus delaying the traffic. After all, methought, there are advantages in having lived near the rose. At a small station, the name of which I forgot to note down, we were stopped by signal, and had to shunt in our turn. The station-master showed me a telegram from Señor Domingo Godoy (who had just resigned the Premiership), asking him to stop me, as he wished to say good-bye. He also was travelling special, but was going to Santiago. He shortly arrived, and we lunched together, finally departing upon our respective routes with mutual good wishes. Later on we were stopped again. This time a telegram from Talcuhano, stating that the sea was too rough to communicate by boat with the *Liguria*, which had been permitted to go on to Coronel, to which port I must also proceed.

At the town of Concepcion I was met by the Intendente, Señor San Fuentes, whose guest I remained for the night. Next morning I was present at an inspection of the garrison, numbering 5,000 men, and was especially pleased with the spruce appearance of three batteries of horse-artillery. Señor San Fuentes (a nephew, I learnt, of the Congress bugbear) and a large party of officers accompanied me to Coronel. On the way we passed over a splendid iron bridge, a mile and a quarter in length, which spans the river Bio Bio.

'This,' said the Intendente, 'is another of the tyrant Balmaceda's undertakings.'

A grand piece of engineering, truly!

At Coronel there was the *Liguria* right enough. Many of the passengers had come ashore upon learning that she would have to await the arrival of the special train, and it was proposed to make an excursion to Lota to see the locally-famous gardens there. But some of the ship's officers objected to any further delay, alleging that the captain was already chafing under the detention.

'There is plenty of time, gentlemen,' said Señor San Fuentes grimly. 'I have not done with the *Liguria* yet.'

The gardens are pretty, but somewhat too much in the Rosherville style for my taste. Indeed, the pavilions, ornamental work, etc., are tawdry to the last degree. Lota by no means justifies its fame.

Upon boarding the *Liguria*, the captain was in a state of hardly-suppressed fume. The Intendente had got hold of some report that the ship was taking a consignment of jerked beef for transhipment to a rebel vessel in the Straits. The captain protested that it was destined for Monte Video; and finally, over a judiciously produced bottle of champagne, Señor San Fuentes accepted the skipper's solemn assurance and allowed the ship to depart.

I was not exactly a pet on board for the first few hours, especially as I could not refrain from crowing mildly at having all the best of the deal. But all that soon passed over. Captain Hamilton turned out to be a capital fellow; and as for the purser, he was simply a paragon, and a model for all others.

We had quite a diplomatic crowd on board:

Señor Salinas, late Intendente of Tarapacá, and now bound upon some complicated financial mission to Paris and Berlin; a young gentleman named Poirier, who was bound for Mexico as nothing less than Chilian Minister to that republic; Señor Asta Borruaga, who was being sent to combat the wily Señor Pedro Montt in New York—besides a dozen or so more, secretaries to legations and diplomatic stop-gaps, bound for I forget how many different places. The strangest thing was that, of the lot, only Poirier and Borruaga spoke English, or indeed any other language than Spanish. What imaginable use such monolinguists could possibly be in foreign legations was a problem I abandoned as insoluble. However, they were a very pleasant set, upon the whole.

Magellan Straits, which we entered upon July 2nd, are seen at about their best at this time of the year, when winter has fairly set in. Our first views were decidedly the prettiest, and, *sui generis*, it would be hard to conceive aught lovelier. The weather was bright, clear, and frosty; the water smooth as glass. Upon either side, as we glided swiftly along, were densely-timbered black-green forests, extending often down to the very water's edge. Behind rose tier upon tier of mountains covered with snow of dazzling whiteness, and set, as it were, with glaciers which reflected the rays of the sun like so many huge clusters of diamonds. The foreground of blue water and the background of blue sky (I hope the terms are correctly applied —they read oddly) completed Nature's masterpiece of winter landscape. I wondered if any painter would have the hardihood to tackle the Straits scenery between Cape Pillar and Punta Arenas upon a clear day in July.

At Punta Arenas (Sandy Point) some mails were landed, and a number of the inhabitants invaded the ship with very ill-smelling guanaco-skins for sale, which were freely purchased, and subsequently as freely thrown overboard. \ I secured some pretty nuggets, proof positive of the auriferous character of the district.

East of Sandy Point the scenery falls off greatly, the timber becomes scantier, the foreground flat and sandy, and the back-lying hills smaller. Still, the snowy coating lends beauty to what in the summer time must be a sufficiently dreary prospect. As we neared Cape Virgins, the funnels of a steamer were seen upon the Atlantic side of the low-lying portion of the promontory in such close proximity to the shore as to induce Captain Hamilton to believe that she must have grounded. He accordingly bore down to render assistance. Upon nearer approach, groups of persons were discerned upon the snow-covered slopes, and the flames of huge bonfires gleamed brightly even in the sunlight. The German ensign, reversed, had been hoisted upon the top of a lighthouse at the extremity of the promontory, and vast piles of cargo were stacked upon the shore. Clearly a shipwreck, and clearly also these people must be taken off. The *Liguria* hove to as close to land as possible, and the chief mate put off, I accompanying him to interpret. We soon learnt that the vessel was the *Cleopatra*, owned by a Hamburg company, that she had struck on a sunken rock unmarked in the chart the previous day, and that she had been run aground to save her from foundering in deep water. But assistance they would not accept, either in the form of rescue for themselves or salvage for the cargo. They had, they said, communicated with Punta Arenas by means of a cutter, and would await the arrival of aid from that port. No women were to be seen, but it was evident that many of the people were passengers. There accordingly remained nothing to be done but pull back to the *Liguria*, which at once proceeded on her voyage. Upon rounding the Cape we got a full view of the *Cleopatra*, which was breaking up very fast, and the sea for a considerable distance was littered with wreckage and cargo. Captain Hamilton stated that most of it would drift back ashore at the next flood-tide, and would probably afford some nice pickings for the native inhabitants.

The *Liguria* reached Monte Video upon July 8 after a smooth and eventless run. Here we had the best part of a day to stretch our limbs ashore and look up old friends. With my usual fatal facility for dry nursing, I took one of the Secretaries to Legation under my wing, and had been in the society of the friends aforesaid to the very last moment consistent with catching the ship's tender, when my protégé took it into his head to fall down in a fit. At first we all thought he was dead, and sent messengers off for a doctor and an undertaker. They arrived together. The medico said the patient would perhaps come round by-and-by, and insisted on his removal to the hospital. But this I would not hear of. Dead or alive, that secretary was the property of the Chilian Government, and must be restored to his superior on board ship. The undertaker broadly protested that the fellow was as dead as Pharaoh, nor do I doubt that he would forthwith have proceeded to bury him, but for the doctor's hesitation to pronounce life extinct.

Time was pressing, so I cut the matter short by requesting the man of coffins to send four of his men with a stretcher to carry the patient down to the wharf. This was accordingly done, and having with great difficulty and at a cost of £6 secured a steam-launch, I finally deposited my hapless charge on board just as the ship was about to start without us. Whatever the fit was, it was a bad one. The poor fellow did not recover consciousness for nearly eighteen hours.

Nothing of the smallest interest occurred during the run to Rio de Janeiro, where we arrived upon the 12th. Here, although we had but a few hours to stay, everyone made it a point to go ashore, as passengers always do, to wander about the very uninteresting and unsavoury streets of the Brazilian capital. I took my party (no more secretaries; ladies this time) to Carson's Hotel, where, knowing the 'son of the house,' we fared sumptuously. From the Chilian consulate came the news that the *Errazuriz* was at last clear of French ports and on her way, to be followed immediately by the *Pinto*. This threw the diplomats into a frenzy of excitement, and when we returned on board, how the corks popped and the *vin d'honneur* flowed in celebration of the glad tidings! But I placed no reliance upon a wicked rumour current next morning, that more than one ambassador mistook the floor for his bunk, and finished the night under the table.

Bahia was reached upon the 16th. This time I made a solitary expedition, and can confidently recommend the Hôtel des Etrangers, situated a couple of miles out of town, for an excellent breakfast, and the very funniest waiter I ever met. For facial expression, for repartee, and for powers of mimicry, I doubt if his equal exists. His very colour was unique; the most highly-polished ebony could scarce vie with it.

I gave my order in Spanish, my Portuguese being of the weakest. He replied in such good Castilian that I concluded he must know something of Cuba, and spoke to him of Havannah. He had never been there.

'Surely,' I said in English, 'you are not American?'

'No, sir,' he replied, in the same tongue and without a trace of foreign accent; 'I'm a German.'

To hear a full-blooded negro lay claim to Teutonic origin was somewhat startling, and I proceeded to expose the imposture; but I couldn't. He spoke German like a Berliner—very much better than I did. The intense enjoyment depicted on his sable visage at my evident bewilderment amused me vastly. It said plainly: 'Try a few more languages, and see who will give in first.' I ordered an omelette, and weighed the chances. Just then he passed me, as I supposed, on his way to the kitchen, throwing and catching three eggs juggler fashion. By some mischance he missed one, and, trying to save it, missed also the next. Both fell shattered upon the floor. He stood looking so comically at the *débris* that I laughed aloud, to his evident satisfaction.

'Comme je suis maladroit!' he chanted, in exact imitation of the refrain of one of M. Paulus' *café-concert* songs. 'Mais, après tout, monsieur sait très-bien que *pour faire des omelettes il faut bien casser des œufs!*' And away he ran for more eggs.

I could not leave the mystery of this dark-hued polyglot unsolved, and asked him to explain. He did so in English.

'You see, sir, none of us remember our parentage from the start. My earliest recollections are of Natal, and the only father and mother I ever knew were Germans. I suspect they adopted me as a baby; but, anyhow, they were good parents to me, and I was a son to them. The old man had been a professor of languages, and so, what with what he taught me and knocking round the world a bit, I can tackle most of them; and whilst you are having your coffee, I'll show you the sort of people I sometimes wait upon here.' And this original genius kept me in roars of laughter at a series of vocal impersonations which McCabe himself could not have surpassed. And this phenomenal 'darkie' was content to grin his way through life as a waiter in a Bahia hotel! Truly, 'tis a strange world, my masters!

From him I purchased a monkey and four parrots, and took them on board. I had this menagerie on my hands until I reached London, when I gave away the lot. *Memo for travellers:* never be seduced into adding birds, beasts, or fishes to your *impedimenta.* They are infinitely (the word is all too weak) more trouble than they are worth.

Between Bahia and Pernambuco I find but one entry in my diary : ' B—— still on high horse, and carrying on with the Cub.' Taxing my memory, I recall that B—— was our most charming lady-passenger, and that the 'Cub' was fifteen years my junior, and (what women call) good-looking. I must have been jealous when I wrote that memo.

My diary further informs me that ' the *Liguria* arrived at Pernambuco upon the 18th. Some of our crowd went ashore. I, knowing the hole, refrained.'

July 28th found us at Lisbon, where quarantine regulations absolutely prohibited any shore-going; but the presence of the *Errazuriz* evoked fresh bursts of Chilian enthusiasm. Some officers came off from the cruiser, but, carefully watched by Portuguese launches, could not come on board; conversation was consequently carried on at a disadvantage. It appeared that the poor *Errazuriz* had been knocking about Europe, trying in vain to pick up a working crew of engineers and stokers, especially the latter. France, England, Germany, Spain, and Portugal had successively blocked her at all ports. All our diplomats volunteered round abuse of the said Governments, but that did not carry counsel. Then I was appealed to, and I tendered cynical advice:

'You will never get your stokers here. Go round to one of the Morocco or West African ports and hire a hundred niggers; they may last long enough to see you through. If not, try St. Vincent; and if that fails, stoke yourselves.'

Captain Hamilton did not hesitate to characterize this counsel as 'barbarous.' I think he was right, and, were I not a slave to truth, would not publish it; but somehow my sympathies were all with the President, who had all Europe against him. I advised the course which *I* would have pursued had I been commander of the *Errazuriz*.

I did not land at Bordeaux, where many of our passengers left us, because Captain Hamilton courteously consented to call at Plymouth. There we arrived upon August 1st, and I bade farewell to the good ship *Liguria*. How is it, by the way, that one feels regret at quitting one's late ocean home, instead of feeling unmitigated joy at the prospect of *terra firma* once more? Is it some ill-defined feeling of gratitude towards the gallant vessel which has borne us so speedily and so safely across the wilderness of waters? I think it is. Anyhow, I believe that most persons feel this regret. Certainly in my case there was superadded the sorrow of saying 'good-bye' to genial Captain Hamilton, Mr. Phillips, the paragon of pursers, and Dr. Boyce, the very prince of physicians.

Home, sweet home! Ay, after all, there *is* no place like it. To feel one's foot once more upon English soil, to hear around one the sounds of one's native tongue, and to know that, within measurable distance, a tankard of 'bitter' is to be had upon demand — these are feelings which must have been floating (in a converse sense) in Byron's mind when he penned 'My native land, good-night!'

The usual rudeness, of course, at the Custom-house. Nothing will ever alter that. Why go through the farce of asking 'Have you anything to declare?' if, upon a reply in the negative, every single article of baggage has to be rummaged at the caprice of a person called Snooks, of alcoholic visage? This is the sort of gratuitous insult which, during some twenty years of travel, I have never been subjected to outside of England. And it is reserved for the 'free trade' mother country to levy a duty of two shillings upon a monkey! Home, sweet home!

CHAPTER X.

THE TRIUMPH OF THE REVOLUTION.

'Back from the Grave'—Smart Paragraphing—News from Chile—The Cumming Incident—The Invasion—A Close Shave—Barbosa the Rash—The Battle of Colmo or Concon—The Attack upon Viña del Mar—Strategy—The Insurgent Army receives Accessions—Balmaceda a Bad Strategist—The Battle of Placilla—Results—*Sauve qui peut*—The *Lynch* caught Napping—A 'Revel of Fiends'—How the Triumph was celebrated in Santiago—Balmaceda vanishes—Señor Montt and the Rump—'Convey, the Wise it call'—A Model Correspondent—Balmaceda's Alleged Suicide—Prospects of Future Peace—The Trouble with the United States—How to bring about a Conservative Reaction—Conclusion.

IT must be confessed that I did not arrive in London in such good spirits as I had started upon my South American expedition six months before. The uncomfortable feeling of a *coup manqué* hung over me. I felt that I had been running my head against the stone wall of public opinion, and need not feel surprised if a few bruises were the result. Not for one moment did I doubt the justice of the conclusions at which I had arrived and which I had advocated, but it is distinctly depressing to find one's self in a minority of one. The British public is prone to believe in the existence of bloodthirsty tyrants and merciless despots, and had unhesitatingly accepted Balmaceda as an almost unexampled combination of both. Such a first-class bogie-man is, moreover, always a godsend to the smaller fry of the press which follow in the wake of their ponderous contemporaries, and love nothing so dearly as to tear yet another scrap from the corpse of a reputation. And thus, as I was not prepared to add to the already-published list of atrocities which had done such yeoman's service for 'extra-special editions,' but was, on the contrary, quite ready to give the lie to the entire miserable chronicle of lies, I found myself, from a Chilian news point of view, a great deal worse than useless.

From my landlady I received a greeting almost worth while coming back for. The good old creature had long ago given me up for lost. It appeared she had abandoned her *Daily Telegraph* in favour of the *Times*, in order to get some news of me.

'They did print a few letters, which I knew must be from you,' she told me, 'because they were from their "Special Correspondent." I read every word of them, and made out that you didn't think much of them revolution chaps. Then you wrote that you were going upon some blowing-up business, and that's the last I heard of you. However, thank God, you're safe back again; which it *did* ought to be a lesson to you not to go shoving yourself again into foreign folks' throat-cutting. And what's more, there's been very hard things said about you in 'most all the papers. My old man he reads them down at the Workmen's Club, and he's told me often that the way they was abusing you was something awful.'

'Oh yes, Mrs. W——,' I answered her, 'I know all about that. You see, the Fleet Street penny-a-liners knew far more about the merits of the question than I did, as was but natural, considering they had the whole nitrate interest to coach them.'

'Yes, sir, I suppose so,' assented Mrs. W——; 'though I don't quite see the use of sending you all that way to find out things that were already fixed up, as a body may say, in London. But there's one bit of print as I think you ought to take up. My old man cut it out of a paper called the *Hawk* (which he'd have been fined had they caught him at it), and gave it to me to keep. I'll fetch it in half a minute.'

In something more than the covenanted time, Mrs. W—— reappeared with the 'bit of print' in question. It was from the *Hawk* of June 2nd, and as about the most outrageously-worded comment upon the action of an *absent* man which has ever fallen under my notice, but at the same time, in substance, reproducing the yelp of many publications *sui generis*, I quote it:

'I am not surprised to hear that English residents in Santiago are annoyed at the sympathy shown by some of their fellow-countrymen for President Balmaceda. I think the *Times* correspondent has a good deal of responsibility in that respect. He was sent out there specially to report on the state of affairs ; evidently he has come under Balmaceda's spell, for his telegrams read very much as if he was " nobbled," or his messages edited in Chile. It must be the latter ; the tyrant is master of the posts and telegraphs ; letters are examined by his minions, and if they contain anything supposed to be in opposition to his wishes are suppressed. The Lisbon correspondent of the *Times* acts as a very wholesome check on his Chilian *confrère*, and has let a lot of light into the President's doings, and the reign of terror which he has instituted. The wonder is that Balmaceda has not been assassinated long ago. He is extremely careful of his person ; his mother, I believe, cooks all his food to prevent him being poisoned.'

'I' is quite right in feeling no surprise at the annoyance of the English nitrate agents in Santiago. 'I' is furthermore correct in saddling the *Times* correspondent with ' a good deal of responsibility in that respect.' And he *was* sent out there specially to report on the state of affairs. He did so. But he neither ' fell under Balmaceda's spell,' nor was he ' nobbled,' nor were ' his telegrams edited in Chile' ; they correspond verbatim with those which he sent. The adoption of the latter theory is clearly a 'hedge' (to adopt 'I's' sporting phraseology) against the libellous 'nobbling' suggestion. The light let into the President's doings and the reign of terror by the Lisbon correspondent of the *Times*, was the light reflected from the news-factories at Buenos Aires, the plan being that the contents of the Buenos Aires journals were epitomized and telegraphed on to London by the said Lisbon correspondent. It *is* truly a subject for wonder that Balmaceda escaped assassination; but either the Orsini bombs sent out were defective, or unskilful artistes were employed. Chilian ladies are not cooks. The President partook of the same dishes as the other members of his family and his guests, and, moreover, his *chef* was a very good one.

Is all this, by the way, what the reading public now accepts as 'smart' paragraphing? To stab a brother journalist, absent, and therefore incapable of retort, and to join in the general howl against a ruler engaged in a life-and-death struggle upon a question of the merits of which the paragraphist evidently knew no more than did the mule I rode across the Cordillera—and this upon the testimony of a correspondent at *Lisbon:* is this really what the race for sixpences has culminated in? *Mais passons.*

Before quitting Chile I received promises from certain of my friends of occasional letters to keep me informed of subsequent events. In London, moreover, I have had access to much other Chilian correspondence, chiefly favouring the revolutionary party. And over and above these sources of information there have, of course, been the telegrams and letters published in the press. It has therefore not been a difficult task to follow the struggle, at least in its main incidents, to its bloody and temporary conclusion. The first letter from which I shall quote extracts was written at Santiago under date July 14th:

'Since your departure, several events of importance have occurred, but almost all of them sad in their results, and some terribly sinister in design, as, indeed, are most of the revolutionary proceedings. Certain capitalists of Santiago, whose names are something more than suspected, entered into relations with a half-breed (*mestizo*) Englishman of Valparaiso, one Ricardo Cumming, and offered or sent him $300,000 in order that by means of treachery and dynamite he might bring about the destruction of the *Imperial*, the *Lynch*, and the *Condell*. This miserable fanatic Cumming got hold of some Austrians and Italians, gave them some money, and finally offered them $30,000 for each vessel blown up by dynamite. These persons, acting in concert with one Sepulveda, who had engaged as a steward in the *Imperial*, managed to get aboard and to stow away behind the bolster on Sepulveda's bunk an infernal machine containing several pounds' weight of dynamite, with time-fuze and everything ready to set it off in the ship's hold. With equal success they contrived to get similar infernal machines on board the *Condell* and *Lynch*, supplemented by quantities of dynamite neatly stowed away in large loaves of fresh bread from which they had removed the crumb. Bread thus prepared is, it seems, known as "Greek bread" (*pan griego*). You see to what cowardly extremes the Chilian revolutionists resort. Fortunately, however, for the Republic and the vessels, one of the Italians bribed into this plot betrayed his accomplices to the authorities, who discovered the infernal machines, the dynamite loaves, and the other appliances, half an hour before the time agreed upon for the explosions.

'The chief quartermaster of the *Imperial*, who also belonged to the conspiracy, did himself justice and hanged himself in his cabin. Cumming, an Austrian named Politio, and Sepulveda (a Chilian), having been tried and convicted, and having confessed their guilt, were shot the day before yesterday in Valparaiso, for the trifling offence of having attempted to blow up the squadron and to assassinate the crews, numbering 600 men, who were aboard.

'This execution was worked up into a political scandal. Several members of the *corps diplomatique*, headed by the British Minister, whom I believe you know (though I am not certain whether he accompanied them personally), requested and obtained an interview of President Balmaceda, in order to intercede for the life of Ricardo Cumming, in the most imperious manner, even carrying their audacity to the point of threatening Balmaceda with the personal reprisals he might have to suffer should the revolution triumph. The President haughtily refused a pardon, observing that the fate of traitors and assassins did not depend on him, and that mercy in such a case would be complicity in their guilt. He added that he was much surprised that the diplomatic body (four members of which were then present) should come to intercede only for Cumming, who was a gentleman and rich, and not also for the others, who were poor wretches whose very names they did not know, any more than they had known the names of the crew of the torpedo-boat who had been shot for treason committed under the instigation of gold supplied by Santiago capitalists. For none of these had the diplomatists interceded, and yet they now did so for an Englishman, Cumming, the head of a most horrible conspiracy. That as for the threats of personal reprisals made to a Chilian President, whilst he was amazed to hear them uttered by a diplomatic Minister, they were in no possible sense a sufficient reason to make him fail in his duty, for that as President of Chile he had staked both his life and his fortune ever since the 7th of January, when the revolution broke out.

If he lost both, they would be sacrificed for the Fatherland, like his other efforts for the well-being of the country.

'Now, what do you think of foreign diplomatists in Chile? And what would the Queen of England have replied to a foreign Minister in a similar case?

'The other principal event has been an engagement at Vallenar between 300 Government troops with a somewhat superior revolutionary force. The result was a total rout of the rebels, who lost more than half their number in killed and wounded. This happened upon the 9th instant. . . . .'

Of other letters which I saw at this time I cannot give extracts, as they were not addressed to me. Coming from revolutionary sources, they were generally fairly moderate in tone politically, and spoke of the final outcome of the struggle as very dubious, the chief hope of the insurgents being in the superiority of their leader (Körner) and of their rifles, added to the all-important co-operation of the fleet.

A Santiago letter, bearing date August 18th, is interesting as having been written but two days before the revolutionary troops landed at Quinteros, and as showing the perfect confidence of the Government Party up to the last moment in its own strength. It is addressed to myself.

'. . . . The Presidency of Don Claudio Vicuña, your good friend and my very good uncle, is now a fact, nothing being wanted save the formal scrutiny by the Senate upon the 30th instant.

'The war, although showing but a poor prospect for the revolutionists, is not over yet. They talk very big about a forthcoming disembarkation of their troops and of a great battle, but I believe these are all "Portuguese yarns." They have contented themselves so far with following up their dastardly dynamite campaign like so many cowardly Russian Nihilists. During the past few days they have made repeated attempts to blow up several bridges in the south, such as those at Lontua, Lircay, Teno, and Putagan; and they have tried dynamite upon the San Pedro tunnel between Santiago and Valparaiso. But all this without other result than the shooting of six or eight of their number, which will probably scare away the others.

'To-day the *Esmeralda* fired eight shots upon Valparaiso, but at a distance of 18,000 metres, more or less, so that the shots fell into the sea. From which it may be inferred that they were merely some signal, or that the ship wished to show us that she still carries guns.

'I have been laid up with neuralgia, and thus debarred from taking part in the hard-fought debates in Congress upon the proposed constitutional reforms. . . .'

Judged by the light of the events which immediately followed, this letter is a pitiful illustration of overweening confidence, almost apathy, upon the Government side, and of timely energy upon the part of the insurgents. The formal ratification by the Senate of Don Claudio Vicuña's election never came off: had the rebels allowed the 30th to slip by without taking action, the Presidency during the next five years would have been legally and definitively settled. The dynamite attempts were, of course, made to cut off railway communication, and so prevent the troops in Santiago from supporting those in Valparaiso, or the numerous large bodies down south from helping either. The shots fired from the *Esmeralda* were signals to let revolutionary partisans ashore know that the hour for the final struggle was at hand. And meanwhile the new Congress was tranquilly discussing constitutional reform ! What a *sauve qui peut* scatter those debates ended in a couple of days later !

The accounts of the short, bloody, and decisive campaign which commenced upon August 20th do not materially disagree, but whereas the revolutionists attribute their victory to the superior fighting powers of their men and to the skill with which they were led, the Balmacedists unhesitatingly attribute their defeat to the repeating-rifles with which most of their foes were armed, and to the deadly havoc wrought in their ranks at the battle of Concon by the fire from the rebel war ships. That both sides fought desperately is evidenced by the fact that, out of rather less than 26,000 combatants, 2,700 were killed and 4,800 wounded.

Early upon the morning of the 20th, the revolutionary transports, twenty in number, and escorted by the *Cochrane*, *Esmeralda*, and *Magellanes*, suddenly appeared in Quinteros Bay, distant, as I have elsewhere stated, about thirty miles by sea from Valparaiso to the north. The *Cochrane* remained at Quinteros to cover the disembarkation of the troops, whilst the other two war ships proceeded towards Valparaiso to cut off the *Lynch* and the *Condell* should they attempt to leave harbour. Being a foggy morning, two small Government torpedo-boats which were out upon patrol duty did not discover the whereabouts of the war ships until, the fog lifting, they found themselves right under the *Esmeralda's* guns. It was a touch-and-go affair for the *Aldea* and *Quale*, but their smallness and speed enabled them to get safely back into port. Clearly the *Condell*, the *Lynch*, and these small torpedo-boats should at once, at all hazards, have been let loose amongst the transports. With their high speed, they stood an excellent chance of dodging the men-of-war; in any case, it was not likely that all four would be sunk without inflicting serious damage. But this was not done; the rebels were allowed to land unmolested, a task which they had accomplished by nightfall. The force thus disembarked consisted of 8,600 infantry, 600 cavalry,

800 Naval Brigade men, three batteries of field-artillery, and a battery of twelve Gatlings of the Gardner model, together with a corps of engineers —in all about 10,600 men. By this time, of course, the Government was fully informed as to the situation, and decided upon opposing the overland march of the rebels at a place called Colmo, twelve miles south of Quinteros. By this selection Balmaceda's generals secured the advantage of being enabled to take up a strong position upon high ground, with the river Aconcagua running between them and the enemy. Their only fear was lest the insurgents should decline to attack upon such apparently disadvantageous terms. If they *should* attack, their defeat was regarded as a foregone conclusion.* The Government forces numbered 8,000 infantry, 950 cavalry, with twenty-two field-guns, and were led, in two divisions, by Generals Barbosa and Alzerreca, between whom there unfortunately existed considerable ill-feeling. President Balmaceda was himself nominally Commander-in-chief, but, not being a soldier, naturally, subject to his express orders, left everything to his military chiefs, and had, indeed, not yet left Santiago. It was calculated

* It is clear, now that fuller information is to hand, that both Balmacedist generals entirely underrated the quality of the invading troops. Balmaceda's distinct orders were not to fight at less odds than three to two (and this recalls vividly to my mind my last interview with him). But Barbosa's fiery temper outweighed such injunctions. ' *Canalla !*' he exclaimed, ' I shall sweep them into the sea !' A late Congressional account, moreover, describes his troops as ' scarcely 8,000 tired, hungry, dispirited men.'

that, when defeated, the insurgents would necessarily fall back upon Quinteros, where they would be cut to pieces before they could re-embark. Additional troops were upon the way from Santiago. The beginning of the end appeared to be in sight.

But in these calculations two fatal errors had been made. The position supposed to be so strong was within easy range of the sea, and of the guns of the *Esmeralda* and *Magellanes*. The firmly-believed-in superiority of the Government troops, man for man, was a delusion; the insurgents were better trained, better armed, better led, and were animated by the conviction that their only hope of safety lay in winning. The Aconcagua was their Rubicon; once they crossed that, they must do or die.

The invaders started from Quinteros at daybreak, and came within artillery distance of the Government forces at nine o'clock. They were formed in three brigades, under Colonels Frias, Vergara, and Enrique Cantos, the uncle of the last-named, also a Colonel Cantos, commanding-in-chief, assisted by the Prussian strategist, Colonel Körner. An advanced guard of Balmaceda's force, consisting of two regiments of infantry and a battery of artillery, occupied some rising ground just beyond the river; whilst, behind, the main body was spread over a line nearly four miles in length.

At 11 a.m. the left wing of the insurgent army

commenced the battle by directing a heavy cannonade against the Government advanced guard, and in a few minutes the artillery upon both sides was hard at work. Then the *Esmeralda* and the *Magellanes* came in close to the mouth of the river, and commenced a furious cross-fire upon the advanced guard, also with deadly effect. The latter small force stood to its guns and its ground bravely for two hours, and, by some fatal blundering or difference of opinion amongst the Balmacedist leaders, was left unsupported. Then their fire slackened somewhat, and seeing this, Colonel Cantos ordered a general advance to storm the position. Through the icy waters of the Aconcagua dashed the insurgents, horse and foot, and up the steep ascent they charged with cries of ' *Viva el Congreso !*' under cover of their artillery in the rear and of the war vessels' cross-fire. Reinforcements were now hurriedly sent forward from Balmaceda's main body, and a terrible struggle ensued. It was a case of ' Greek meeting Greek ' —of Chilian against Chilian ; and for an hour the Balmacedists, favoured by the ground, held their own. But at the end of that time numbers, backed by artillery, prevailed, and the advanced guard, reduced to a few hundred men, fell back, being compelled to abandon their guns, which the victorious insurgents at once turned against Balmaceda's main body. Had the Government leaders now responded by a general down-hill advance, supported by *their* artillery, it is probable that the Congressional troops, fatigued by their late attack, would have been driven pell-mell into the river Aconcagua, nor could the insurgent batteries or war ships have ventured to fire when once hand-to-hand fighting commenced. But, instead of so doing, the President's army remained entirely upon the defensive—the very worst use that excitable Chilian soldiers can possibly be put to. I have over and over again heard their officers declare that one Chilian attacking is worth two defending ; and yet, upon this occasion, this seemingly recognised fact was wholly ignored by those very leaders.* Colonel Cantos, at all events, profited by it, and pressed his men forward, the artillery still thundering away in the rear, and the war ships dropping shell after shell into the Government position. After two more hours' fighting, Balmaceda's lines broke and retreated, abandoning eighteen field-guns and a large supply of ammunition to the victors. Upwards of 2,500 Government troops were left upon the field, and of these nearly one-half were

* The Chilian soldier is a peculiarly-organized fighting machine. He is by race more than three parts Auracanian, than which no more indomitable nation ever existed. He is pre-eminently and literally bloodthirsty, and he loves to see blood flow from wounds inflicted by his own hand. He uses the rifle, and even the bayonet, as it were, under protest, and can hardly be restrained, when at close quarters, from throwing down his fire-arms and hurling himself upon the foe knife in hand. An Englishman attached to the Ambulance told me that after the battle at Pozo al Monte scores of men lay locked in the death-grip, their knives plunged into one another's bodies.

killed. The slaughter in some of the regiments was terrific. Thus the Temuco regiment lost 520 men out of 600. The San Fernando regiment fared even worse, losing 550 out of 600. These were the troops which so long defended the advanced position, and it will be confessed that they did their duty well. Colonel Körner himself, a staff-officer during the Franco-Prussian War, subsequently declared that he had never heard of, much less witnessed, such bloody work as took place in this battle. Besides the killed and wounded, nearly 2,000 men were taken prisoners, and these all volunteered or were impressed into the insurgent army. The losses upon the side of the victors were considerably less, 1,100 men being placed *hors de combat*, of whom 360 were killed. Such was the battle of Colmo or Concon.

So soon as news of the disaster reached Santiago, the President made strenuous efforts to despatch reinforcements to Valparaiso, and ordered the southern garrisons to hasten up to the capital. But now were seen the results of the dynamite tactics spoken of by my correspondent. Acting in consort with the invaders, and counting the time very exactly, the revolutionary emissaries so wrecked the railway-lines as to render a rapid despatch of troops from the south impossible, and Balmaceda had practically only the garrison of Santiago available. This force, to the number of

AFTER THE BATTLE.

about 6,000 men, was sent to the front, he himself announcing his intention of accompanying the southern reserves to Valparaiso, and of commanding in person at the inevitable decisive battle. Meanwhile his generals were bidden to act entirely upon the defensive, pending his arrival.

Upon August 22nd the revolutionary army made a determined attack in force upon Viña del Mar, a watering-place five miles east of Valparaiso. This township being strongly fortified, and possessing an almost impregnable stronghold known as Fort Callao, the *Esmeralda* and the *Cochrane* assisted in the bombardment. But here the Government artillery more than held its own; and as the nature of the ground did not favour an assault with infantry, the Congressional leaders found themselves compelled to retire. This was claimed as a victory by the Government, and inspired renewed hopes amongst its supporters. The President thought so highly of the repulse that, over-sanguine as ever, he did not hesitate to inform the world that the insurgents had got themselves into a trap from which escape would be impossible. And, indeed, had he been able to advance his reserves rapidly from Santiago, and act in consort with General Barbosa's forces from Valparaiso, the situation of the invaders would have been extremely critical. But Colonel Körner knew his business too well to be thus caught. Upon the 24th he fell back upon Salto, about fifteen miles eastward of Viña del Mar, where there is a wide railway-bridge spanning an impassable chasm. This bridge was cut, and thus rail-communication was effectually cut off between Santiago and Valparaiso. A desperate and novel attempt was made to prevent the destruction of the bridge by the despatch from Llai-Llai of an ironclad train bearing artillerymen and Gatling guns. But the artillery of the insurgents proved too strong, and the train was forced to retreat.

The reader will understand that the failure to capture Viña del Mar having rendered a direct advance upon Valparaiso impossible, it had been decided to make a detour and to attack the maritime capital from the back. This detour involved a march nearly due east as far as Quilpue (twenty-five miles), a south-easterly slant to Las Palmas (twelve miles), a westerly course to Placilla (fifteen miles), and a straight march north upon Valparaiso (seven miles). Quilpue was accordingly occupied upon the 25th, and then the troops rested all day, starting at midnight for Las Palmas. This is a superb country seat belonging to Don Claudio Vicuña, the President-elect; and, as may be supposed, it suffered pretty severely at the hands of the invaders. The extensive stud-farm was forthwith converted into a shambles. Of this stud-farm poor Don Claudio had always been especially proud, and he had spared no expense in securing the very best cattle and sheep procurable in England. Alas! prize Herefords and costly merinos were ruthlessly slaughtered, and when even the appetites of 12,000 hungry men had been satisfied, the butchery was continued from sheer spite. One report which has reached me states that the château itself was pillaged and burnt down; but this act of vandalism, occupied as the house was by the revolutionary leaders, I cannot bring myself to believe.

The army remained at Las Palmas all day upon the 26th, and was joined by 400 cavalry which had deserted from the Government, and coolly informed Colonel Cantos that they had only awaited a favourable opportunity for murdering their commanding-officers to do so. A nice precedent, truly, for a Commander-in-chief to condone!

The marches were all made at night, for some not very apparent reason; and accordingly at midnight the troops started for Placilla, near which they encamped upon the 27th, upon a farm known as Las Cadenas. It was then decided to attack the Government troops next day, they occupying a strong position upon the heights overlooking the village of Placilla. From deserters it was ascertained that they numbered about 9,000 men. The revolutionary army had swollen to 12,000, in addition to the enormous advantage given by the field-guns captured at Colmo.

Meanwhile the President had mustered about 7,000 men, with three batteries of field-guns, but only to find his communication by rail with Valparaiso cut off. Yet additional reinforcements were coming up from Concepcion, and if he could get within striking distance before the decisive battle all might yet be well. But at this juncture he displayed a fatal want of decision. His rail-communication was still open up to within twenty-five miles of Valparaiso. There was nothing to have prevented him from making a detour, as the revolutionary army had done, and debouching upon Viña del Mar, whence his road to Valparaiso was but a five-mile march. And he had had four clear days to do this. Yet the plan seems never to have occurred to him or to his advisers ; and absolutely nothing was done. The Congressional leaders were perfectly well aware of the possibility that Balmaceda might reach Valparaiso by imitating their own tactics, and hence resolved to attack the Government army at Placilla, before reinforcements should arrive. It is known that a strong difference of opinion existed between the Balmacedist generals, Barbosa and Alzerreca, as to the advisability of accepting battle with inferior numbers and inferior artillery ; but as both, together with nearly their whole staffs, were killed, the merits of the dispute will probably never be known. Of the battle itself, the following description, from the pen of a Congressional staff-officer, is the best which I have seen :

'Long before daybreak on the 28th, the first and third brigades were in motion, marching in the direction of Placilla. The third brigade was posted on the right wing, (the first on the left, while the second was to occupy the centre. Owing to the undulating ground, the first and third brigades were able to get into place without being perceived by the enemy. The latter were posted on high ground overlooking the Placilla plains, occupying two miles in length. Their artillery was massed in the centre, overlooking the village, with infantry posted on the slopes below in front of the artillery, as well as all along the heights. On their extreme right was posted another battery of artillery. The cavalry were well out of sight in reserve. This arm fatally neglected their duty before the battle, not a scout being out to observe the enemy's movements. About a quarter-past seven the enemy opened an artillery fire on the second brigade, who were advancing across the plains, having been the last to leave the camping-ground. These the Government forces mistook for the leading columns of the Opposition army. The second brigade, however, advanced at the double, and quickly got into their position; the right and left wings at the same time advancing and opening their fire on the enemy caused the fire to become general, and at half-past seven exactly the battle began. The Iquique regiment on the left, ably seconded by the Constitution regiment, were the first to show in the battle. Step by step they could be plainly seen ascending the hill, driving back the enemy's infantry, and getting nearer every minute to the enemy's artillery, which was thundering away without ceasing from the top of the hill. All this time the right wing had been engaging the enemy's left, and soon began to advance. After about an hour and a half's fighting, the Government left was in such danger that the guns in the centre were turned round, and began firing at the Opposition right wing, which was already outflanking the enemy, the infantry holding the Opposition left wing in check. At this period of the battle the Tarapacá regiment began to suffer dreadfully from the effects of the enemy's artillery fire, which had been suddenly turned to oppose the advance of the right. To their aid were sent the Esmeralda and Pisagua regiments, under the command of Körner, and, by making a long detour, they completely turned the Government left flank, and, with the Opposition successful on their own left, and the steady advance of the second brigade in the centre, there was nothing left but to send the cavalry forward, who, climbing up the steep hills by the road and on all sides of the heights, came unexpectedly on the shaken infantry at the top, and turned their defeat into utter route, cutting off the retreat of the two generals, Alzerreca and Barbosa, who were both killed, the latter preferring death to surrender. By half-past ten the battle was over, 3,000 men having been taken prisoners. The Government besides must have lost 1,000 killed and about 1,500 wounded, while the Opposition losses are put down at 400 killed and nearly 1,000 wounded. The battle being over, the victorious troops were quickly reorganized, and the army, preceded by the cavalry, started on its march to Valparaiso, a distance of seven miles from the battle-field. All resistance being now at an end, there only remained to take possession of the town, which was accomplished at one o'clock, and by five o'clock the whole army were in peaceful occupation. Half an hour later the *Almirante Cochrane* anchored in the bay for the first time since the outbreak of the war.'

Of course, as soon as the news became known in Valparaiso of the defeat of the Government troops, there was a rush of leading Balmacedists to place themselves beyond the reach of Congressional vengeance, and such foreign war ships as happened to be in port were invaded by eager applicants for safe asylums. The Americans had heretofore stood well-nigh alone in evincing sympathy with the cause of the President, and had given practical proof of this sympathy by prohibiting the despatch of arms to Iquique from United States ports, and by a subsequent determined effort to capture the arms-freighted *Itata*. They had, indeed, been almost as avowedly partisans of Balmaceda as the British war ships had been of Congress ; and had they been represented by any other living man than Mr. Patrick Egan, as Resident Minister, their moral support would have carried far more weight than it did. For reasons too well known to need repetition here, this ill-chosen representative has for many years stood beyond the pale of British society, and the mere fact of his being, even as the mouthpiece of the Washington Government, upon the Presidential side, very greatly intensified the British feeling, both in and out of Chile, against Balmaceda. However, the United States cruiser *Baltimore* was recognised by the fugitives as their safest place of refuge, and thither very many betook themselves, amongst others Captain Fuentes of the *Lynch*, which had been mainly instrumental in sinking the *Blanco Encalada* upon April 23rd. Knowing that their lives would not be worth one minute's purchase if caught, he and his officers had left the *torpedera* moored near the jetty, with a scratch crew of twenty men, who had orders to surrender the vessel when summoned to do so. But no such summons came. The Congressional troops no sooner saw the execrated 'devil's ship' than they opened a murderous rifle-fire upon those on deck. The unfortunate crew soon realized that they were doomed men, and in desperation replied with the Gatling guns. So hot was the fire from shore, however, that nothing on deck could live. Five tried to escape in a boat, but were riddled almost immediately. Two poor wretches swam for their lives, but foolishly climbing upon the mooring-buoy, were promptly 'potted.' Finally, all were killed except two, who hid in a stoke-hole, and contrived to swim ashore at night. The other *torpedera*, the *Condell,* had previously put to sea, still under the command of Captain Moraga, whilst the *Imperial* was known to be cruising in northern waters, in happy ignorance as yet of recent events. I may anticipate so far as to state that both vessels subsequently surrendered in the Peruvian port of Callao.

After many hair-breadth 'scapes, Don Claudio Vicuña, the President-elect; Señor Julio Bañados Espinosa, Prime Minister; Senator Alfredo Ovalle V.; Admiral Viel, Intendente of Santiago, and a few other leading supporters of the late Government, managed to get aboard a German man-of-war, and although the Congressional leaders tried hard, upon various pretexts, to get hold of them, the German Admiral, by direct command of the Emperor, peremptorily refused to give them up. The editor of the Valparaiso Government organ and several others were less fortunate, for, being caught, they were summarily shot, without even the semblance of a legal trial. My friend Mr. Loewenstein, also a Balmacedist editor, and English, was saved by his nationality. As for the populace of Valparaiso, it *viva'd* and cheered the victors just as it had, four months previously, *viva'd* and cheered the destroyers of the *Blanco Encalada*. Nay, its enthusiasm was now more genuine, since it was allowed free license to pillage the houses of known Government adherents. The following graphic account of the behaviour of the mob *eight hours after Valparaiso had been occupied by the revolutionary troops,* taken from a letter published in the *Times* upon October 26th, from an enthusiastic Congressional adherent in Valparaiso, tells its own tale. And this, he adds, is but one of the 'terrible nights' which ensued.

'Masses of lurid smoke, and showers of sparks, and tongues of flame poured upwards into the still clear sky. Every now and then, across the open space visible to us, figures rushed wildly, and sometimes fell, as we heard the rattle and saw rifles flashing with dire suggestiveness. Presently the firemen's bells tinkled along the street leading to the square, one side of which was roaring with eddying flame and the fall of roofs and timber. Then the cracking of shots increased, the mob, which was bent on plunder, actually opening fire on the engines as they vainly attempted to take up their positions. Meanwhile, by the flaring light of the conflagrations, shops were being burst open and emptied of their contents, no lock or padlock being proof against the riddling with rifle-bullets to which they were subjected. With many of the rioters, no doubt, plunder was the main object, but a large proportion of those engaged in the fiendish mischief of these nights acted in a spirit of mere reckless devilry. To speak of the scenes then taking place as "a revel of fiends" is

RUINS IN VALPARAISO.

no exaggeration of language. People whose houses were situated in the broader streets, in the neighbourhood of the lanes crowded with the dens of infamy, describe how both men and women came out from these haunts in the more open spaces, and as they danced frantically the *cueca*, the national dance to which the lower-class Chilians turn by a sort of instinct in their excitement, every now and then one of those armed with rifles would suddenly raise his weapon, and as a piece of mere wanton sport shoot down, it might be, the unfortunate woman who was gesticulating opposite to him, or perhaps one of the comrades who was accompanying him in his debauch. It has been calculated that by daybreak on the morning after the decisive battle from 300 to 400 corpses were strewed about the streets in the main body of the town, and that perhaps fifty of these were the mangled remains of women.'

There was no such revelling of fiends in Balmaceda's time, at all events.

In Santiago the news of the total rout of the Presidential troops was received with the wildest enthusiasm — never during Chilian history had such an opportunity for wholesale plunder, raping, and destruction presented itself. Balmaceda's difficulty as to what he should do with his men was speedily solved by the men themselves, who, throwing discipline to the winds, joined with the mob in the work of devastation. The police, powerless against the revolted soldiery, either joined in also or threw away their uniforms. A division of Congressional troops speedily arrived, but, so long as only the property of Balmacedists was being destroyed, made scarcely a pretence of restoring order. The houses of all supporters of the late Government, from those of the President and of Don Claudio Vicuña to those of their most insignificant adherents, were wrecked, and in many cases burnt to the ground.

Balmaceda disappeared. In vain he was sought for, hunted for; nowhere could he be discovered, and the belief gained ground that he was attempting to cross the Cordillera into Argentine territory. Indeed, an apparently well-authenticated report stated that he had been shot in the snow in an altercation with his muleteer.

The Congressional leader, Señor Jorje Montt, at once assumed the office of President, the Rump of the old time-expired Congress forming itself provisionally into the legislative body known as the *Junta*, or Assembly. It was announced that fresh general elections would be held as soon as possible, meaning, of course, as soon as the Balmacedist governors, intendentes, and other officials should be replaced by Señor Montt's nominees. And these elections were to be quite 'free.' Of course; as free, possibly, as they had been at the last voting. Certainly not more so—probably a good deal less.

Then began the game of confiscation. By what shadow of right a self-elected ' President' and the tag-end of a Congress, whose legal existence had expired three months before, proceeded to annex the goods, chattels, and bank balances of their defeated political opponents is a hopeless and useless question to inquire into. Whatever can be urged in justification thereof might with equal legal weight secure a general amnesty for the inmates of Dartmoor. They had not even precedent to go by, since the late Government had carefully refrained from injuring or stealing the property of the enormously wealthy Congressional partisans, with the exception of certain horses requisitioned for cavalry and artillery purposes.

Upon September 18th Balmaceda's tenure of the Presidency legally expired, and upon the 19th the news went forth that he had shot himself in the Argentine Legation at Santiago. At this period the outside world was almost entirely dependent upon a highly-imaginative correspondent of the *New York Herald* for its Chilian news, and he certainly 'kept the pot boiling.' But a few days previously he had telegraphed a circumstantial description of Balmaceda's escape to a foreign man-of-war, disguised as a drunken sailor, and he had specially emphasized the histrionic skill displayed by the fugitive President on the occasion; an eye-witness could not have been more exact. The suicide version he also telegraphed *in extenso*, together with farewell letters alleged to have been written by Balmaceda. Subsequent telegrams confirmed the intelligence; but the body would seem to have been buried with uncalled-for secrecy and speed. By the time this book is published the exact truth will be known, but upon the date on which I write these lines (October 26th) I confess to still entertaining doubts as to the ex-President's demise. It is clear that the best possible way of checking inquiry and pursuit would be by announcing the hunted man's death; and it is clear also that no indisputable evidence of his death has as yet been adduced. The nearest approach to such evidence is contained in a letter said to have been left in charge of Señor Uriburu, the Argentine Minister, and of which the following is a *resumé*. It is addressed to his three brothers. After stating that his term of office was ended that day, he said he had reviewed the whole affair, and had arrived at the conclusion that he would be no longer able to continue in his asylum in the Argentine Legation without compromising his protector, Señor Uriburu. He expressed the fear that his enemies were about to bring about a tragedy which would damage the Argentine Legation. He disdained making any further attempt to escape. He had intended to give himself up, but, owing to his belief that the insurgent leaders would respect nothing, he had altered his mind and would make a personal sacrifice. This course was the only one left him to lessen the misfortunes of his friends. He had written letters to Señor Claudio Vicuña, Señor Bañados Espinosa, which would be sent in charge of Señor Uriburu, and had asked the last-named to deliver to Señor Eusebio Lillo for publication a document which would prove of historical value. 'Europe,' the writer proceeds, 'will then comprehend my conduct. There are moments in one's life when its sacrifice is the only course left to a gentleman of honour. I set about the final act of my career with a calm mind. My death may alleviate the rage of my enemies against those who supported me. Watch over my children. I have charged Espinosa to write a history of my administration. I never told Emila that his wife should lend her assistance to his task. The distance from this world to the other is less than we imagine. We shall see one another again, when we shall be without the grief and bitterness which now surround us. Watch over our mother. Befriend our friends.'

Of course if this letter (dated September 18th) be genuine, it is highly probable that the intention of suicide implied in the 'personal sacrifice' was carried out; but the reference to the late Prime Minister as 'Espinosa' instead of as 'Bañados' looks more like the work of a foreign than of a Chilian hand.* However, time will tell.

* A somewhat curious old Spanish custom survives in Chile, of adding the mother's maiden name to the patronymic. Thus the name of the Minister in question is Julio Bañados. But his mother's family name being Espinosa, he is known as Julio

The outlying garrisons had, of course, no option but to place themselves at the disposal of the victorious Congressional authorities. Such of the officers as could made their escape; the rest were thrown into prison, for the crime, apparently, of having remained loyal to the legally-established Government. One unfortunate, an especial friend of mine, Colonel Carvalho, commanding the forces at Coquimbo, got aboard a British steamer bound for Callao; but at Iquique, where the vessel called, an armed party came on board and forcibly removed him, the protection of the Union Jack being apparently reserved for rebels. Needless to add that the splendid army at Coquimbo never had a chance of firing a shot, and the regiments stationed there were the very-flower of Balmaceda's troops.

- The triumph of the revolution has been viewed in Europe as a guarantee for future peace and progress in Chile, and Chilian stocks at once rose from 74 to 91. Upon what this hopeful hypothesis is based I do not know. In a previous chapter I have gone at some length into the condition of political parties in the Republic, and to that chapter I would ask the reader to refer. The victory of the insurgents means the victory of the Clericals, the aristocratic (for want of a better term) *Montt-Varistas*, and the plutocrat *Conservadores*, aided

---

Bañados Espinosa, commonly written Julio Bañados E. Where but one name is employed in speaking to or of a person, the first or second is used—never the third.

by dissatisfied factions of the Liberal Party. The object striven for has been accomplished. Balmaceda has fallen. But what next? Into whose hands is the administration to pass? Who are to enjoy the loaves and fishes of office, Liberals or Conservatives? The acting 'President' is Jorje Montt, son of Manuel Montt, who for ten years (1851-61) governed Chile with a rod of iron in conjunction with his chosen Prime Minister, Varas. In his day also a revolution was attempted, but was crushed with pitiless severity. He was the great apostle of government of the masses by the classes, and his political descendants, the Montt-Varistas, revere his policy. \ It may be possible for the three sections of the Conservative Party to act in some sort of unison, but how is it possible for the Liberals to bow their heads to the Conservative yoke? Now, with all the influence which the existing position of Señor Montt as acting President confers, the Conservatives in the recently held elections have secured but thirty-seven seats in the Chamber of Deputies, as against fifty-five won by the Liberals, whilst in the Senate the Liberal vote is still more preponderating. The election of a new President has not yet even been mooted, but sooner or later it must be done. Will he be Conservative or Liberal? If the former, how can he, with a Liberal majority in Congress, govern upon Conservative principles without overriding the Chamber, as Manuel Montt openly did, and as

Balmaceda is said by his enemies to have done? If the future President be a Liberal, as he almost certainly will be unless force be brought to bear upon the electors, how will he govern in the teeth of a strong Conservative minority, aided, as before, by discontented or disappointed Liberal factions? The man does not live who could reconcile these factions, simply because the loaves and fishes are not numerous enough for all, and the ' outs ' will be in chronic opposition to the ' ins.' Upon this rock of attempted unification of the national Liberal Party Balmaceda came to grief, and so, assuredly, will any succeeding President, were he the veriest miser of public money, who shall attempt the same task.

For a short time, no doubt, the newly-elected Congress will be unanimous enough in plundering Balmacedist adherents and undoing the legislation of Balmaceda's last Congress. But then will begin the struggle for supremacy. Quite possibly Señor Montt will prorogue the Chambers until June, and so have a free hand for arranging the details of the inevitable Presidential election. If not, the contest will commence earlier; that is all.

As I write these concluding lines, there would appear to be a possibility of serious trouble arising between Chile and the United States. At least one American sailor, Regan, has been murdered, and several more of the crew of the *Baltimore* savagely assaulted by sailors of the Chilian fleet, aided and abetted by the Valparaiso new police. Moreover, an impression prevails that the authorities have deliberately connived at these attacks. Why, it may be asked, should Señor Montt and his advisers expose the country, still palpitating from the effects of the late bloody civil war, to the danger of a war with a power so overwhelming as the United States? Well, as a matter of *national* policy it would be ultimately most disastrous; but as a matter of *Conservative* policy it would temporarily serve a turn, especially if it be done quickly. Señor Montt, and the Conservatives generally, must now see clearly that, although they figure so prominently as leaders of the revolution which deposed the Liberal leader, Balmaceda, the Chilian people is ungrateful enough to remain Liberal when it comes to the ballot-boxes. They may, furthermore, be credited with sufficient judgment to realize that their only chance lies in regaining the popular affections by some dashing *coup*. Now, the great Chilian national idol is Captain Prat, who lost his wooden ship, the *Esmeralda*, his whole crew, and his own life, in an insane attempt to fight the Peruvian ironclad *Huascar*. The Americans are just now absolutely detested in Chile, and any statesman bold enough to defy the American squadron would bid fair to depose Prat in the popular estimation. Besides, the American ships now in Chilian waters are no match for the Chilian fleet. The *Baltimore* and *San Francisco* are very fine cruisers, but they are not ironclads. Two smaller American war ships are also within hail. But the Chilians have available two ironclads, three first-class cruisers, five well-armed wooden corvettes, two torpedo-catchers (my old friends, the *Lynch* and *Condell*), and several torpedo-boats. As regards fighting qualities, the Chilians have given abundant proofs of their courage ; nor was I much impressed by the large percentage of negroes which I saw amongst the crew of the *Baltimore*. Finally, Chilians cannot be expected to understand Great Britain's policy in dealing with great Powers ; it is commonly understood that a deadly international feud exists between England and the United States, and the wish might easily father the thought into believing that the *Warspite* would be dragged into the quarrel. I do not venture to hazard a conjecture as to how the difficulty which has arisen will be settled. Most probably, I suppose, an apology will be made and an indemnity paid. But I firmly believe that, were the soul of Napoleon in the body of Señor Jorje Montt, a popular naval war would be hazarded as the only possible means of bringing about a Conservative reaction.

My task, such as it has been, is done. I have endeavoured to chronicle a dark chapter in Chilian annals by the light of such individual powers of judgment and observation as I possess. Other pens will doubtless treat the same questions from entirely different aspects. And this is quite in the fitness of things. My chief regret is that I cannot see the silver lining to the cloud which so many others have seen reflected from the revolutionary bayonets. My chief sorrow is that so many persons endeared to me during my stay in Chile are dead or in exile.

NOTE ON THE CONSTITUTION AND POLITICAL PARTIES OF CHILE.

THE CHILIAN CONSTITUTION.

(*Extracts bearing upon questions at issue between President and Congress.*)

ARTICLE I.—The Government of Chile is popular-representative.

ART. XIII.—The legislative power is vested in the national Congress, composed of two Chambers, one of Deputies, the other of Senators.

ART. XVIII.—The Chamber of Deputies is composed of members elected by the departments by direct vote.

ART. XX.—The Chamber of Deputies shall be wholly renewed every three years.

ART. XXIV.—The Senate is composed of members elected by direct vote of the provinces, at the rate of one senator for every three deputies.

ART. XXVI.—Senators shall be renewed every three years (*with certain modifications*).

ART. XXXVI.—The functions of Congress are (*principally*)—

To approve or reject annually the Supply Bill for the expenses of the public administration submitted by the Government.

To approve or disapprove a declaration of war proposed by the President.

To pass special temporary laws to restrain the liberty of individuals or of the press.

Art. XXXVII.—Only by virtue of a law can—
Taxes be imposed or removed.
The expenses of administration be annually fixed.
The forces by land and sea be regulated as to number.
Debts be contracted, or previously-incurred debts be sanctioned.
(Expenses are decreed for eighteen months only, as are likewise the land and sea forces fixed.)

Art. LII.—Congress shall commence its ordinary sessions upon June 1st of each year, and shall close them upon September 1st.

Art. LIII.—When convoked to an extraordinary session, Congress shall occupy itself with the business for which it is convoked, to the exclusion of all other business.

Art. LVII.—Before concluding its ordinary sessions, each Chamber of Congress shall annually elect seven members to form the Constitutional Committee, which shall form a single body, and whose functions shall expire on the 31st of the following May.

Art. LVIII.—It is the duty of the Constitutional Committee—
To watch over the due observance of the constitution and of the laws.
To bring under the President's notice such statements as may conduce to this object. And if these statements hinge upon the evil-doings of the authorities immediately dependent upon the President, and he shall not pay heed thereto, it shall be understood that the President and the Minister in fault accept full responsibility for such conduct of inferior authorities.
To give or withhold its approval with respect to the actions of the President.
To request the President to convoke Congress to extraordinary sessions should circumstances, in its judgment, render such course necessary.
To render an account of its stewardship to Congress, to which it is responsible.

Art. LIX.—A citizen, with the title of 'President of the Republic of Chile,' shall govern the State, and is the supreme chief of the nation.

ART. LXI.—The President of the Republic shall continue in the exercise of his functions for a period of five years, and cannot be re-elected for the ensuing period.

ART. LXIII.—The President of the Republic shall be elected by electors nominated by the people by direct vote. ⱽThe number of electors shall be three times the number of deputies returnable by each department.

ART. LXIV.—The nomination of electors shall take place in departments upon June 25th in the last year of a Presidency. The electors must possess deputy-qualifications (*i.e.*, enjoy all rights of citizenship and of franchise, and have an income of at least $500 a year).

ART. LXV.—The electors, assembled upon the ensuing 28th day of July, shall proceed to the election of a President.

ART. LXXX.—The President-elect, on taking office, shall take the following oath, in the presence of his predecessor and of both Houses of Congress: 'I, N. N., swear by our Lord God and the Holy Gospels, that I shall faithfully discharge the office of President of the Republic; that I shall observe and protect the Catholic, Apostolic, Roman religion; that I shall maintain the integrity and independence of the Republic, and that I shall safeguard and cause to be safeguarded the constitution and the laws. And so may God help me and protect me; and if not, may He call me to account.'

ART. LXXXI.—To the President of the Republic is entrusted the administration and government of the State; and his authority extends to everything having for its object the preservation of public order internally, and the external security of the Republic, observing and enforcing the constitution and the laws.

ART. LXXXII.—The following are the especial functions of the President:

> To take part in making laws as sanctioned by the constitution; to approve and promulgate them.
>
> To issue decrees, regulations, and instructions which he may deem advantageous towards the execution of laws.
>
> To prorogue the ordinary sessions of Congress for a period not exceeding fifty days.

- To summon Congress to extraordinary sessions, with the approval of the Council of State.
- To appoint and remove at his pleasure all Cabinet Ministers and their subordinates, the Councillors of State of his selection, Envoys, Consuls, and other agents abroad, Intendentes of provinces, and Governors of towns.
- To appoint the judges both of higher and inferior courts, upon the recommendation of the Council of State.
- To dispose of the sea and land forces, organize them, and distribute them as he may deem advisable.
- To declare one or many places in the Republic in a state of siege, in case of foreign attack, with assent of the Council of State. In case of civil strife, such declaration resides with Congress; but if the latter be not in session, the President may declare one or more places in a state of siege, with assent of Council of State, and for a specified time.

ART. LXXXIII.—The President of the Republic can be impeached, (only within one year of quitting office) for all acts of his administration in which he may have seriously compromised the honour or the security of the State, or have openly violated the constitution.

ART. CII.—There shall be a Council of State composed in the following manner:

Three members shall be elected by the Senate, three by the Chamber of Deputies, and five by the President, who shall preside at the Council.

The other Articles need not be quoted, as they do not touch upon disputed grounds.

POLITICAL PARTIES IN CHILE.

It has been said that Chile has never been a Republic in aught save name. The natural division of parties under a really Republican *régime* would be into Republicans and Democrats. In Chile the rival parties are broadly grouped as Conservatives and Liberals. Neither Conservatives nor Liberals are united in political ideas. The former are split into three sections; the latter into four. And these sections at the period of the outbreak of civil war may be enumerated and defined as follows:

CONSERVATIVES.
- *Montt-Varistas*, who believed in aristocratic government.
- *Clericales*, who advocated government through priestly influence.
- *Conservadores*, who held what may be termed Conservative opinions, without extreme views.

LIBERALS.
- *Liberales del Gobierno*, who approved Balmaceda's efforts to reconcile all shades of Liberal opinion by distributing, as far as possible, the loaves and fishes of office all round.
- *Nacionales*, who scouted this policy as unfair to supporters of the old Liberal Party which had returned him to office.
- *Sueltos, i.e.*, Free Lances who went, each faction, for its own hand. Hence there were as many varieties of *Sueltos* as dissatisfied leaders of cliques.
- *Radicales*, who were out-and-out Democrats, and came to view Balmaceda's policy as (to quote Señor McIver, a well-known public man) 'favouring a Conservative reaction.'

In the end, the *Liberales del Gobierno* found the other Liberal sections arrayed against them as well, of course, as the Conservatives. And hence the political dead-lock.

APPENDIX A.

THE TRANSANDINE RAILWAY.

THE traveller will, in the not distant future, be spared the task of crossing the Andes on muleback; and this, to many, will be a source of unmixed satisfaction. Those whose business takes them frequently to and from Buenos Aires and Valparaiso are apt to grow weary of the slow-moving *macho*, and to inveigh against the discomforts of the mountain *posadas*. But the tourist can generally enjoy a somewhat rough 'outing,' provided it be compensated for by sublime scenery and novel experiences, and to him I speak words of warning: 'Contrive your trip within the next two years, or you will miss the mule part of the programme, and be unable to narrate to your grandchildren how you crossed the Cordillera' (for the railway is going through, not over, the highest peaks). To me it is matter for considerable surprise that the trip across the South American continent so seldom enters into the plans of my globe-trotting fellow-countrymen, nor have I the slightest hesitation in affirming that no one could ever return disappointed from such a tour. The difficulties and dangers which formerly existed have disappeared before the skill and energy of the engineer, and perhaps were the route more generally known, more travellers would enjoy the opportunity of beholding Nature at her grandest and most sublime.

But it is not only the tourist who reaps, and will reap, the advantages conferred by the Transandine Railway. The business man and the speculator (ever upon the look-out for a 'good thing') also look forward to the completion of the gigantic undertaking with keen interest. Indeed, I have been asked more questions relative to the progress and prospects of the iron road, destined to connect the Atlantic with the Pacific, than about even Balmaceda and the sinking of the *Blanco Encalada*. And this is why, in the interests alike of intending travellers and of intending investors, I append a short descriptive account of the enterprise.

Buenos Aires is nearly 850 miles distant from Valparaiso, of which 760 miles are in Argentina and 90 miles in Chile. The traveller does the first 430 miles of the journey by the Buenos Aires and Pacific Railway, as far as Villa Mercedes. Here the line of the Argentine Great Western commences, terminating at Mendoza, 220 miles further on. At Mendoza the Transandine ascent commences, and for 110 miles the line (not yet completed) belongs to an English company, which purchased the concession from Messrs. Clark, still retaining the services of these gentlemen as contractors for the work. At the Chilian frontier this English-owned section meets the final Chilian section, which runs to Santa Rosa de Los Andes, a further distance of 40 miles, and which is still owned by the Messrs. Clark. From Santa Rosa to Valparaiso is a distance of nearly 54 miles, covered by the Chilian Government line. The entire distance from ocean to ocean will consequently be accomplished by five different railway lines. The line to Mendoza has a gauge of 5 feet 6 inches. The Transandine lines (Mendoza to Los Andes) are 3 feet 3 inches in gauge. And the Chilian Government gauge is 5 feet. So that passengers and cargo will have to be transferred twice on the journey.

Mendoza is 2,376 feet above sea-level, and Santa Rosa 2,704 feet; but the lowest pass between the two towns attains an altitude of 12,467 feet, and consequently an elevation of nearly 10,000 feet has to be overcome. To add to the difficulty, the ascent from the Chilian side is three times as steep as upon the side from Argentina; and it was at first believed that a considerable detour would have to be made, involving, probably, frequent use of the 'zigzag' system adopted in New South Wales in crossing the Blue Mountains. But the introduction of what is known as the 'Abt' system rendered this deviation unnecessary. This 'Abt' system overcomes steep gradients by means of a longitudinal rack laid between the rails and strongly bolted to the sleepers. The locomotives are provided with toothed wheels, which work in this rack in such a manner that six teeth are constantly engaged, and a firm grip thus secured. Gradients as high as 8 per cent. can thus be easily surmounted. The 'Abt' plan will be used for a distance of 12 miles upon the Chilian side, and the last 10 miles approaching the summit from the Argentine side.

It will readily be understood that the engineering difficulties upon a line crossing ranges abounding in mountain torrents, and passing an altitude far above the winter snow level, are enormous. Many large bridges of the strongest and most costly description have to be provided, Nature having, however, supplied one (and an extraordinary phenomenon it is) at Puente del Inca. The track has to be of the most solid character, often, indeed, a mere ledge cut out of the mountain side. And the tunnels would long ago have disheartened less daring pioneers than the Messrs. Clark. Of these the longest will be 5,540 yards, passing through the summit of the Cordillera, 2,000 yards below its highest peak, from the Argentine side. Following this will come the Calavera tunnel, 4,100 yards long, upon the Chilian side, and then the Portillo tunnel, which will have fair claims to be regarded as the most remarkable example of railway mining in the world. It will be 1,840 yards in length, in the course of which it will make a double spiral turn, corkscrew fashion, to overcome the excessively steep gradients, one terminus being 440 feet lower than the other. Two other tunnels, one 1,395, and the other 1,207, yards long, will follow in succession until El Juncal (7,218 feet above sea-level) is reached. When one reflects that these five tunnels, to say nothing of several shorter ones, mean perforating more than 14,000 yards of solid rock, one is fain to admit that the task is a stupendous one. Drilling has been found necessary, and has to be effected under every possible disadvantage. In the great tunnels of Mont Cenis and St. Gothard drilling machinery was also used, the motive power being air compressed by the aid of steam-engines and water-power. But in the Andes absolutely no fuel exists near the summit, and the cost of transport from the nearest source of supply would be ruinous. Water-power, indeed, exists abundantly, but at considerable distances from the sites of the proposed tunnels. How utilize it? It has been done by adopting a system of electrical transmission, which has been found to answer admirably. Is there not something grand about modern science, which can thus bring one great power of Nature to overcome the obstacles thrown in the path of progress by Nature herself? All the machinery had to be conveyed, of course, on muleback. The weight of iron pipes made it necessary to substitute steel ones, of 20-inch diameter and of thicknesses varying with the pressure of different portions of the conduit. The water, forced along at considerable pressure through these pipes, is used for driving Girard-turbines, each of 80 horse-power at 700 revolutions per minute, and working a dynamo giving 135 ampères at 400 volts. From such installations the power is transmitted by copper cables, specially insulated, to the points where the drilling operations are in progress.

The line is now available from Mendoza to Punta de Las Vacas. Upon my trip, it will be remembered, it only went as far as Uspallata. So that, actually, the only mule-riding involved is between Las Vacas and Juncal, about 40 miles. At Juncal a carriage may be procured to Santa Rosa.

It may be stated that the Transandine line should, according to first estimates, now be completed. But the disastrous financial troubles in Argentina, followed by the outbreak of civil war in Chile, have so far retarded the works that, at the very least, two years more will be required to finish them, the tunnels being the chief source of delay, coupled with the still-existing difficulties in the way of securing sufficient capital to press matters on to completion. And here, naturally, the pertinent question arises: Will the line pay? One can only estimate the comparative probabilities.

When once the Transandine line shall have been completed, the systems which go towards forming the Transcontinental Railway will enter into competition with the sea-route *via* Magellan Straits, both as regards passengers and freight. At present the charge for a first-class fare by steamer from

APPENDIX A.

Buenos Aires to Valparaiso is £40, the time occupied averaging fourteen days. When the railway is through, however, the first-class fare would not exceed £10, of which £5 would represent the sum paid to the Transandine lines. The time would be about sixty hours, probably considerably less. Of course the steamships would have to lower their fares, but the gain in time would still be an important factor in favour of the railway.

At present, as has been stated elsewhere, the Cordillera is passable for but five months in the year, during which time about 8,000 persons cross it on muleback. It may fairly be assumed that this number would be at least doubled were the line completed, and, moreover, the journey could be performed all through the year. Upon this assumption, about 38,000 persons would cross, paying £190,000 per annum to the Transandine lines. Again, the cattle trade between Argentina and Chile (*viâ* Uspallata) now aggregates 50,000 head annually, the losses suffered during the rough and pastureless journey being enormous, and several months' fattening being necessary to fit the survivors for market. The railway will obviate these losses and delays. It is proposed to charge £2 per head, so that, even at present numbers, a gross income of £100,000 may fairly be expected from this source.

It is estimated that about 2,000 tons of goods will cross monthly from Mendoza to Santa Rosa, and *vice versâ*. This, at £4 per ton, should yield £96,000 a year. Considerable traffic is also expected from the silver and copper mines of the Argentine Andine provinces. This, together with carriage of produce and sundries, may reasonably be estimated at £30,000 per annum. The profits from mail-service are not taken into account.

The total estimated gross earnings would thus amount to £416,000 per annum, of which, allowing 60 per cent. for working expenses, £166,400 would represent net income. The guaranteed interest on the preference share and debenture capital amounts to £133,870, leaving a credit margin of £32,530.

One other important point remains to be noticed. The New Zealand Government proposes to establish a mail-service, *viâ*

Magellan Straits, with London, and some time ago invited tenders for the construction of the necessary vessels. It would obviously be more expedient to run the mail-ships between New Zealand and Valparaiso, whereby not only would trade spring up between Australasia and South America, but, by means of the Transcontinental railway, a saving of eight or nine days would be effected *viâ* Buenos Aires. It would, moreover, be a pleasant alternative route for colonists visiting England, or for Englishmen proceeding to the Australasian colonies, and would probably be well patronized.

Hence it would appear that, from every point of view, the Transandine Railway will do good work, and will start with excellent prospects as the final link between the Southern Atlantic and the Southern Pacific. Most assuredly, if ever undaunted courage in overcoming obstacles deserved success, Messrs. John and Matthew Clark should reap it in full measure.

APPENDIX B.

THE VALUE OF TORPEDOES IN NAVAL WARFARE.

EVER since the introduction of the Whitehead torpedo as a perfected factor in naval warfare, expert opinions have differed widely as to the advisability of continuing to construct costly ironclads, which apparently lie at the mercy of these submarine monsters. The contest had previously lain between size of guns and thickness of armour-plating, each additional inch of muzzle diameter being met by a corresponding increase in armour; and as it has been found that there is a limit to the size of guns, so far as their effective working at sea is concerned, and that this limit does not exceed the potential resisting-power of a ship's sides, the advocates of heavily-armoured ironclads held their own in the discussion, and floating fortresses of the *Nile* and *Royal Sovereign* types continue to be added to our fleet. But to the potential destructive power of the torpedo there is practically no limit; the most powerful war ship afloat would, if smitten fairly by one of

APPENDIX B.

these deadly missiles, disappear under water within a few minutes. Indeed, an ironclad is more at the mercy of a torpedo than is an unarmoured vessel, the superior buoyancy of the latter offering at least the chance of sufficient time to save the crew.

The opponents of the costly, heavily-armoured type of war ship emphasize the folly of constructing a vessel costing three-quarters of a million sterling, when three or perhaps four unarmoured and (so far as torpedoes are concerned) safer ships could be built for the same money. The value of the ironclad as a battleship against other ironclads, or against forts, is not disputed; but it is held that the risk incurred from torpedoes more than outweighs the fighting advantages.

To this the advocates of the armour-plating system retort that ironclads of the most powerful type are absolutely indispensable to a modern fleet, which without them would be powerless to act against a hostile squadron or to come within range of a fort; that the risk resulting from torpedoes would have to be run were it even far greater than it is, and that precautions are available to minimise this risk.

There cannot, it would seem, be much doubt that this latter view is the correct one. The idea of opposing a fleet of unarmoured ships, however numerous, to even a moderate squadron of ironclads is, upon the face of it, preposterous, to say nothing of the forts. Armoured ships are essential. They have a terrible and unseen foe to guard against; but they must do it as best they can, and take their chance. Moreover, that chance is a very much better one than alarmists seem disposed to believe.

I think that too much importance has been attached to the sinking of the *Blanco Encalada*. The ill-fated flag-ship was taken completely unawares. Her commander displayed a want of caution, which many persons would regard as criminal negligence. I may mention that a telegram from me appeared in the *Times* upon April 21st, stating that the *Condell*, *Lynch*, and *Imperial* were starting to attack rebel ships in northern ports, and that I was accompanying the squadron. This telegram was at once repeated from London to Iquique, and appeared in

La Patria of that town upon the 22nd. The northern ports being all in telegraphic communication with Iquique, it is inconceivable that the news should not have been sent along the coast. Yet the commander of the *Blanco* (Captain Gonie) and his principal officers left the ship anchored in Caldera Bay, without netting, without patrol-launch, without even her electric search-light in use, to enjoy themselves at a banquet given on shore in honour of Señor Jorje Montt's saint's day. A very sad St. George's day it proved, when, at early dawn, the flagship went down with well-nigh all hands on board. And, even despite this gross carelessness, her crew had timely warning of the presence of the *Condell*, upon which they opened a fire sufficiently hot to have driven her off without having succeeded in her object; but they never thought of looking for her consort, the *Lynch*, upon the other side, which vessel, stopping dead-short at pistol-range, launched the torpedo which did the work of destruction. Surely this cannot be accepted as a fair test of ironclad against torpedo vessel, or as a precedent for the future. With the example of the *Blanco Encalada* before their eyes, few captains, it may be assumed, are likely to follow in the footsteps of Captain Gonie.

Two points are especially worthy of note in connection with this Caldera affair. Torpedoes, unless very skilfully handled, are very uncertain in their action. The first one discharged from the *Lynch* went straight to the bottom; the second steered wide; the third (No. 811, I think it was) had always borne a bad name at practice, but on this occasion behaved admirably. Of three torpedoes discharged from the *Condell*, all missed the mark, most likely because the *Condell* was travelling when they were sent. To insure accuracy of aim it would seem that both torpedo vessel and ship should be stationary; but this, like snipe shooting, may be merely a matter of skill and practice, of which neither Moraga nor Fuentes had had much.

As regards beating off or sinking the attacking boat or boats, it is, on the other hand, fair to note that the *Condell* and *Lynch* were doing work for which they were not originally intended. Both are torpedo-catchers—that is, vessels designed to protect ships from torpedo-boats, not themselves to attack ships. At

APPENDIX B.

torpedo range (limited to 600 yards, and very uncertain at more than half that distance) they offered a target for the *Blanco's* guns, which the diminutive torpedo-boat proper would not have afforded. It seems probable, indeed, that a man-of-war could not safely rely upon her guns against a simultaneous attack by several of these deadly launches.

A war of words is now raging between torpedo makers and those who manufacture the anti-torpedo metal netting, designed to encircle a ship crinoline-wise. Torpedists claim to have overcome the netting by increasing the velocity of the torpedo, and by providing it with a projecting knife capable of severing the strongest crinoline now in use. Whereto the netting makers reply that the crinoline can be increased to any required degree of strength. In this dispute the torpedists have apparently the best of it, since there must be a near limit to the weight of the netting with which a ship could hamper herself, whereas it is not easy to foresee where the penetrating power of a torpedo will stop. Nets, it is to be feared, will ere long be of little value.

The success attending the attack made by the *Lynch* and *Condell* has naturally directed considerable attention towards vessels of this type. Here, again, opinions differ. Most of the British naval officers whom I consulted appeared to view them with something very like contempt. The notion of a British war ship being in any dread of a couple of torpedo-catchers was very generally scouted. They were, I was often assured, useful merely as a sort of police-boat, to keep a sharp lookout for and sink torpedo-launches; and had they to deal with the *Warspite* or the *Champion*, they would very soon disappear from the scene. Upon the other hand, Captain Schley and most of the officers of the *Baltimore* held the two vessels in high estimation, averring that, with their speed and destructive power, they should, in resolute hands, give a good account of a hostile squadron.

To me, personally, it seemed rashness, justifiable only by necessity, to employ them, as they *were* employed, for attacking purposes. They appeared to be mere boxes of delicate and complicated machinery, which was continually in imminent danger of breaking down. Their steam-tubes needed repairs after every trip. The chief engineer of the *Condell* told me that he never knew at what moment enough of these tubes would burst to leave the vessel like a duck with a broken wing. At Caldera, although none of the *Blanco's* shots struck her, the concussion caused by replying with her own Hotchkiss guns burst sufficient pipes to reduce her speed to seven or eight knots an hour. Outside Pisagua, in the encounter previously spoken of with the *Huascar* and *Magellanes*, her engines had to be stopped before it was deemed safe to fire. Both the *Condell* and the *Lynch* had, it is true, been very badly handled since the English engineers left them at Buenos Aires; but surely bran-new vessels intended for warfare ought to be able to stand rough usage for a few months, at all events. And machinery which is liable to break down when guns are discharged is, as one would suppose, sadly out of place in a war vessel.

But apart from this, and given the most skilful engineering, it is not clear where the advantage of this class of torpedo-boat may be assumed to lie. As mere torpedo-catchers they are unnecessarily large, since one torpedo-launch can perfectly well tackle another. Moreover, they are themselves fitted with torpedo-tubes. Is it proposed to sink torpedo-launches by means of torpedoes? If so, the idea has never yet been formulated, nor does it seem to be a very sensible one.

As fighting-ships, they are little better than floating coffins. They are, of course, unarmoured, and it would be difficult for a shot to strike one of them without smashing up some of the ubiquitous steam-gear or machinery. Should a missile hit one of the five torpedoes, which, with their tubes, take up considerable space on deck, the vessel would at once be hoisted with her own petard. Taken all round, a more unsatisfactory way of risking one's life than cruising in a torpedo-catcher in wartime, I cannot well imagine.

It was never made clear to me why some use was not made of the three regular torpedo-boats or launches lying throughout the war in Valparaiso. A torpedo discharged from the *Aldea* or the *Quale* would be just as deadly as one fired from the *Condell*, whilst from their small size, their high rate of speed, and their flushness with the water, they would have offered an extremely difficult target for a ship's guns. So far as I could make out, they were kept in port in order to protect it from attack; but this did not seem necessary, because, in the first place, the forts were numerous enough and powerful enough to have blown the entire rebel fleet out of the water; in the second place, a bombardment of Valparaiso, even if practicable, would have chiefly damaged the property of sympathisers with the revolution; and lastly, the shipping was entirely foreign owned. Just before starting upon the third cruise up north, a petition, signed by several officers of the torpedo-catchers and of the *Imperial*, was sent to the President, asking that at least the *Aldea* might be allowed to accompany the squadron, manned by volunteers. But the request was not complied with.

In this connection, it is to be remarked that torpedo-boats are not intended for service out of port, although men-of-war carry launches fitted with torpedo-tubes, for use should occasion offer. Vessels of the *Aldea* type cannot, with crammed bunkers, carry more than eight to ten hours' coal, and would run considerable risk of being swamped in a heavy sea. But north of Coquimbo heavy seas are almost unknown, and to Coquimbo the *Aldea* might have been towed by the *Imperial*, choosing fair weather for the run. Once in calm northern waters, the torpedo-boat might, keeping in touch with the *Imperial*, have lain in wait for outgoing ironclads at night, or have paid nocturnal visits to ports with possibly destructive results.

The limited coal space and unseaworthiness of small torpedo vessels have apparently caused them to be relegated almost entirely to coast and harbour defence. Modern battleships are fitted with torpedo gear, and are expected to do their own torpedo work. If, however, we draw a mental picture of a modern naval battle, it is impossible to overlook the enormous advantage which the assistance of a flotilla of torpedo-boats would bring to the side owning them. Such a flotilla could not accompany a squadron to any considerable distance from shore, in the turbulent seas of the northern hemisphere; the boats would need to be carried, and only launched during an engagement. The only way to accomplish this would be by constructing a torpedo-boat store-ship of considerable speed, capable, at the right moment, of discharging a flotilla of the destructive launches. The construction of such a vessel presents no difficulty. The only subject for wonder is that it is not already in existence, if, indeed, the *Vulcan* may not claim to be such a ship. The presence of such a flotilla would place the enemy's ships in a situation of peril, from which escape would seem to be impossible. For the crews of the torpedo-boats the service would be one of extreme danger also. A proportion—possibly a large proportion—of the launches would be sunk, but some of them would assuredly get within torpedo range, and would dearly avenge their consorts. It would be desperate, almost forlorn hope, work, but such considerations do not weigh one single grain in modern warfare, and the race of naval heroes is not yet extinct. Torpedo work must infallibly be the especial field for the reckless, dare-devil element in a navy which in former times used to man the boats in 'cutting-out' operations. Given a torpedo, the means of launching it, and the knowledge that if the missile but strikes an enemy's ship that ship is doomed, and, unless the records of the past wholly belie the exploits of the future, the task will, over and over again, be accomplished. Englishmen, thank God, have never been backward where danger was to be incurred and glory won, and our gallant tars are little likely to fall astern of the heroic traditions of the service. But let not England, on that account, rely too much upon the, at best, uncertain results of individual pluck acting upon the spur of an emergency. Let her realize that torpedoes are essentially the weapons best fitted for the hands of absolutely fearless men, and that the greatest danger which threatens her maritime superiority lies encased in the terrible tubes. A few store-ships, each one carrying a small flotilla, could not fail to play an important part in the offensive and defensive naval operations of the future, and should be constructed without delay. The manning of torpedo-boats should, furthermore, be recognised as service of special danger, and volunteers, therefore, would be fairly entitled to extra pay and privileges.

APPENDIX C.

CHILIAN CHARACTERISTICS AND CUSTOMS.

As a race, the Chilians may fairly be said to take the lead amongst the nations of South America, a fact which may be traced to several clear and well-marked causes. Their ancestors, centuries ago, came chiefly from the hardiest of the Spanish communities, the Basques and Biscayans; the aboriginal inhabitants of the western sea-board of the continent were, perhaps, the most indomitable, virile tribes of which American history furnishes a record, the famed Araucanians, and with them the early settlers intermarried freely; the mountainous character of the country itself tended to beget those qualities of physical vigour and sturdy independence distinctive of hill-dwellers all the world over; the climate, temperate and bracing, did not favour those habits of indolence and listlessness so distinctive of the Spanish races in warmer regions; the very soil, fruitful under good husbandry, was not of the sort which 'tickled with a hoe, laughs with a harvest.' And thus, from fathers to sons, the Chilians have been an industrious, manly, frugal people. The epithet commonly and lovingly bestowed by them upon their native land speaks for itself: 'Poor Chile' (*pobre Chile*).

Chilians are essentially good-natured and hospitable. It is rare to hear ill-natured remarks made, even by girls speaking about other girls. For instance, the word 'ugly' (*feo*) is never used with respect to human beings, and our term 'plain' has no exact equivalent. Where it is clearly impossible to describe a person as handsome, he or she is spoken of as 'very sympathetic.' Almost all the young ladies of my acquaintance were wont to refer to each other as *muy simpatica*, in a sort of interrogative fashion; whereto I, knowing the unwisdom of praising one daughter of Eve in presence of another, used to assent with an ambiguous smile. Nor did it add to my personal vanity to overhear myself mentioned, a dozen times in the course of an hour, as 'muy simpatica' also! But then I deserved it, and the pretty girls didn't.

When a native has emphasized the fact that he is *Chileno*, further evidence of his excellence is held to be superfluous; which is my mild way of hinting that Chilians have an uncommonly good opinion of themselves. But, after all, is not this common to all peoples? I don't think that Englishmen, at all events, are very backward on this score, even admitting the satire in H.M.S. *Pinafore* to be unduly severe. Besides, the *Chileno* is quite ready to admit the existence of good qualities in foreigners, and he has a very especial admiration for the English.* The names of Lord Cochrane, O'Higgins, Lynch, McKenna, etc., are held in high honour as those of distinguished founders of Chilian greatness; whilst our great naval heroes are almost as famous in Valparaiso as in London. I had frequently heard the statement questioned, before I visited Chile, as to the *bona fides* of the Chilian boast, that 'they are the English of the South.' I made it a point to verify this as often as I could, and the almost unfailing reply was: *Es cierto, señor; somos los ingléses del Sur.* Sundry U.S. scribes have attempted to substitute 'Yankees' for 'English;' but I do not think that the officers and crew of the *Baltimore* would endorse the amendment. It is a noteworthy fact that children of English parentage, born in Chile, are (in exact analogy with the historical precedent of early English settlers in Ireland) *Chilenis Chileniores*.

Implicit confidence in the future of the little Republic is an article of national faith. That Bolivia and Peru must sooner or later be annexed is regarded as inevitable, as also that a slice of Argentine territory (the provinces of Mendoza and San Juan, for choice), and, at least, a fair moiety of Patagonia will some day follow suit. National ambition is, it may be presumed, the natural outcome of national self-confidence.

Education is held in deservedly high esteem by those of more advanced and modern views; whilst by the Conservatives and, above all, by the Clericals it is regarded with considerable

* Into no foreign language with which I am acquainted can the word British, used as a noun, be translated. The Welshman, Scotchman, Irishman, or Colonial, becomes an Englishman as soon as his foot touches alien soil. British is reserved exclusively for home consumption, unless, indeed, we admit the Americanism 'Britisher' as a semi-foreign modification of the rule.

APPENDIX C.

distrust, as being radically inconsistent with Government *by the classes for the masses*. So far as the bulk of the people is concerned, education can scarcely be said to have taken strong root; but the higher classes are, as a rule, remarkably well-informed. As one result of this, political controversy is confined to the latter, and in perhaps no other country is it more freely indulged in. Chilians of all classes love argument, from the *roto*, who affects the *argumentum ad hominem* pointed by his ready *cuchillo*, to the Senator, who is never so happy as when he is denouncing a political opponent, or expounding his views of national progress.

Judged from an English stand-point, women must be regarded as occupying a backward position. National usage tends to deprive them of all liberty of action. Hampered by an extremely severe code of etiquette, the Chilian young lady has but few chances of studying that most interesting of all subjects to the female mind—the male sex. She sees, and is seen by her father's guests; but courtship must be carried on in a roomful of people; a *solitude à deux* would be regarded as a scandalous impropriety. English girls resident in Chile are working manfully to emancipate their dark-eyed sisters, and, as there are signs of lawn-tennis coming into vogue, perhaps freer times are in store for the pretty señoritas. They make, however, admirable wives and mothers under the existing social code; and the absence of the independence, not to say audacity, of the modern Englishwoman, is not without a certain charm of its own. The Chilian women are the backbone of the church, as, indeed, women appear to be in other countries. The average Chilian seldom troubles to put in appearance at church; but his womankind must go, and that too under most depressing millinery conditions. Bonnets are absolutely prohibited, being replaced, for church-going occasions, by the black *manta*, a shawl worn hood-fashion upon the head and long enough to conceal the dress. Of this manta it is difficult to speak in terms of reprobation too strong. Perhaps the assurance that it makes a pretty girl plain, and a plain girl downright ugly, will be deemed sufficient. It certainly reduces church-goers of whatever rank to the same sumptuary level, and may, for that reason, be of value in increasing the attendance. But why Chilian ladies, who upon all other occasions dress elegantly enough, should consent to descend to the level of their kitchen-maids upon Sunday, I could never understand. Strangest of all, Chilians admire, or profess to admire, this fearsome garment. Perhaps if the *padres* could persuade men to wear the national *poncho* upon the Lord's Day, they also would attend the services. Of the clergy, by the way, I know nothing except that common report does not credit them with the possession of all the apostolic virtues.

The houses are built in the old-fashioned Spanish style, the rooms being arranged in the form of a quadrangle round a court-yard called the *patio*. For tropical climates this plan answers well enough, but for Chile the English system would answer far better. In particular, Chilian architects do not recognise the necessity for windows to every room, and absolutely ignore fire-places. Hence it is customary in the winter-time to dine in overcoats and furs; and I have known a lady excuse herself from playing upon a three-hundred guinea pianoforte in a most palatially furnished drawing-room, upon the ground that her fingers were numbed with cold. The universal belief is that fires are most unwholesome. And every time I quoted English experience to the contrary, I was met by the retort: ' Yes, but then everyone knows that half the people in England die of consumption!'

One soon gets used to Chilian cooking, which, indeed, is rapidly becoming Gallicised. Of specially Chilian dishes, which one meets everywhere and always, may be mentioned *cazuela*, a chicken broth flavoured with many vegetables; *puchéro*, boiled beef; and *porótos* (called in Spain *judías*), haricot-beans, which latter are the staple food of the peasantry and labourers. In good houses the *ménus* are of inordinate length, and that guest must be hard indeed to please who cannot find at least half-a-dozen dishes to his taste. Sweets are served in great variety. Chilian wines are excellent. I recall one called *Urmeneta*, a hock of rich flavour and bouquet, as of exceptional merit. A liquor called *Chicha*, a sort of wine-cider or unclarified champagne, is much esteemed as being very wholesome. It is, at all events, very strong. Pisco, a white-grape brandy, is the best of the locally-made alcoholic beverages. There would seem to be a great future in store for the Chilian wine-industry. But, of course, even there, the European vintages hold their own as *vins de luxe.*

To sum up. I do not think it possible for a healthy and healthily-minded traveller to carry away with him aught save good opinions of Chile and the Chilians, and he must be indeed sadly *antipatico* if he fail to leave behind him many and sincere friends. My best wishes will, at all events, ever be forthcoming for the future prosperity of the bonny little Republic, a prosperity well-assured, if the Chilians themselves will but bear in mind that political intrigues are death-blows to national welfare, and that he is the true patriot who sacrifices personal ambition upon the shrine of the public good. Let but the countless factions of political parties disappear or harmonize, and it will be possible with a well-grounded feeling of hopefulness to re-echo the national cry, *Viva Chile !*

THE END.

BILLING AND SONS, PRINTERS, GUILDFORD.

www.ingramcontent.com/pod-product-compliance
Lightning Source LLC
Chambersburg PA
CBHW031854220426
43663CB00006B/625